AFRICANS IN BRAZIL
A Pan-African Perspective

ABDIAS DO NASCIMENTO
ELISA LARKIN NASCIMENTO

Africa World Press, Inc.
P.O. Box 1892
Trenton, New Jersey 08607

Africa World Press, Inc.

P.O. Box 1892
Trenton, New Jersey 08607

First Printing 1992

Cover Design by Carles J. Juzang

Book design and typesetting by Malcolm Litchfield
This book is composed in Janson and Benguiat

Library of Congress Catalog Card Number: 91-74122

ISBN: 0-86543-238-4 Cloth
0-86543-239-2 Paper

CONTENTS

Preface by John Henrik Clarke v
Introductory Note xi

1 Memories from Exile: the Making of a Brazilian Pan-Africanist (Lisbon, 1976 and Rio de Janeiro, 1991) 3
Appendix: Nascimento's Inaugural Speech as State Secretary 70

2 Pan-Africanism, Negritude, and the African Experience in Brazil (Miami and Dakar, 1987) 81

3 Africans in South and Central America: Members of the African World (Accra, 1988) 119

Bibliographic Essay 169
Notes 177
References 187
List of Chapter Subtitles 197
Index 199

PREFACE

Pan-Africanism is an old dream that resurges in the minds of most Africans living outside of Africa in every generation, while being consistent in many forms in all generations. This dream is most persistent in its reoccurrence at periods of extreme difficulty in the life of the Africans in their respective homes away from home and forced exile from Africa. If this seems like a contradiction, it must be acknowledged that much of the life of Africans living outside of Africa is both a contradiction and an enigma reinforced by an enigma.

Most Africans living outside of Africa are the products of the same historical events with variations depending on their respective slave masters, or colonizers. There is now a need to look at Pan-Africanism holistically. After a general view of Pan-Africanism, it is also a necessity to look at the many manifestations of Pan-Africanism under different historical pressures and in different places.

This book by Abdias do Nascimento and Elisa Larkin Nascimento is a document that focuses on a particular kind of Pan-Africanism and how it manifested itself under pressure and what it says about the plight of the Africans in Brazil, the largest African nation, in population, outside of Africa. This subject has been part of a number of books dealing with Brazil and Africans in what has been referred to as the "New World."

Pan-Africanism and South America: Emergence of a Black Rebellion by Elisa Larkin Nascimento (Mrs. Nascimento) discusses Pan-Africanism in South America with some emphasis on Brazil.

Maroon Societies: Rebel Slave Communities in the Americas (1973), edited by Richard Price, deals with revolts against conditions

Africans faced in forced exile. This resistance was clearly a manifestation of Pan-Africanism.

In an unpublished work on the subject, "Pan-Africanism: A Brief History of an Idea in the African World," I have given the following definition:

> Pan movements are not new in the world. These movements existed long before the use of the preface "Pan" was a part of a group's organizational name. Any movement by an ethnic group to recover and reclaim their history, culture, and national identity, after a period of slavery, war, or migration, forced or otherwise, can be called a "Pan" movement.
>
> The largest number of these movements existed in the United States, a nation of immigrants. In this country these movements were mainly historical and cultural societies whose objective was to preserve the history of the United States and the respective history of each immigrant group.
>
> Pan-Africanism, often thought of as a movement conceived and developed by the Africans living outside of Africa was, in fact, a world-wide movement affecting Africans in every part of the world. An operational definition of Pan-Africanism is long overdue. Generally, we think of Pan-Africanism as a twentieth-century phenomenon conceived and developed by Africans living outside of Africa. In fact, Pan-Africanism is a world-wide movement that used different approaches depending on the political climate of the countries where African people lived in large numbers. In Africa itself, Pan-Africanism was often expressed through armed resistance to slavery and colonialism.
>
> There is a need for an operational definition of Pan-Africanism that will explain its many manifestations in different places under different circumstances. All over the world Africans were fighting to restore what slavery and colonialism had taken away from them. No matter what their circumstances were their objective was the same. Slavery and colonialism strained, but did not completely break, the cultural

umbilical cord between the Africans in Africa and those who, by forced migration, now live in what is called the Western world. A small group of African-American and African-Caribbean writers, teachers, and preachers, collectively developed the basis of what would be an African-consciousness movement over one-hundred years ago. Their concern was with Africa, in general, Egypt, Ethiopia, and what is now called the Nile valley.

In the years before the emancipation of the slaves in the United States and in the Caribbean Islands these "free" blacks had barely mastered their conqueror's language; however, in spite of their lack of formal training their first writings reflected a concern for Africa as their homeland. The great African-American scholar W.E.B. DuBois describes the situation in this manner:

> From the fifteenth through the seventeenth centuries, the Africans imported to America regarded themselves as temporary settlers destined to return eventually to Africa. Their increasing revolts against the slave system, which culminated in the eighteenth century, showed a feeling of close kinship to the motherland, and even well into the nineteenth century they called their organizations "African" as witness the "African Unions" of New York and Newport and the African churches of Philadelphia and New York. In the West Indies and South America there were even closer indications of feelings of kinship with Africa and the East.
>
> From a speech, "The American Negro and the Darker World," by W.E.B. DuBois, delivered in New York City, April 30, 1957.

The book, *Pan-Africanism: New Directions in Strategy*, edited by W. Ofuatey-Kodjoe, is an historical view of different manifestations of Pan-Africanism away from home and in Africa itself. It is a many-dimensioned historical view of the subject. This approach was much needed and long overdue. The origin of Pan-Africanism is often viewed with a study of slavery, its impact and aftermath. What is needed here is a serious study of the slave-buyers and the slave master, their buying customs and the method they used to control their respective African captives. The slave masters in the Caribbean Islands and in South America generally bought slaves in large lots and held these lots together. Seemingly they were of the opinion that they could work them better that way. And in the main, this was true. However, they had missed an important dimension of slave organization: Slaves who were taken from a specific area in Africa maintained a cultural continuity. This cultural continuity would later be a facilitator in the most successful slave revolts in history.

In the English colony that became the United States, the slave-buying and the slave maintenance custom was different. They generally bought in small lots and often broke them up. If a slave master bought ten slaves early in the week and was short of cash that same week, he would sell five or more of his slaves. Therefore, slavery in the United States operated figuratively, like a brokerage house.

In the United States the slave master feared every aspect of African culture, religion, and custom. They immediately outlawed the drum and all African musical and spiritual instruments. They outlawed the practice of any form of African religion. This process forced upon the African in the United States a special culture of discontinuity from which they have not recovered to this day. When a people's cultural continuity is broken, they automatically break their loyalty system. A loyalty system is essential to holding a people together.

Some elements of African culture and custom were retained in spite of the conditions. The patterns of black speech in the United States have many African similarities. In my own research on the Africans' reaction to life and death, I have noticed these similarities while making a comparison between funerals in New Orleans and in rural Alabama and Georgia, where I grew to early manhood. It is necessary to live in both places for an extended period in order to notice these similarities.

This book by Abdias do Nascimento and Elisa Larkin Nascimento is mainly the reflection of a Brazilian Pan-African activist. Nascimento has for many years been the main contact between the Africans in Brazil and the Western world and Africa itself. He has challenged the concept that Brazil is a nonracist society, and he has shown that some of the same prejudices exist against Africans in Brazil as against Africans in the United States and in the rest of the Americas.

Brazil itself deserves special attention over and beyond the subject of Pan-Africanism. The uniqueness of the Brazilian case is that Brazil is an African state with a smiling white minority forever announcing nonracialism and practicing none of it. Some Africans have been lulled to political sleep by the forced dialogue of Brazil's nonracialism. Their belief that they have no color problem is their most tragic problem.

This book removes the mask of pretense from the face of Brazil in order that the revolutionary nature of Brazilian Africans of the past can be seen, in order to project the possibility of a revolutionary future that will make African Brazilians full citizens of their country and full members of an African world union in formation.

There was an extensive abolitionist movement in Brazil. Some Africans played major roles in this movement. Professor Asa Davis, in a paper delivered at the University of Ife (Nigeria), July, 1976 (*The Proceedings of the Conference on Yoruba Civilisation*, edited by I. A. Akinjogbin and G. O. Ekemode) calls our attention to the activity of a Brazilian-African abolitionist of Yoruba descent, Luiz Gama. He quotes the following to prove his point:

> I once said that national slavery had never produced a Terencius, nor an Epictetus, or even a Spartacus. There is now an exception to be made: slavery among us produced Luiz Gama, who had much of Terencius, of Epictetus, and of Spartacus.

Preface

This book calls our attention to the fact that there is a need to study the life of Luiz Gama and other black Brazilian abolitionists and to look at the resistance movements in Brazil, in Bahia and in Palmares, as a form of Pan-African manifestation.

The book helps us understand the status of the Africans and Brazilians in their relationship to the Pan-African Movement that for at least 100 years has reverberated throughout the African world.

John Henrik Clarke
Professor Emeritus, African World History
Hunter College

April 1991

INTRODUCTORY NOTE

Since the first publication in the United States of Cheikh Anta Diop's work in 1974, there has been a rapid increase in the quality and quantity of literature in English on the African formulation, or reformulation, of African history. African researchers, whose weight has become ever greater in the broad context of scholarship, are increasingly concerned with the international dimensions of the African world.

Among African Americans in the United States, African cultural and historical consciousness has grown and developed considerably. At the same time, the so-called Hispanic population in the United States, which contains many Africans, has insisted upon its own visibility and has placed a growing emphasis on the African dimensions of its specific cultural manifestations.

One expression of this general African cultural consciousness is the growing and active practice of African religious worship in the United States today. Many of these African religious communities have their origin in South and Central America and the Spanish-speaking Caribbean—the region generally referred to as "Latin" America.

The combination of these developments has called attention to the dearth of material available in English on the African experience in this region, written from the African-American viewpoint. In keeping with a balanced regional perspective, we use the term term "African-American" here and throughout the text in reference to Africans not only in the United States, but in all the Americas.

This book is part of the present authors' continued attempt to contribute to filling this void. Recently, the publication of the volume *Orishas: the Living Gods of Africa in Brazil* (Nascimento, forthcoming) furnished the English-speaking public with an African-Brazilian artist's view of the rich and beautiful heritage of African religious culture in Brazil, essentially the same heritage that informs most Afro-American religious practice in the United States.

In the present volume, for the first time in English, the autobiographical essay of an African-Brazilian activist in Pan-African affairs is accompanied by essays containing his contributions to recent African world events at which he represented the region and, in particular, the second largest African population in the world, that of Brazil. Thus, Chapter 2 consolidates the texts of Abdias do Nascimento's presentations at the 1987 preparatory meeting of Fespac (the Festival of Pan-African Culture), held in Dakar, and at the Conference on Negritude and Afro Cultures in the Americas held in Miami that same year. Chapter 3 contains the texts delivered at the 1988 inaugural sessions of the annual lecture series instituted by the W. E. B. DuBois Centre for Pan-African Culture in Accra, Ghana.

The book closes with a bibliographic essay that reviews the literature existing in English on the subject of the African experience in Brazil and in the South and Central American and Spanish-speaking Caribbean region as a whole. This essay is not intended to be an exhaustive analysis of available information, but rather a general guide for the reader interested in identifying the broad issues under consideration in the field or in looking for further sources on these themes.

Aside from the authors' participation in the African world events involved, this volume arises essentially from the development of the Department of African-American Studies at Temple University in Philadelphia, under the leadership of Dr. Molefi K. Asante. This Department has pioneered, not only in the sense of instituting the first doctoral program in African-American Studies, but also in bringing to an academic institution a worldwide perspective emphasizing the need for research, diffusion, and integration of knowledge on hitherto neglected aspects of the African world experience. It was in this spirit that the department invited Professor Abdias do

Nascimento to Philadelphia as a Visiting Scholar in 1990-91, an invitation that facilitated the preparation of these volumes.

The Ogunic barrier-breaking force of Molefi Asante combined with that of Kassahun Checole, who has dedicated his energies to the creation and consolidation of an independent African publisher with the same goal of expanding and developing African world perspectives. The combination of these creative forces made possible the publication of these works.

The authors are especially grateful to Daniel I. Larkin and to Margaret J. Larkin for their thoughtful reading of the manuscript, their valuable suggestions, and their unwavering support, in various forms, throughout the process of preparing this book for publication. The suggestions made by the editor, Patricia Allen, were also very helpful.

While the present essays have been updated, reflecting some major contemporary trends and events in Afro-Brazilian activism and intellectual expression, the story of Africans in Brazil, and to a greater extent in the region of South and Central America and the Spanish-speaking Caribbean as a whole, remains to be told. Conventional academia's ignorance, distortion, and depreciation of its importance and dimensions has led to the loss to history of many of this saga's major events and protagonists, left unregistered for lack of means or interest. We hope that the publication of these works will unleash a larger demand for volumes penned by Africans from throughout the region.

Elisa Larkin Nascimento
Rio de Janeiro, Brazil
January 1991

AFRICANS IN BRAZIL

1

MEMORIES FROM EXILE

The Making of a Brazilian Pan-Africanist

(Lisbon, 1976 and Rio de Janeiro, 1991)

This essay is based on Abdias do Nascimento's contribution to the book *Memórias do Exílio: Brasil 1964-19??* (Vol. 1) (Lisbon: Editora Arcádia, 1976), a collection of interviews with and memoirs by Brazilian political exiles, edited and coordinated by Pedro Celso Uchôa Cavalcanti and Jovelino Ramos, under the patronage of Paulo Freire, Abdias do Nascimento and Nelson Werneck Sodré. Nascimento's interviews were taped and edited by Clóvis Brigagão in Lisbon, Buffalo and New York in 1975 and 1976. The text has been updated and edited by Elisa Larkin Nascimento, who also adds an Epilogue, furnishing a brief sketch of more recent activities and events, in most of which she herself participated.

Born in Exile

My position in this interview is the most paradoxical one possible. Here I am, talking to white intellectuals, children of the elites that have been oppressing people of my color in Brazil for four hundred years. For this reason and others, I have to make it clear from the beginning that my situation is different from yours. My exile is of a different kind. It didn't start in 1968 or 1964, or at any other time in my life. Now, more than ever, I understand that I was born in exile, and my parents and grandparents as well: descendants of African people brought by force to the exile of enslavement in the Americas.

I am not an opponent simply of the military regime set up in 1964, because all Brazil's governments have been against Africans.[1] In fact, all Brazilian political factions have always discriminated, overtly or subtly, against Africans. The liberals are distantly paternalistic. The right is openly racist. The left is deaf, dumb, and blind when it comes to the specific situation of African Brazilians and contemptuous of our cultural tradition. The Marxist left, in particular, basically agrees with the legalism of liberals who think they can solve the whole problem with a pat legal declaration that "all are equal before the law." Doubtless they mean the law of white magic. The only difference is that the Marxists define legality in terms of class. To them also, "all are equal before the law—of the proletariat." Watch out if you dare to be different!

Obviously, I am aware that these political currents have distinct and differing positions. But regarding the specific concerns of African Brazilians, they come together and complement each other in the effort to destroy African roots and to mold African-Brazilian people and their culture according to European paragons. I didn't get this out of any books. Quite the contrary. I have much to tell in these memoirs!

Childhood

At the time, I didn't know exactly why, but I had some kind of protest inside me from when I was a child. My mother, Georgina Ferreira do Nascimento, was a sweetsmaker, cook, and seamstress. At times she was also a wet nurse for the children of coffee barons. On those occasions she would take us with her from our town of Franca, São Paulo State, into the countryside. We little black kids would hang around the plantation, playing that old role: protégés of small white mistresses. My brothers would get little nothing presents and be happy. Me, I would receive any gift with suspicion. Something told me there was an unpleasant game going on in those relationships.

There were seven of us, all apparently well-adjusted in "white" Brazilian society. I was one exception; the other was Ismênia, my only sister, whom I don't like to talk about. As an adult, she killed herself. Undoubtedly, she wasn't "adjusted" either.

My father, José Ferreira do Nascimento, was a shoemaker who, in spite of long, hard, and underpaid workdays, still found time to play classical guitar in a small local band. Sometimes he accompanied the silent movies that played at the Santa Maria Theater. My parents' relationship was rich, lasting and loving. I never heard them quarrel. Only much later would I realize that domestic violence and fights could be part of married life. After my mother died, when I was about sixteen, my father stayed single and raised my younger brothers and sister by himself.

Throughout my childhood and adolescence, I had a very close relationship with my mother. She gave me all the emotional and material support she could. Especially during the night, while she worked making sweets to sell the next day, we had opportunities for long conversations. During these nocturnal narratives I delved more and more deeply into the saga of our people's suffering. I learned, for example, about my maternal grandmother, who long before had been committed to Juqueri, an insane asylum in São Paulo State. This institution was so horrifying that eventually it became notorious, internationally, as the ultimate example of psychiatric medicine's most perverse mistakes. Later on, my grandmother came to live with us. What agony it was to listen in on her dialogues with invisible beings! I would watch her, trying to penetrate that stare that was fixed on the invisible interlocutor in the world beyond. And although I couldn't see them clearly, I used to make out shadows that would tenuously take shape through the force of her words and then dissolve, revealing ancestors, relatives, brothers, and sisters enslaved in the pain of the whiplash. Even in the hazy naïveté of a child's view, the horrors of the enslavement she had experienced with her family stood out clearly in the anguish of this lunacy that never afforded her a real escape.

Sometimes, while the pot of guava jam boiled, exploding little incandescent flowers that often would burn my mother's strong, round, handsome arms, she would speak of my paternal grandmother, then dead. My father's mother was sexually abused by a Portuguese merchant in Formiga, Minas Gerais State. I know that this event, from which my father's birth resulted, was for him a source of deep shame and distress. In his time, the stigma was strong and heavy against those referred to in discreet whispers as "natural children," the polite euphemism for illegitimate. While my father was still a child in her arms, my grandmother left Formiga in search of hope. They finally settled in Franca, where I was born.

My mother loved me intensely. She vested enormous trust in me, and this sentiment she infused in me has always been my source of inspiration, stimulation, and support.

One event from my childhood remains alive in my memory to this day. There was a little African Brazilian orphan boy, my schoolmate, who was poorer than we. One day, a white woman neighbor was beating the boy, I don't remember why. This happened in the street, in front of our house. My mother, who was always so calm and sweet, took on an unexpected fury and ran fighting to the boy's defense. With this scene, my consciousness of African people's reality in Brazil had its start.

Another Afro-Brazilian experience that made a deep and early impression on me was the story of Luiz Gama. His mother, Luíza Mahin, a freedwoman, was a courageous leader in the famous *Malê*[2] insurrections in Bahia during the first decades of the nineteenth century. Born a free man in Bahia, Luiz Gama was sold into slavery in São Paulo by his own father, a white aristocrat, to pay off gambling debts. Yet, with everything against him, he became a leading attorney and a major abolitionist, fighting slavery in the years before 1888. He invested all the money he earned in the manumission of his African brothers and sisters.

A Young African and the Catholic Church

My father, a practicing Catholic (my mother was different), wanted me to become a priest. I was one of those compulsory Catholics: Sunday school, catechism, first communion, all the traditional religious training. In my opinion, these things just confused our heads.

Easter Week in Franca was impressive, a fantastic theatrical presentation whose catharsis was the Procession of the Encounter on Good Friday. A Lady Mary, her breast pierced by seven swords, and a Christ bathed in blood, suffering under the weight of his cross; all this sharpened my sense of drama. The meeting of the Mother and the Son, the images and the priest's melodramatic sermon, all tinged with scarlet, constituted an unforgettable ritual. My imagination would shoot off on the paths of mysticism.

Only much later, as a young adult, did I feel sufficiently motivated, spiritually, to take on monastic life. First, I looked into the Franciscan order. They were a pack of racist Germans. They would accept me on the condition I remain a "lay brother," and not aspire to being ordained. I told them, "You mean be pageboy to a priest? Not me!" But I hadn't given up yet. I went to the Augustinians, with my friend Rodrigues Alves. These were Spaniards. It was the same story all over again. They advised us to have Christian humility and other virtues they didn't practice in relation to us. It wasn't until much later, when I was introduced to Candomblé, my ancestors' religion brought to Brazil by enslaved Africans, that I dedicated myself seriously again to religion.

Education and Profession: the Case of Dr. Petraglia's Boy

Had I wanted to, had I been a domesticated white man's boy, I would have made myself a very successful little personal career without ever leaving Franca. At thirteen, I was already teaching primary school and working as an accountant on plantations and farms in the area. As a shoemaker, my father barely managed to make 100 mil-reis (about 10 dollars) a month. The mayor of the town made 500 mil-reis. I made 300 mil-reis. For almost any black child, this was already the conquest of the sky; he would need no more in life. But not me. Never would I conform to the petty little rules of the town, or let myself be made into the exceptional Negro: "... yes, he's black, but he's smart, a black boy with a white soul!"

I was always distant, wary. I went to high school almost against my father's will. He was afraid of the risks involved in life's ventures beyond familiar boundaries. He often pointed out the story of Dr. Petraglia's adopted son: "Remember Dr. Petraglia's boy, the black one? He went to medical school, became a doctor, and ended up hanging himself." The young man had gotten a degree in medicine, but he was frustrated in the end because nobody wanted to go to a Negro doctor. My father would recall the story to convince me that I shouldn't go to school. In his view, knowledge could only bring me suffering, frustration, and suicide. And in the context of the straitjacket that Brazilian society is for Africans, this was often the case. But I was proud of what I already knew and I wanted to go on, to learn more. My mother encouraged this and arranged for me and some of my brothers to get scholarships to decent schools.

Another case in point: one day I was offered a new job as a rural accountant. The man who came to pick me up ordered me to sit in the back of his truck, with the crates of chickens. Naturally, I refused. Any white schoolteacher and accountant would deserve to be treated with respect, but this character threw me in the back of the truck as if I were another crate of chickens. Well, I wasn't. I took my bundle of clothes down, and right there in the middle of the town square I told him where to put his job. Never would I submit to that kind of "employment" and its insults.

Enlistment, Hope in the Big City and Bad News from Home

I needed to escape the limitations of this stagnant small-town situation, permeated by classic colonial atmosphere and anti-African provincial attitudes. In 1930, I decided to join the Army and left my astonished family, bound for São Paulo—the big city, opportunity and progress. As a naïve, idealistic adolescent, I could hardly imagine that neither the Army nor the big city held much more hope for Africans than smalltown Franca.

When I signed up for the Army at sixteen, I was stationed at Quitaúna barracks, Second Group of Heavy Artillery, near São Paulo, capital city of São Paulo State. Later that same year, after the 1930 Revolution, in which Getúlio Vargas first took power, I was transferred to the Fourth Infantry Regiment, also at Quitaúna. Then, right after the 1932 Constitutionalist Revolution, I was transferred again to the Second Regional Sanitary Formation, in São Paulo city itself, and was finally discharged from that unit in 1936. It was only then that I left São Paulo State for Rio de Janeiro.

One day, a few months after I enlisted in the Army, a telegram arrived from Franca calling me home urgently. It was my mother. When I had left Franca she was already ill, but she had never stopped making and selling her sweets and her famous homemade gelatin. She had become worse. The barracks happened to be on alert, which meant that no one could get out. All leaves had been cancelled. What could I do? I didn't spend much time thinking about it; I went AWOL. When I arrived in Franca by train and got a taxi at the station, I asked the driver to take me to Rua Líbero Badaró, where we lived. Unintentionally, he gave me the news: "You mean the house where the lady just died?"

The tension I was under intensified and closed down on me like a set of steel doors. During the taxi ride, I recalled the moment I had left Franca: my mother's goodbyes, how I left her behind quickly so I wouldn't see her cry. As the taxi turned the corner, my own tears were coming down in torrents. During my only other visit home from the Army, it had been almost unbearable to watch my mother dragging herself through the streets of the town. The entire right side of her body, arm, leg, tongue and so on, had been paralyzed by thrombosis. The family had to keep on living, and there was no time or money to spend on the health of this mother of seven children. She shifted the weight of her basket to her good arm, the left one, and kept on selling her sweets and gelatin. My father earned a third of what we could survive on, though he worked like a slave.

When I arrived home, my heart was dry and hard like a stone. My mother's body lay in a box in our meager sitting room. I knelt by her and stayed there, motionless, until the burial. From the large numbers and high social rank of the guests, it looked like some dignitary's funeral. Far from being proud of such a well-attended burial, I was outraged, because a good many of the people who accompanied my mother's martyred body were responsible for her early death and my family's hard life. There they were, the beneficiaries of our neo-slavery: the town's white elite, typical paternalists, who showed up only to ease their own guilty consciences at the expense of my mother's funeral. My impulse was to run them out of there with a horsewhip.

When I got back to the barracks, I was met with the compassion and support of a young African-Brazilian lieutenant (what a rarity!) named Alfredo Corrêa. Not only did he refrain from punishing me for going AWOL, but he also offered me a job in the Third Battalion's "House of Order," which meant that I went straight from being a soldier in the field to office work. This gave me a relatively privileged position.

The Constitutionalist Revolution broke out in July 1932, pitting São Paulo State against Getúlio Vargas, who, since his victory at the helm of the 1930 Revolution, had been governing the country arbitrarily with no constitution. During this period, I met and formed a lasting friendship with Sebastião Rodrigues Alves, then a corporal, who would prove to be a constant and dedicated militant of the Afro-Brazilian cause. We were both discharged from the Army in 1936, for resisting against racism, and our common struggles and fast friendship would not end until Rodrigues Alves' death in 1985.

In the Army: the Search for Direction

At sixteen years old, when I enlisted in the Army, I was a country boy, completely ignorant and naïve. I had no access to information or orientation in political matters, but I was full of enthusiasm and desire to act. It was very risky to participate in any Afro-Brazilian or other kind of movement, because soldiers were not allowed to get involved in politics or any activity of a social nature. Even so, in the barracks I used to hand out copies of the *Red Lantern*, the Communist party's clandestine newspaper, and I founded a paper called *The Recruit*, which circulated a few issues.

Basically, these things happened in a confused way. I did them in the complete absence of contact with anyone politically experienced or informed. I was a soldier, ready to obey orders, even to shoot at the people from the *Red Lantern* or the National Liberation Alliance[3] if the officers gave the order. There was no choice. I had no information, no context, no reading material. It was a dead end. But I was always searching. I couldn't just stand there, immobilized, with all that energy, that inner need to find my way, to get out of that rat trap. But, where to go? Which side to take?

In retrospect, it would be easy to say that the correct choice was the left. But it's not that simple. With me, everything is and always has been complicated. In the course of things, I tried all the options and I had just as much trouble with the left as with the right. During that confusing time, before I was out of the Army, I had clandestinely joined the Integralist movement![4]

I was dishonorably discharged from the Army after a fight at the entrance of a nightclub (the Majestic, on Aurora Street in São Paulo), where my friend Rodrigues Alves and I were barred on racial grounds. This was in February 1936. We made it a good fight. The nightclub's receptionist got beat up, and so did the Police Commissioner for Political and Social Order, Egas Botelho, who endorsed the anti-African measure. Rodrigues Alves and I disappeared into the night. It happened to be Carnival, with huge crowds out dancing in the streets. But, finally, we were found. There's always an informer.

One morning, while we were still asleep in our rented room, the police surrounded the boarding house with a brutal war apparatus. They had enough forces for a search and destroy mission against an entire guerrilla army, let alone two young soldiers. They took us by force and dragged Rodrigues Alves and me through the streets of São Paulo like two black Tiradentes.[5] Beating us all the way, they took us to the infamous Investigations Office on Gusmões Street, which was the very portrait of horror.

To this day, my breathing stops and my blood turns cold in veins, when I recall how at least thirty prisoners were piled up in a cubicle designed for no more than eight people. I tried to balance myself on the lid of the communal latrine, which was simply a hole dug into the floor. Almost at every instant a prisoner would have to use the latrine, and I would move over as far as I could, forced to watch the operation from very close quarters. The stench inundated the entire atmosphere, which was already sinister because of the semi-darkness and the noise of a huge fan which ventilated next to nothing, but in compensation produced a greasy, monotonous, maddening din. We never knew whether it was night or day, since the sunlight did not penetrate that darkness, torn at intervals by tormenting cries that cut through space. They would indicate that one more prisoner was being "scientifically" interrogated.

After being kept in this dungeon for some weeks, to "learn our lesson," Rodrigues Alves and I were brought before General Almério de Moura, commander of the Second Military Region (São Paulo). Our saving piece of luck was that, while still a soldier, I had studied for a year, in 1935, at the Alvares Penteado School of Administration and Finance. The General decided that, as students, we would not be sentenced to prison but dishonorably discharged from the Army.

After being forced out of the Army, we spent a good deal of time roaming the streets of São Paulo, with no money and no place to call home. Despite the lack of a prison sentence, we were continually persecuted by the police.

I remember an incident in São Paulo around this time, when we were hungry, out on the streets, and had no money. We resorted to all sorts of tactics to survive. The Italian invasion of Abyssinia was the big news item of the day, and Rodrigues and I were constantly defending the Abyssinians. Our strategy was this. There was an Italian vendor who sold candies and snack foods on a convenient street corner. I would engage him in heated debate over Abyssinia's occupation, and while he was wildly gesticulating and exalting the heroism of the Italian nation, Rodrigues Alves would sneak behind him and pilfer a few items for our lunch.

Finally, the situation became untenable. In 1936, I moved to Rio de Janeiro. This was my first trip outside São Paulo State. Afterwards, though, I travelled back and forth between Rio de Janeiro and São Paulo on frequent visits of various durations. In Rio, I worked for newspapers, first as a proofreader, then as a reporter. I also went back to studying economics, which I had begun at Alvares Penteado School in São Paulo, and took a degree from the University of Rio de Janeiro. Once again I became involved with the Army. I registered as a cavalry student at the Center for Preparation of Reserve Officers. And once more I found myself dishonorably discharged, when I was arrested as a student in 1937 for protesting against the New State dictatorship. So ended my military career. There was a time later when I tried to enlist in the Air Force and be a pilot, but I was denied entrance, on racial grounds.

Brazilian Black Front—the Thirties

My first experiences in the Afro-Brazilian movement were in São Paulo, while still in the Army, in the ranks of the Brazilian Black Front (*Frente Negra Brasileira*—FNB). Some of the Front's leaders had been working since the 1920s to articulate an Afro-Brazilian movement. There was the proposal for a Congress of Black Youth in 1928, in São Paulo, which never materialized. It wasn't until 1938 that I and five other Africans organized the first major Afro-Brazilian youth meeting, the Afro-Campineiro Congress, in Campinas, São Paulo. In 1950, the Black Experimental Theater (TEN) held the First Congress of Brazilian Blacks in Rio de Janeiro.

In São Paulo in the late twenties, the people and ideas were already there, but not until the beginning of the thirties did the movement become institutionalized in the form of the Brazilian Black Front. Among its founders were Arlindo Veiga dos Santos, Isaltino Veiga dos Santos and José Correia Leite, and as a mass movement it was the most important organization that African Brazilians had created since the abolition of slavery in 1888.

The Front held large rallies and protests against race discrimination in public places, the objective being to integrate Africans in Brazilian society. It fought against the barring of blacks by hotels, bars, schools, barbers, clubs, the Civil Guard, police departments and so on. In this sense, it was similar to the civil rights movements in the United States. As I recall, the Brazilian Black Front did not go far beyond this kind of demand, a perspective which I would criticize today.

I couldn't be very deeply involved in Front activities, because I was serving in the Army, whose disciplinary rules prohibited any participation in political or social activities. My participation in the Front was more symbolic and in spirit. But I remember *The Bugle of the Dawn*, the FNB's newspaper, which printed news and commentary about Marcus Garvey, the great Jamaican, and the African-American movement he unleashed in the United States under the slogan "Africa for the Africans, at home and abroad."

Despite the language barrier and the poverty of means of communication, the Brazilian Black Front kept alert to African freedom movements in other countries. It was a vanguard whose goal was to prepare African Brazilians to assume an economic and political role in Brazilian society, and to win black representation in the National Congress, a goal which it never achieved during its existence. The movement spread from São Paulo to other states with significant African populations: Bahia, Pernambuco, Rio Grande do Sul, Rio de Janeiro, Minas Gerais, and Maranhão.

In 1937, with the installation of Getúlio Vargas' New State dictatorship, the Front was closed down, along with all other existing political organizations.

Like any other mass organization, the Brazilian Black Front had its internal problems of ideology and leadership. Actually, this fact is a good indication of its vitality. One of its leaders, Arlindo Veiga dos Santos, was involved with the New Patriots' Movement (*Movimento Patrianovista)*, a rightist organization, while José Correia Leite was a socialist. This polarization led inevitably to the split which later occurred. However, I don't believe the incident had anything to do with the Communist Party.

The Footing: an Example of Brazilian Racial Democracy

Sometime around 1938, in the midst of the New State dictatorship, I joined a delegation of Africans from São Paulo on a mission to the nation's capital, then in Rio de Janeiro. In São Paulo city, there used to be a custom called the *footing* (yes, the name was in English) on Direita Street, in the downtown business district. A number of Africans would get together and walk up and down the street, taking up the sidewalks and adjacent streets as well. It seems there were complaints from the local merchants against those Negroes who blocked the view of their storefronts, albeit the *footing* took place on Sunday, when shops were closed. It was a strongarm government, and Police Chief Alfredo Issa banned this romantic Afro-Brazilian Sunday entertainment. So we formed a committee to take our protest to Rio de Janeiro, then the nation's capital. The group was composed of Fernando Góes (journalist), Rossini Camargo Guarnieri (poet), José Galdino (officer of an Afro-Brazilian recreational club), and me. The newspapers, then under strict censorship, couldn't publish anything except an article by Osório Borba, which managed to "get past" the censors. It wasn't worth much, except to show the courage of Osório Borba.

Integralism, Communism, and Prison

In Rio de Janeiro, after 1936, I continued my activities in the Integralist movement, which I had increased considerably in São Paulo after leaving the Army. The themes that attracted me to the Integralist movement were nationalist and anti-imperialist ones, the fight against capitalism and the bourgeoisie. It was an important stage in my life.

The Integralist movement was where I first began to understand, in an articulate way, my country's economic, social, and political reality and the implications of its international context. Integralist youth groups studied very hard and very seriously. I met and came to know people of rare quality like San Thiago Dantas; Gerardo Mello Mourão, the great poet whose fraternal friendship has crossed the years with me; Roland Corbisier; Rômulo de Almeida; Lauro Escorel; the late Jaime de Azevedo Rodrigues, courageous Brazilian ambassador to a European country, who gave up his diplomatic career after the military coup of 1964; Hélder Câmara, later Recife's famous bishop, whose progressive works on behalf of the poor prompted the military dictatorship to ban his name from being mentioned publicly; Ernani da Silva Bruno, the historian from São Paulo; Francisco Luiz de Almeida Salles; Ricardo Werneck de Aguiar; Antônio Galloti; Mario Mazei Guimarães; and many others. I came to know the Integralist leader Plínio Salgado quite well, since I worked in his office, and there was a time when I was quite friendly with him.

In the Integralist organization, I was separated from the Afro-Brazilian movement, and so I maintained two parallel activities. As soon as I witnessed racism within the Integralist movement, I left it for good.

I recall one incident by way of example. Along with Garrido Torres, I was organizing a campaign for the institution of Economics as an autonomous Faculty in the Brazilian university system. The campaign consisted primarily of reports and interviews with personalities in education and economic science, published by the Integralist paper *The Offensive*. As it turned out, the paper would print the written material but infallibly would cut my image out of the photographs where I appeared with the interviewees. This was largely the work of the paper's Portuguese editor, Vitorino, a typical Salazarist Portuguese.[6]

The reactionary aspects of the Integralist movement are clear in retrospect, but those of us who joined at the time did so for very different reasons. It is easy for today's historians, social scientists, and young self-important leftists to degrade and berate those of us who once had ties with Integralism, no matter how explicitly we may criticize its errors or renounce our former association. These people don't understand what the movement meant in its historical context and have no better basis upon which to attack others than the long-buried convictions of the past and their own self-righteousness.

In December 1937, I was arrested with a group of university students. We were leafletting against the Vargas dictatorship and United States imperialism. At this point, I experienced the police brutality of Felinter Müller and Emílio Romano,[7] in whose hands I found myself suffering the same physical, mental, and moral aggressions and torture as other political prisoners. After a short time at the infamous police headquarters on Relação Street, I and five other companions in civic adventure were sent to the prison on Frei Caneca Street. From there, we were taken periodically to the National Security Tribunal,[8] where we were tried and convicted. I was held prisoner in the Frei Caneca penitentiary until April of the following year.

An interesting thing happened in prison. A group of students, all of us ex-Integralists, became friendly with various Communists, ideologically the archenemies of Integralism. Among them Captain Trifino Corrêa, arrested during the 1935 *Intentona* revolt. At first it was a tense, dramatic encounter. But very quickly the atmosphere changed. We became friendly and formed a kind of seminar on Brazilian Studies, where each of us spoke on a chosen topic. I contributed with a piece of research on roads and cattleways as Brazil's first means of communication during the colonial period.

We could often see the "Knight of Hope," Luis Carlos Prestes,[9] sitting in the sun on the patio of the chapel where he was held. I already knew Prestes from an earlier, very impressive occasion. As a reporter for the newspaper *O Povo*, I had covered Captain Prestes' trial by the Supreme Military Tribunal as the leader and main architect of the *Intentona*. It was a terrifying sight when he would show up in the courtroom all covered with blood. Prestes would turn to the officer-judges and, in an energetic and authoritative tone, denounce the guards who had beaten him in such a cowardly way just minutes before.

I met with Prestes other times, much later, at friends' homes or small meetings. I spoke with him enough to be able to testify to the complete absence in him of any positive attitude regarding African-Brazilian people's aspirations. Naturally, in classic Brazilian fashion, he "sympathized with" or could even declare "support" for our movement, but definitely he did not understand the specificity of our struggle.

Afro-Campineiro Congress

After being released from prison, I returned to São Paulo in 1938. For some time I was in hiding there, from police persecution. Although I had left the Integralist ranks, the political police were constantly on my back. They would detain me for a few hours and then let me go. Their goal was a simple one: general harassment. The Integralists came to my aid, arranging for a hiding place in a house in São Paulo's Brooklin neighborhood, if I'm not mistaken. It was during this period that my right ear became badly infected. I couldn't come out of hiding, but the ear was swollen and very painful. With no money for a doctor, I went to my old friend Francisco Luis de Almeida Salles, who took me to an ear, nose, and throat man and solved my ear problem.

Then I went to Campinas, São Paulo State, home of Geraldo Campos, a childhood friend from Franca and companion in the Rio de Janeiro penitentiary. On May 13, anniversary of an abolition that never really happened, we opened the Afro-Campineiro Congress, which we organized with the help of Nelson Omegna, the sociology professor at the Normal School. The Congress was held at the Arts and Sciences Institute of that pretentiously racist city. Omegna also edited a newspaper that published pieces about the Congress and articles we wrote about the Afro-Brazilian situation.

Sharing the work involved in organizing the Congress were Geraldo Campos, Aguinaldo Camargo, Agur Sampaio, João Gualberto, Jerônimo (the typesetter) and me. For one week the various aspects of African-Brazilian people's living conditions were discussed: economic, social, political, and cultural. The most important thing for me was one session in which the Congress organizers swore an oath to return to Africa one day to make our contribution to the liberation struggle of the Black Continent, our ancestral home. Much later, I tried modestly to do my part. From the Sixth Pan-African Congress in Dar-es-Salaam, Tanzania, to Ile-Ife, Lagos, Accra, Dakar, Bissau, and Luanda, I made the effort to participate in African world affairs.[10] Perhaps the crowning moment of this Pan-African experience was when I went to Windhoek in March 1990 for the independence celebrations of Namibia, Africa's newest nation.

After the Afro-Campineiro Congress, I came back to Rio de Janeiro and finished my degree in economics at Rio de Janeiro University. The next year, 1939, I lived again in São Paulo, where I went to work for some time as a bank accountant and manager. In this job, I travelled to the rural areas of São Paulo State, serving at local branches in Garça and Vera Cruz, until that world of business deals among coffee and cotton barons suffocated me, and suddenly I astonished colleagues and superiors by resigning, abandoning bank books and accounts to breathe once more the breeze of Rio de Janeiro's beaches.

Back in Rio, I joined in the creation of the Holy Orchid Brotherhood and embarked on a series of travels and adventures with the group. My next major activity in Brazil would be to create the Black Experimental Theater (TEN) in 1944. This is one of Brazil's most well-known black movements, essentially because it was the first to join antiracist civil and human rights demands with concern for the recovery and promotion of African cultural values and identity as a tool for building Afro-Brazilian consciousness.

Origins and Antecedents of the Black Experimental Theater

I was already an adult, but I knew very little about the theater. I had enjoyed it ever since childhood, in Franca, when the theatrical effect of the religious processions I earlier described so caught my imagination. I also used to watch the puppet theater and always had a hidden desire to participate in the New Year's shows produced by the grade school I attended. Yet I was never chosen to do so, because of my color, of course. But they never had the honesty to say why.

I used to go to the circus, where there was generally a "pantomime," meaning a play, to close the show's second act. Inspired by the circus, I used to get together all the kids in the neighborhood in my back yard and produce shows. We all danced, sang, and clowned around. There was no assignment of roles. Everyone did a little of everything.

To me, as a child, theater meant the circus, or else the vague image of my father getting ready to dance in the folklore festival called counterdance. He would go out to the fields to gather leaves of *pita*, a plant with long fleshy leaves. He would mash the leaves thoroughly, squeezing out all their juice, and what was left were very white, fine fibers to make long hair and beards.

When I left the bank in São Paulo State and returned to Rio de Janeiro, around 1940, the Holy Orchid Brotherhood banded together in what was to be a lasting bond of friendship and solidarity. It was a group of Argentine and Brazilian poets: Efraín Tomás Bó, Godofredo Tito Iommi and Juan Raul Young, all three of Argentina; from Brazil, Gerardo Mello Mourão, Napoleão Lopes Filho, and myself. We made a long adventurous trip along the entire Amazon river, to Ucayale at the base of the Andes, sustained not by money (we were destitute) but by creative energy and group spirit.

We went on to Lima, where we saw a production of Eugene O'Neill's play *The Emperor Jones*. The show brought back to me all those childhood theatrical instincts. Most of all, I was indignant to see a blackfaced white actor, Hugo D'Evieri, playing the title role of Brutus Jones. There is a substantial African population in Peru, so obviously this was one more form of anti-African discrimination, just as in Brazil, where Africans entered theaters only in the real-life role of janitor. This was when the idea occurred to me of creating a black theater in Brazil. I committed myself to embark upon the project when I returned home.

For a few years, we lived in Lima, La Paz, and then Buenos Aires. In Lima, aside from rediscovering the theater, an event which proved so important to my future, I also gave lectures on the Brazilian economy at the famous Peruvian university, the Universidad Mayor de San Marcos. Along with the other Orchid brothers, I also had a memorable meeting with Haya de la Torre, the founder and leader of the famous opposition political movement APRA, which was underground at the time. This did not prevent us from being invited by the President of the Republic, Manuel Prado, to lunch at the Palace. The Vice-President, Larco Herrera, gave us very special treatment. We published articles and essays in his newspaper *La Crónica*, which guaranteed our basic living expenses. More than that, Larco Herrera was a patron of the arts. One time, for example, he took us to the first rehearsals for the début of a Peruvian vocal phenomenon, Ima Sumac, whose accompanying orchestra was conducted by the Maestro Vivanco.

At the time of my stay in Bolivia, Godofredo Iommi had returned to Buenos Aires, while Efraín Bó and Napoleão Lopes had decided to go north to Colombia, Central America, and Cuba. Juan Raul Young and I ventured into the interior of Peru, to Arequipa, where the bedbugs in one hotel ran us out. We decided to spend the night on the benches of a park, lulled by the scent of its roses, until the morning came and we could take the boat that crosses Lake Titicaca and then the train to La Paz. The altitude (about twelve thousand feet) left me sick. My face was swollen to the point of deformity, lips cracked, breathing short. La Paz definitely did not mean peace to my health. I had to get out. Before leaving, though, we saw a play at the city's major theater: *Bodas de Sangre*, by Garcia Lorca. The nation's President, an Army Major, was in a balcony right next to us. Nevertheless, the play went on and the performance was excellent.

Buenos Aires was important to the development of my theatrical sense, because there I watched plays with a critical eye, thinking about the theater I would someday create in Brazil. I saw several productions of the Teatro del Pueblo, directed by Hugo Barleta. At the end of these productions there were very fruitful dialogues among director, actors, technicians, and audience. I learned quite a bit from those debates at the Teatro del Pueblo, and also from the activities of another Buenos Aires experimental theater group, La Mascara.

In 1942, I headed back to Brazil. After a few days in Montevideo, where the pangs of homesickness began to hit me after such a long absence, I was excited by the prospect of going home. But my enthusiasm soon suffered a nasty blow. It was as if Brazil wanted to make sure I had no false illusions about where I stood, even in the first moments of homecoming. The welcome I received from my country was to be barred by a smalltown nightclub in Jaguarão, Rio Grande do Sul. I was not to be allowed on the dance floor because of my "low color," I was told.

The Convicts' Theater

When I arrived in São Paulo, another surprise awaited me. For the same racial incident of 1936, which they called disciplinary (the one that triggered my first dishonorable discharge from the Army), I was now sent to prison, having been sentenced *in absentia* at a "trial" held while I was abroad.

The idea of creating the black theater was still hot on my mind, but the São Paulo penitentiary was famous for its impenetrability and severe treatment of prisoners. So I decided to try founding a convicts' theater. This venture was a real test of my ability to deal with a sensitive and delicate situation. I would have to take advantage of the publicity surrounding the name and progressive philosophy of the penitentiary's new director. The São Paulo press and rumors inside the prison were saying that this physician, Flamínio Fávero, would radically change the prison's methods of dealing with convicts. As a Protestant pastor, Dr. Flamínio Fávero would human-ize the institution, known as a steel and concrete fortress. Why not try the theater idea on him?

My first tactic was to enlist the support of a very active and intelligent fellow prisoner, Pericles, number 4349 if I recall correctly. He was convicted of embezzlement. He knew the Penal Code inside out, and legal bureaucracy as well, so he was very useful to a great many convicts whose habeas-corpus petitions and other legal documents he drafted.

Number 4349 liked my theater project. The new director, Flamínio, was unusually accessible and received us for an interview. Very courteous, he listened attentively to our proposal. Right then, he approved of and encouraged the idea, authorizing us to begin work immediately. Number 4349 and I divided up the tasks at hand: I took on the artistic orientation, choice of repertoire, training of actors, and directing of plays. Number 4349 was left with the responsibility of coming up with the materials and means of producing the shows: making sets and costumes, building a stage, obtaining props, and so on.

The Convicts' Theater was an extraordinary and fascinating experience. I urged fellow prisoners to write plays, and we put on two productions: an historical drama about the proclamation of the Brazilian Republic, and a musical comedy satirizing the prison system. For the first time, I found myself directing actors. We also formed a prisoners' band. All our shows were warmly received by the prison audience.

I finally got out of prison, after a long, hard legal fight for habeus corpus, which the Supreme Federal Court finally conceded.

Creation and Success of the Black Experimental Theater

My experiences on return to Brazil had only increased my determination to create a black theater organization. The goal would be not only to produce plays, but also to use the theater as a weapon to fight for the improvement of the quality of life for African Brazilians. I had to take one step at a time, though, and initially I would need support from other intellectuals.

As soon as I was released from prison, I looked up a few writers in São Paulo. My friend Fernando Góes introduced me to Mário de Andrade and others. There wasn't much receptivity to the idea of founding a black theater group. Mário de Andrade, one of Brazil's greatest writers, was a typical product of Brazilian racial ideology: one of those mulattoes who spend their lives passing and would never admit to any African identity. Intellectually, they are strictly European and feel horrified or threatened by any initiative asserting Afro-Brazilian cultural identity. Obviously, I was looking for support in the wrong place.

But there was something in the air in favor of the idea. Around that time, an article was published in one of São Paulo's newspapers, signed by Galeão Coutinho, discussing the need for a black theater in Brazil.

I decided to try creating my black theater in Rio de Janeiro. The first meeting was held at the Café Amarelinho in the Cinelândia area of downtown Rio. Aguinaldo Camargo, Wilson Tibério, Theodorico dos Santos, José Herbel, and Rodrigues Alves all participated. Shortly afterward, a white theater man named Paschoal Carlos Magno, just back from Europe, gave a lecture at the Brazilian Press Association or the Ministry of Education and spoke of the need for a black theater. At this point, we could predict that the same old scenario of cooptation would evolve. So we met again at the old Phoenix Theater to announce publicly that the Black Experimental Theater was already a reality.

Our next meeting was held at the home of Aníbal Machado, a writer from Minas Gerais State whose door was always open. He supported anything worth doing. As we spoke, he picked up the phone and called Carlos Lacerda, then editor of the major daily *O Jornal*.[11] Lacerda encouraged the idea and published news items about the project, but we couldn't get off the ground. Where would our theater function if we ourselves didn't even have a place to live? After a lot of wandering around, looking, asking, we finally obtained access to parts of the National Student Union (UNE) building on Flamengo Beach Street. When business closed down for the day at their restaurant, around 7:00 or 8:00 p.m., the black theater people would get together there. Ironides Rodrigues, a law student, took on the task of giving literacy classes; after all, theater people must know how to read and write. Attorney Aguinaldo Camargo, who was a fantastic person, extremely intelligent, and undoubtedly one of the best actors Brazil has ever produced, gave courses in general culture. Recruitment was quite eclectic. We wanted people without training or experience, since theater experience for blacks usually meant sexually-exploited stereotyping, soap-opera melodrama, or degrading clowning. People like domestic servants, maids, and underemployed workers came down from the *favelas*[12] perched on the hills. Many a white mistress became very upset with us: putting outrageous ideas in her servants' heads!

The Black Experimental Theater (TEN)[13] was founded in October 1944, and in November we were already participating in a play written by Stela Leonardos called *Palmares*, produced by the Brazilian Students' Theater. It wasn't exactly black theater, but it had a scene based on the Republic of Palmares, founded by Africans in the sixteenth century.[14] Aguinaldo Camargo played Zumbi, and another two hundred TEN actors and actresses, among them Natalino Dionísio and Fernando Araújo, played the black Troy's rebellious people. After only one month's existence and very little rehearsal time, we faced a huge responsibility, with so many people on stage and three leading roles. We came out of the test very well.

From the beginning, we were racially open, accepting whites as soon as they accepted the premises of our theater. Some of them wanted to help, but most came with paternalistic attitudes: "You don't have the know-how, this is a technical problem." When I decided to start us off with a production of Eugene O'Neill's *The Emperor Jones*, these expert "advisors" were shocked. "You don't have the stamina for that play! You'd have to have a great actor and an outstanding director. Where will you find them in your group?"

Real support came from Eugene O'Neill himself. From his sickbed in San Francisco, he wrote us a moving letter, encouraging us in what we were doing and waiving royalties.

It was around this time that I first met with President Getúlio Vargas. Paschoal Carlos Magno, a leading personality in the Rio de

Janeiro theater milieu, had arranged a meeting of the President with theater people. It was held at Catete Palace in Rio de Janeiro, then the seat of the national government. As one of the speakers, I gave an account of the creation of the Black Experimental Theater. After this, the dictator-President pulled me over to a corner, and we looked through the windows to the gardens outside. He put his hand on my shoulder as if we were old friends, saying my name intimately: "Abdias, . . . " But I was all on my guard, because I had never found myself chatting with presidents before, much less *this* president, whose politics I had fought from the very beginning. Getúlio displayed the smiling, friendly face of someone who wanted to help.

"Abdias," he said, "all this stuff you're saying isn't very objective yet. You need to put your ideas together better." (I was talking about black people's social advancement, integration, and similar issues.) Getúlio was practical. He phoned the Mayor of the Federal District (city of Rio de Janeiro) and ordered that the Black Experimental Theater's first play be staged at the Municipal Theater. The Municipal meant the cream of reactionary high society. Black people didn't set foot inside it as actors or audience. The only Negroes in there were the janitors, and they came in after the curtain was down and the audience gone.

There was a lot of gossip and intrigue by fancy ladies trying to keep our premiere out of the Municipal Theater. They said they needed it for a show in honor of the Allied victory in World War II. But we stood firm: "It's the President's order!" We wanted to fight Nazi racism at home. So, on that one day, 8 May 1945, we put Eugene O'Neill's masterwork on stage.

Despite the nonbelievers, TEN's first production was a resounding success. It was a historic night for Brazilian theater and for the Afro-Brazilian struggle. We made a good start against difficult odds. It was chaos at the Municipal Theater; we had no rehearsal time, no money for sets. But although they were improvised from cheap cotton, the sets were extraordinarily beautiful and effective, thanks to the gracious collaboration of the famous artist Enrico Bianco. He was there just to help, in solidarity with our idea. Abigail Moura's incredible music made magic in the theater. Other collaborators were Ricardo Werneck de Aguiar, who had translated O'Neill for us; photographer José Medeiros; dancer José Silva (known as the Sorcerer from the Congo); Sadi Cabral in the part of Smithers; and Arinda Serafim as the Old Native Woman. Serafim was an amazing woman, very strong, an illiterate domestic whose dedication and outstanding leadership were essential to the Black Experimental Theater's creation.

I remember one detail of that unforgettable night. In the setting of the scene inside the Emperor's mansion, there was a gong that Aguinaldo Camargo, as the great Emperor Jones, sounded to call his servants. Once, when he hit it, the gong fell, and I had to hold it in place backstage, in an excruciatingly painful position, unable to move until the end of the act. But the gong sounded on cue, and the show was a huge success.

In the same production at the Municipal Theater, before the drama of Brutus Jones began, we staged a reading of three fighting poems by authors from the African Diaspora of the New World: *Always the Same*, by Langston Hughes of the United States; *Menina de Favela (Slum Girl)* by Aladir Custódio of Brazil; and *Negro, Hermano Negro* by Regino Pedroso of Cuba. These texts were read in a dramatic chorale, with four soloists: myself, Aguinaldo Camargo, Ilena Teixeira, and Ruth de Souza. Thus, our very first public presentation had a radically leftist tone, unmistakably supportive of progressive world politics. Predictably, Brazilian "progressives" did not reciprocate that support. Later, under their usual pretexts accusing us of "racism" and "fascism," they did their best to destroy and discredit us.

It was the hope of many to destroy the Black Experimental Theater on our first night. The major daily *O Globo*, for example, had published an editorial attacking us and labelling us a "Palmarist group trying to create an artificial problem in Brazil, using the footlights' glitter." Unfortunately for *O Globo*, the critics applauded us, including its own Henrique Pongetti, who was full of praise, emphasizing the profound seriousness of the initiative.

We raised serious controversies, particularly later, when we produced my play *Sortilege (Black Mystery)* on the stage of the same Municipal Theater. Reactionary journalists like Paulo Francis and Luisa Barreto Leite tried to silence our denunciation of the racism at the roots of Brazilian society, calling us "racists" and "Nazis." But in the end, the attacks as well as the praise were positive. The Black Experimental Theater was born with vigor and vitality, full of the accidents and energies of life. A reading of volumes like *Black Experimental Theater—Testimonies* (Nascimento, 1966), *Blacks in Revolt* (Nascimento, 1982), and *Plays for Blacks and Prologue for Whites* (Nascimento, 1961) illustrates the truth of this statement more completely.

The Afro-Brazilian Democratic Committee

By the end of the war, the Black Experimental Theater was operating in the space loaned by the leftist National Student Union (UNE), in part of the building owned by that organization on Flamengo Beach Street. But we needed a tool for political action. Our first goal was to work for amnesty for the political prisoners of Getúlio Vargas' New State dictatorship. We didn't want to involve the TEN in political work, so in 1945, Rodrigues Alves, Aguinaldo Camargo, and I created the Afro-Brazilian Democratic Committee. An open organization, with Africans and non-Africans participating, the Committee nonetheless explicitly assumed an Afro-Brazilian perspective and identity.

This position, emphasizing African values, caused a lot of irritation among certain groups and individuals, especially after political amnesty was won that same year, 1945. Ideological arguments began to prevail at our meetings. At one point, the Committee's majority belonged to the UNE camp (we did meet at their building). We Africans, who had founded the organization, suffered a frontal attack from the non-African majority. Instead of discussing matters of substance, they started to use my Integralist past as a password of confrontation. One time, they demanded a public confession and retraction from me. I refused. I had nothing to say in any session of forced self-criticism. There was nothing in my past to regret or repent. I was not about to submit to leftist whitemail.

I came through that episode and left it behind me. However, it changed me. It is difficult, painful, to learn the lessons of life not by putting on or taking off the green shirt of Integralism, but by tearing one's own skin. I had suffered racism in the Intregralist ranks and had denounced fascism. I was not going to submit to another fascist maneuver now.

So UNE's bosses threw the three of us out, indicting us as racists. The real error was theirs. They wouldn't admit that Africans have their own specific problems, their own ideas, and their autonomous struggles in Brazilian society. We would have to give in to the correct line determined by people alien to our situation, our history, our needs. It's an abominable and absurd abuse: they use Africans when they need our support or our numbers, but they refuse to recognize or deal with our people's specific needs. This situation went to such extremes that an African like Raimundo Souza Dantas had the nerve to state publicly at one of the Committee's meetings that he had been sent into the organization by the Communist Party with the intention of recruiting us all. In fact, the Committee died out soon after we were expelled, because those who remained had nothing to do with African life in Brazil.

Years later, one of those UNE officers, attorney Paulo Mercadante, had the integrity to confess to me that the UNE people in the Committee had had us thrown out under Communist Party orders that had come from outside the country.

TEN: Headquarters and Censors

In the context of the incidents involving the Afro-Brazilian Democratic Committee, it wasn't long before the Black Experimental Theater was also kicked out of the UNE building. We took up the challenge and rehearsed in open air on the streets, by the pillars of the Ministry of Education and Culture building in downtown Rio. This problem of office and rehearsal space plagued us from the beginning of TEN's theater work to its end in 1968, when I came to the United States. People would ask, "Where is TEN's office?"

I would say, "Right here," and point to the little briefcase I carried under my arm. The home of the Black Experimental Theater was that folder full of papers, photographs, documents, news clippings. It was our archives and our institution.

When I opened that briefcase, TEN's business hours would begin. At the beginning, this would happen at the Café Amarelinho, later at Café Vermelhinho, or else on the eleventh floor of the Brazilian Press Association (ABI). I would give interviews, hold try-outs, appointments, rehearsals, all in this unique "office." During the Kubitschek administration, when Paschoal Carlos Magno was cultural advisor to the President, he almost managed to get us a house. But the School of Choral Music also requested the building, and Education Minister Clóvis Salgado decided in its favor. We tried to get a plot of land in Brasília, which was just being built. But Israel Pinheiro and the owners of the new Federal capital gave out land to anyone and everyone except dispossessed Africans. In the new capital or the old, it was always the same story: Africans' place is out in the morning dew.

At one point a good friend of mine, Thiers Martins Moreira, was director of the government's National Theater Service. He told me that his boss, Education Minister Clemente Mariani, a mulatto banker from Bahia, used to whisper into Thiers' ear: "Don't you support that Negro theater. We should do away with it, is what we should do. You should be trying to figure out a way to do that discreetly." This kind of behavior is typical of the ruling class in Brazil. They show surface sympathy to your face or in public, but they kick your ass from behind. We got around them, though. Forced out of UNE headquarters, we functioned for a while in the attic of the Phoenix Theater, thanks to Bibi Ferreira.[15] It wasn't very accessible, nor did it accomodate the activity and numbers that UNE could, but it was all that was possible.

People who worked with TEN didn't earn any wages. We had a hard time just surviving. Arinda Serafim, among the first of us, as well as Ruth de Souza and Marina Gonçalves, did the hard work of domestic servants. Aguinaldo Camargo was a lawyer. Lea Garcia, Ironides Rodrigues, Claudiano Filho, and Haroldo Costa were students. I myself, and an infinity of others, were workers without jobs, all of us living on the edge. João Elísio, an outstanding personality in this group, was a teacher of ceremonial dance who came from the religious houses of Candomblé in Caxias.

The Black Experimental Theater was constantly in conflict with the Censorship Bureau. In Ricardo Werneck's translation of *The Emperor Jones*, for example, there was a phrase that went something like: "Good God, I'm scared shitless!"[16] Now we couldn't say that. When the censors got through with it, we ended up with, "I am afraid."

My own play, *Sortilégio*, written in 1951, was held up by the censors for several years before it was finally released for production and publication (Nascimento, 1957).

Around 1948, a real problem came up with the play *Black Angel*, by Nelson Rodrigues.[17] Initially, the play was banned for dealing with a subject taboo to official Brazilian Culture. After a long battle waged by the author, in which we participated, *Black Angel* finally was released by the censors. Later, when it was considered for presentation in an official season sponsored by Rio de Janeiro's local government at the Municipal Theater, the authorities required that the African-Brazilian hero, Dr. Ismael, be played by a white actor in blackface. In the end, they did not produce it. Finally, the play was staged by the Maria Della Costa company, directed by Ziembinski.[18] I'll never understand why, but they put a blackfaced white man on in the leading role. It was a tragic incident from the artistic point of view, and simply criminal sociologically speaking, because it symbolized the artistic lynching of Africans, one aspect of the social genocide that African Brazilians have been suffering for almost five hundred years of building a country for others.

There is no basis for blackfacing white actors in a country with a majority black population. To allege a lack of African actors for parts that require artistic skill is a bare-faced lie. And even people who call themselves progressive, like Paulo Francis, commit the same offense against African Brazilians. In his case it occurred when he directed Antonio Callado's play *Pedro Mico*. While proclaiming his "progressive" perspective, he used to (and still does) attack our movement in his newspaper columns. In this respect, he is a typical product of a racist, reactionary, and genocidal society. Not only did they try to smother a movement that had enormous social and artistic significance, although it was numerically small, but they also did everything they could to destroy me personally. This, in short, is my experience with the so-called "vanguard" or "Brazilian left."

The Black Experimental Theater earned many enthusiastic admirers and inspired the formation of several other black theater groups throughout Brazil. With my authorization, for example, Geraldo Campos founded the Black Experimental Theater of São Paulo. In Rio de Janeiro, a group that had worked with us in Joaquim Ribeiro's play *Aruanda* decided to go on its own and founded the Grupo dos Novos, which would later become Brasiliana. The poet Solano Trindade, also inspired by the example of our theater, founded the Brazilian Popular Theater. Mercedes Batista, who initiated her career with us, founded her dance group after acting as TEN's dance director and after a year of study with Katherine Dunham in New York. In Rio de Janeiro and São Paulo, various groups and shows have turned up, bearing witness to this day that Black Experimental Theater's seed is still germinating. Undoubtedly, the fruits will someday come forth in the form of a strong and irresistible National Black Theater.

The Afonso Arinos Law Against Racial Discrimination

After the Afro-Brazilian Democratic Committee closed down, the Black Experimental Theater organized the National Black Convention in São Paulo in 1945, and then held another in Rio de Janeiro in 1946. At the closing session of the São Paulo convention, we released a manifesto which included, on my suggestion, along with other measures, a demand for a national antidiscrimination law. This document received the formal support of practically all the political organizations and parties existing at the time. It was read by Senator Hamilton Nogueira of the National Democratic Union (UDN), to the 1946 Constituent Assembly. Nogueira made an excellent speech presenting our bill.

During that period, when democracy was being restored after the New State dictatorship, I met with several national political leaders. One example was Octávio Mangabeira, the UDN's leader, to whom I was introduced by R. Magalhães Junior. Slick and sly, the old Bahian politician received me with the apparent sympathy characteristic of professional politicians, but soon started throwing me hot potatoes.

"Just think, in Bahia, when so and so, a black man, died, there was one of the biggest funerals I can remember. All the authorities were there, showing him great respect and high honor!"

"Precisely, your Excellency," I said. "What we want is for Africans to enjoy great respect and high honor while they're still alive."

He and his court of political foxes laughed good-naturedly. He tried to change the subject, but I would turn it around on him and get him by the tail: by the wolf's tail, because Mangabeira was one of those escapist Negroes, like so many other Bahians, who do everything they can to pass for whites and deny their African origin. Like these Bahian whites (*brancos da Bahia*), there are also *mineiro*[19] whites, one of whom is Afonso Arinos de Mello Franco.

Luis Carlos Prestes, Secretary General of the recently legalized Communist Party, supported our proposal of an antidiscrimination measure. I received the letter of support, as President of the National Black Convention. Nevertheless, it was no surprise to me when the Communist Party's Honorable Representative from Rio de Janeiro State, Claudino José da Silva, the only Congressman of African descent, voted against it. He justified his position alleging that the proposed law would narrow the broad concept of democracy! Later on he would confess, at a public session of the National Black Convention in Rio, that he had followed the Party line, voting against projects coming out of a black movement.

Like most Africans who rise to higher social positions in Brazil, this Representative did not think or act with any African consciousness. He displayed the skin color, but no commitment to the history, culture, collective problems, or destiny of the enslaved Africans who built the nation and their descendants. On the inside, ideologically, he saw himself as a European Marxist-Leninist. A person so unidentified with his community could hardly be considered an African-Brazilian Congressman in any meaningful sense of the term.

With all this against it, the antidiscrimination bill was not approved. The Members of Congress agreed, at the time, to reconsider the proposal if and when concrete cases of discrimination occurred in the country. As if there were not already far too many.

Soon, however, an incident occurred that was scandalous enough to be noticed. Katherine Dunham, the African-American choreographer from the United States, was denied entrance to a hotel in São Paulo, despite holding advance reservations. Much later, at a convention held in her honor in 1984 in Chicago, Ms. Dunham and her husband, John Pratt, told me and my wife Elisa the following story: Dunham's secretary, who is white, had arrived at the hotel ahead of her and confirmed the reservation. When Dunham herself arrived alone, suddenly no rooms were available. In order to test and confirm the hotel's position, Mr. Pratt, who is also white, approached the desk alone and obtained a room. Thus, with the discriminatory nature of the hotel's position well defined, they made an appointment with a prominent São Paulo attorney. Having described the incident in full, they received the classic response that racial democracy has always given Africans in Brazil. After a self-important pause and a puff on his pipe, demonstrating the patience of someone accustomed to having his time consumed by unfounded claims of injustice, the attorney explained, "I'm afraid there is nothing I can do for you. We have no legislation against racial discrimination in Brazil, because there is no need for it. In our country there is no racial discrimination."

This happened in 1950, and as a result of the incident Congressman Afonso Arinos de Mello Franco (the "*mineiro* white" mentioned earlier) introduced a new antidiscrimination bill in the House. This measure became known as the Afonso Arinos Law. Actually, it should have been called the "Hamilton Nogueira Law" or the "National Black Convention Law," given its true historical antecedents.

This law restricted its definition of race discrimination to certain instances and punished these practices with extremely light penalties, as misdemeanors rather than crimes.

As President of the National Black Convention, I organized a commission, composed of me and other Convention delegates including Sebastião Rodrigues Alves, José Pompílio da Hora, Aguinaldo Camargo, and Isaltino Veiga dos Santos. We were received by General Eurico Gaspar Dutra, who was then candidate for President of the Republic. He had been Minister of War for many years, so he was very familiar with the Army as an institution. The Convention commission went to General Dutra to protest against the military's discriminatory treatment of blacks. Dutra, who would soon become President, listened to us and responded in his characteristic way, without having to argue the subject. He stated that there were "reserve circulars" restricting Africans' entrance and ascension in Army ranks. At our request, he ordered Colonel Figueiredo, his chief of staff, to furnish us with a copy of the "reserve circular." Many were the times we called upon the Colonel, trying to get hold of the said copy, which never did come into our hands.

First National Congress of Brazilian Blacks

We had already organized the National Black Conventions in 1945 and 1946, and then the National Conference of Blacks in 1949. This conference was a preparatory exercise for the First National Congress of Brazilian Blacks. I presided over all these meetings, which were attended by delegates from various states, representing cultural organizations, fraternal and beneficent societies, religious organizations and authorities, and interested individuals from many different walks of life. During the Conference of 1949, Arthur Ramos[20] made a speech that was a pity not to have taped, for he died soon afterwards in Paris, where he was director of UNESCO. At that meeting we voted on the agenda for the First Congress, drafted by Guerreiro Ramos,[21] Edison Carneiro,[22] and myself.

In May 1950, the First National Congress of Brazilian Blacks took place in Rio de Janeiro, organized by the Black Experimental

Theater. It was a slow process, but we would not rest. The Congress was a landmark in Afro-Brazilian history. For the first time, we Africans discussed our concerns publicly, as masters of our own destinies, not only in the form of academic papers or formal oral and written communications, but more importantly in spontaneous improvisation. This spontaneity and self-determination were the accents that marked the radical difference between this First Congress of Brazilian Blacks and the previous Afro-Brazilian Congresses that had been held in the thirties in Recife and Bahia (see Larkin Nascimento, 1980:20-22). In these, it was the pomp and circumstance of white scholars and scientists that prevailed. They organized and directed everything, while African Brazilians were displayed merely as "ethnographic material," the object of research.

Africans were in charge of the First Congress of Brazilian Blacks, and at various sessions we aggressively confronted the subtle forms of paternalism emanating from "scientists" and other whitenesses. In the latter group we include, among others, the sociologists L.A. da Costa Pinto, Edison Carneiro, and Darcy Ribeiro.[23] Positive contributions of white allies were made by Roger Bastide and Hamilton Nogueira. Ironides Rodrigues, Sebastião Rodrigues Alves, Arinda Serafim, Aguinaldo Camargo, and Ruth de Souza were among the outstanding African-Brazilian participants.

Edison Carneiro was a mistake among us. I had always maintained a friendship with him, paralleled by strong divergence of views on Afro-Brazilian affairs. In Edison's mind, black people's problems were reduced to a mere aspect of class struggle (Carneiro, 1964). To me, this was insufficient. The racial contradiction in Brazilian society looms as the first obstacle, the immediate reality in the daily life of African-Brazilian people. White supremacism keeps them out of the very mainstream society where class contradictions exist.

TEN's Newspaper Quilombo

In 1949 and 1950, we published a newspaper called *Quilombo: Black Life, Problems and Aspirations*.[24] It produced about ten issues. Supposedly it was a monthly, but with neither money nor advertisements, living on loans, it didn't have the means to establish a regular life. Guerreiro Ramos was one person who got into trouble financially supporting the paper. But *Quilombo* had its purpose. We published essays like those by Guerreiro Ramos on sociodrama and psychodrama, Sartre's famous piece entitled *Black Orpheus*, poetry by Carlos Drummond de Andrade, a speech given by Katherine Dunham about the state of disinherited peoples' religious worship, and many other types of articles. There even appeared a chapter of my unpublished novel, *Zé Capetinha*, the final version of which was never finished. We printed little announcements of birthdays, weddings, and anniversaries. We also published biographical sketches of people like Solano Trindade, Edison Carneiro, Guerreiro Ramos, and others.

Quilombo maintained a high level of quality illustrations (photos and drawings), which gave it a fine graphic presentation. It was created with love and care and printed in the offices of the daily *Jornal do Brasil.* We managed to balance readings for intellectuals with material for the general public.

Basically, the goal of *Quilombo*, as its title implies, was to take up the African freedom struggle begun in Brazilian territory by the heroes of Palmares and waged by Chico-Rei, Luiz Gama, José do Patrocínio, Karucango, Luíza Mahin, the martyrs of the *Malê* insurrections and the Tailor's revolt, and so many others in the African history of resistance in Brazil.

Political Endeavors

It had always been painful for me to observe the absence of Africans in my country's politics. This had been particularly so when I read Joaquim Nabuco's statement that Africans alone had built the nation. The image I retained from childhood memories was of my uncle Laureano do Valle working in all the elections as a votehunter for the Republicans or the Democrats (those were the parties at the time), and my father voting by *cabresto*,[25] obeying the local political chiefs' determinations. When Franca sent a Federal Representative to Rio de Janeiro, then the nation's capital, it elected Antonio Pereira Lima, the racist founder of São Paulo's Civil Guard, which barred Africans.

I tried to change black people's political image. I ran for office several times, for the Federal District City Council, for State and Federal Representative. I ran on different party tickets but always lost. One time it was because the Social Labor Party wanted an "ideological voucher," an official appraisal of one's politics taken from police files. It was an arbitrary demand. I went to court and got a "security mandate," a guarantee of constitutional rights, and argued the unconstitutionality of their position. But the court dragged its feet, didn't rule on my petition, and the deadline for candidates' registration went by. So I couldn't run on that ticket.

Another time, we (Rodrigues Alves was my main accomplice) created a Black Affairs Department in the Brazilian Labor Party (PTB) of Guanabara State.[26] This development made a lot of waves, and African Brazilians nominated me to be their candidate on the PTB's slate for Representative. That was an indication of the Black Affairs Department's activity. Everything seemed to be going well. Then all of a sudden something snagged. I don't really know where. Perhaps it was in the Party's regional steering committee. All I know is they cut me out of the ticket. Why? They cited my Integralist past. As if in that sack of cats that was the PTB there had ever been any ideological coherence.

Another time, I tried the more conservative Social Democratic Party (PSD). As far as I was concerned, all these parties were the same in their essential fraud against black people. At the last minute, this one torpedoed me, too. I was running for the City Council. Unexpectedly, Marshall Mendes de Morais, President of Guanabara's PSD, moved me to the slate for Federal Representative, replacing me with his driver, a black man called White Rose. I hardly had a chance at winning a seat on the Council. How could I compete for a federal post? It was all a hoax to bleed out black votes. I didn't contest that election either.

I also had some relations with the Brazilian Socialist Party, and my last attempt before exile was again in the PTB, where I had tenuous ties with Leonel Brizola. In 1962, I ran for the State Assembly and campaigned extensively in the *favelas* in the South and North zones of Rio de Janeiro. I had the support and permanent collaboration of an extraordinary African-Brazilian woman, Marietta Campos, who later would marry the French-Guyanese poet Léon Damas, one of the founders of the Negritude poetic movement, along with Aimé Césaire and Leopold Senghor. My slogan in that campaign was based on the Brazilian phrase *to vote white*, meaning a blank ballot: "Don't vote white, vote Black: Abdias Nascimento." This time I came close to a thousand votes.

Returning from exile in 1981, I worked closely with Leonel Brizola in the consolidation of the Democratic Labor Party (PDT), legitimate successor of the predictatorship Brazilian Labor Party (PTB). As the PDT's national Vice-President, I ran for the National Congress in the 1982 elections, taking office in 1983 as the first African-Brazilian Representative in Brazilian history dedicating his political activity to Afro-Brazilian concerns. In 1990, the PDT nominated me to the Senatorial race, and I was elected Deputy to Senator Darcy Ribeiro. Governor Brizola, on taking office in 1991, created a State Secretariat for the Defense and Promotion of Black Peoples, appointing me as Secretary.[27]

Aesthetics, Christ, and the Black Arts Museum

Before 1950, the TEN had been organizing beauty contests among African-Brazilian women. We were sensitive to these matters, questions of aesthetics. Vaudeville-style theater had always included black and mulatto women as hipwigglers, but when it came time to talk about "Brazilian aesthetics," the judges always displayed Hellenistic tastes. They imported their concepts of beauty from Europe: pure cultural alienation. There were also leftist critics who confused the beauty contests for an opportunity to exploit black women sexually. These people could never understand that the point of these contests was to put a final end to the Brazilian tradition, which had prevailed since colonial times, of looking at African and mulatto women as mere objects of erotic pleasure.

Another controversial project was the visual arts contest we held in 1955 on the theme of the Black Christ. Guerreiro Ramos invented this idea, and I took it up with enthusiasm. A discussion of cultural symbols in their most profound dimension, the religious one, seemed opportune and valid to me. One more attempt at integration, this project was sponsored by such respectable figures as the Cardinal of Rio de Janeiro, Bishop Jaime Câmara, and my friend Bishop Helder Câmara. The Catholic Church has always been very sly with this strategy of incorporating elements of other people's cultures into its own domain.

More than a hundred artists, African and non-African, showed their works. We set up an exhibit at the Ministry of Education building, and the event really messed with Christ's image in Brazil. In a closer approximation to historical truth than his traditional depiction as a blue-eyed Aryan, Jesus began to be portrayed with the dignified appearance of African color and features. Djanira won the contest, with her painting *Christ on the Whipping Post*, portraying Christ as an enslaved African.

One result of this event was the idea of founding a Black Arts Museum, which would come to fruition only later, in May 1968. Its opening was heralded by a course in African art that we held in the auditorium of the National Fine Arts Museum in Rio de Janeiro. This was a very gratifying experience. The auditorium had a capacity of two hundred people and was continually overcrowded with interested students. Several speakers made presentations, among them R. Teixeira Leite, Flexa Ribeiro, Raimundo Souza Dantas, Grande Otelo, Edison Carneiro, Nelson Pereira dos Santos, Adonias Filho, Florestan Fernandes, Alceu Amoroso Lima or Tristão de Athayde, and Thiers Martins Moreira. While it was very well-attended, perhaps it was a bit too eclectic. But I was always on the alert, putting my two cents in where it was needed, to maintain the course's character and identity.

Right after that, with my collaboration, the daily *Morning Mail* put out a series of interviews about the importance of the Black Arts Museum. Its first exhibition of collected works opened on 13 May 1968, at Rio de Janeiro's Image and Sound Museum. The exhibition space was conceded by the Museum's director, Ricardo Cravo Alvim.

Self-Criticism

The Black Arts Museum suffered from a certain ambiguity. It was for, by, and about Africans, but it also had works by non-Africans. The very nature of a museum is static. It is known and visited by the middle class and upwards, appreciated by the "initiates," the "cultured ones." If it were really to fulfill its purpose, our museum would have to be mobile, climb the hills to the *favelas*, visit the rural areas. The artwork needed to be discussed, widely known, enriched with different experiences. The idea was to recognize and respect African art with the African-Brazilian people in mind. We didn't have the financial or material means for this type of aesthetic and cultural revolution.

Nevertheless, I do have reasons for self-criticism. The integrationist perspective, which (for better or worse) had been my orientation since the thirties, essentially implied a certain distance from our people. The Black Experimental Theater, for instance, did put on a few shows in the *subúrbios*,[28] and once in a house of *macumba*, the Afro-Brazilian religion widely practiced in Rio de Janeiro. Those were the most enjoyable moments, with that immediate, spontaneous response. The audience understood everything, participated as an integral part of the show. But they were exceptions. Usually, we played to the traditional theater audience, meaning the white upper classes. It was a mistake to insist on addressing the intellectual milieu. There was the error of wanting to "civilize" oneself, the futile hope of being "understood" by the society's elites. "Integration" meant African culture's effort to be recognized by "Brazilian" society, as if Brazilian society were other than African. Yet the white ruling classes control the means of recognition and prestige. So we circulated in surroundings that were not exactly our own, using the language and the contacts of people who not only exploit Africans economically, but ignore and despise our culture.

The Excluded Ones

Our movement's ambiguous situation in those days, which put us somewhere between the people's aspirations and those of the elite, was most evident on festive occasions. During Carnaval, sometime during the Dutra presidency,[29] Ruth de Souza, Claudiano Filho, and I had invitations to the dance at the Hotel Gloria. It was a fancy, aristocratic ball, but we had invitations, so why not go and have some fun? There we were at the door, invitation in hand, a special invitation at that, and they wouldn't let us in. They said it was because of the banner we were carrying. "So we'll leave the banner outside!"

Our night out turned into a problem. The hotel people kept saying they didn't want us in there, and we kept fighting and arguing. It was absurd! Time went by, and we were still outside the door, making noise. White friends arrived, spoke to us, and left us behind. Everyone could party except us, with our badge of color. One went by and then another: Paschoal Carlos Magno; Michel Simon, that French writer who was very friendly with us; the head of the National Theater Service. Everyone walked in and left us behind.

The next day, I denounced the incident in an open letter to the Chief of Police, which was published in the *Daily News*. Dr. Santana, an African-Brazilian physician from São Paulo, wrote a letter to President Eurico Dutra. In the end, the police officer in service at the Gloria, Agnaldo Amado (who wasn't all that white himself), was deemed the responsible party and was transferred to another precinct. They explained that the punishment was not severe because "he was just following orders."

In another episode, Irene Diggs, an African-American anthropologist from the United States, was barred at the Hotel Serrador in downtown Rio de Janeiro. She was on a cultural mission for the Department of State and had a suite reserved by the American Embassy. But when the hotel employees saw that Negro woman arriving at the desk, they said they had no room. She called a press conference, gave interviews, and the press raised hell. Typically the hotel denied that it had discriminated against Diggs on racial grounds. So journalist R. Magalhães Jr. challenged the hotel to host an African-Brazilian couple for a weekend. I was asked to be the guinea pig, and I said, "I'm not prejudiced. One repentant discriminator is worth a hundred racists in jail."

So, one fine day, there I went with my wife Maria de Lourdes Valle, to check out luxury life at the Serrador. I'm not sure if they thought Negroes were pompous and ostentatious or what, but they received us with the utmost ceremonial courtesy. It was a game with marked cards. I checked in early. At lunchtime, I came down to the Night and Day, which at the time was the most fashionable place for high finance executives and the political cream of Rio de Janeiro. I sat down at a table and along came the maitre d'hôtel, by the name of Freixinhas, as I recall.

Freixinhas: "You can't sit here."

Me: "Why not?"

Freixinhas: "This restaurant is exclusively reserved for the hotel guests."

Me: "Yes? Then it's reserved for me."

Freixinhas: "You are a guest at this hotel? What is your room number?"

Me: "716."

Freixinhas: "Where's the key?"

Me: "Right here."

Freixinhas made a face of utter horror and disappeared down the corridors to try to get to the bottom of this anomaly. He came back transformed, acting like a lady. I could hardly breathe without the waiters running in my direction asking what I wanted. So I thought, "I've got to invent another game, because this one's over." I invited all my friends, African and non-African, to a reception in the hotel's salon. This turned out to be uproar personified. Africans who had never set foot in a hotel started climbing up and down the stairs, using the social elevators, talking loudly. It was scandalous! The management got scared and prohibited my guests from travelling to other parts of the hotel. They could only frequent the salon. This created problems, because among my guests were white politicians and journalists. I have pictures of this scene: City Councilman Tito Lívio; composer Ari Barroso; Carlos Lacerda, who would later be governor of Guanabara state; the artist Santa Rosa, maestro Abigail Moura; actor and attorney Aguinaldo Camargo. Everyone was drinking and laughing. There were speeches, applause, a veritable antiracist rally. The hotel owners didn't know what to do. They must have thought, "This goes to show, we really can't have Negroes in here!"

The Media, the Left, and Africans

The news media are always ready to publish stupid, meaningless stuff about Africans, but they cut out anything serious. Newspapers, magazines, radio, and television may put out a piece of news here or there, but discriminatory and prejudiced attitudes always prevail. At one point, a paper called *The Sun* was founded in Rio de Janeiro, and they asked me to write a column. By the third article they had vetoed me. I was exposing racism in Itamaraty, the Foreign Ministry. It turned out that one of the paper's owners worked in the diplomatic service. The sun was not about to rise for me. Another time, African journalist João Conceição began to publish a column in the *Evening Daily*, also a Rio de Janeiro newspaper. He didn't get through two weeks in the paper; they fired him and cancelled his column as soon as he tried to deal seriously with African concerns.

A similar incident happened at Tupi TV. When I put on *The Emperor Jones* for the Rio de Janeiro television audience, there were so many phone calls protesting against it that the station decided to suspend broadcast of the other plays that had been programmed for the Black Experimental Theater cast. Another time, in a television series, African actor Jorge Coutinho was playing the part of a servant who falls in love with the master's white daughter. They were to be married. There was another avalanche of protest letters and phone calls attacking the character and the station. They had to kill the character rather than consummate this marriage, which was so outrageous to Brazilian racial democracy.

In contrast, explicitly or subtly anti-African material is published off-handedly. Sometimes it's not so subtle. This item appeared in Zózimo's social column in the daily *Jornal do Brasil*, 6 April 1975:

> Monday was decorator Júlio Sena's turn to receive for a black tie dinner, in the annual festival of honor celebrating Dona Maria Cecília Fontes' birthday.
>
> The Largo da Mãe do Bispo [a colonial square in Rio de Janeiro] was decorated with eighteenth century motifs and served by Negro waiters, sometimes playing the role of slaves. The litter in which the boldest guests were carried into the inner rooms had been dug up by the host and used abundantly for entertaining the select few who were present.

Leftist cultural and intellectual circles were not much different. During the struggles of the early sixties,[30] for instance, I worked with the Centers for Popular Culture (CPC) and in the film *Five Times Slum*. African Brazilians were always treated as outsiders. At best, we were the left's "folklore." At worst, we were "divisionists" potentially responsible for the pulverization of working class unity. Basically, the left identified with European ideology, and its "vanguards" belonged to the country's so-called elite. Bossa Nova, for example, used Afro-Brazilian themes as part of its vanguard posture. But when the poet Vinicius de Moraes, leader and symbol of the Bossa Nova cultural trend, decided to write a play developing those themes, he remained faithful to his European aesthetic ideals. Resorting to Greek mythology, his symbol of prestige, Vinicius couched his Afro-Brazilian cultural motifs in the language and contexts of Greco-Roman tradition, creating a *Black Orpheus*.

Blackfaced white actors, Black Christ, Black Orpheus: in the last analysis, they all conspire in the historical rape of my people. African religious culture is rich and alive in our religious communities all over Brazil. We have no need to invoke Greece or the Bible in order to raise it to the status of mythology. On the other hand, Greece and Europe owe to Africa a great deal of what they call "Western Civilization."

For all these reasons, I changed my position. Today, I am

convinced that courting white people to get recognition is wasted time, aside from being the wrong perspective. We must deal with our own needs, without waiting for white people. We can address them afterwards, but first we must define and assert ourselves as Africans. Otherwise we end up being manipulated. This was the case with the Communist Party, among others. They think that to make a statement of African tradition and lifestyle is divisionist. But they're always there, trying to influence our movement and divert it to their ideological line. If they think the Afro-Brazilian question is nonsense, why put their noses in our affairs? The only reason is to try to manipulate us.[31]

Based on my personal experiences and those of my people, it seemed inevitable that Afro-Brazilian mass movements would abandon the integrationist position for one of autonomy and independence. This began to happen in the 1970s, with a new proliferation of Afro-Brazilian organizations. In Rio de Janeiro, we can cite as only three of many examples the Institute for Research on Black Culture (IPCN), student groups linked to the Center for Afro-Asian Studies (CEAA), and the Brasil-Africa Studies Center (CEBA) of São Gonçalo. In São Paulo, many similar groups appeared.

In 1978 in São Paulo's capital city, a young African-Brazilian worker named Robson Silveira da Luz was tortured to death by the São Paulo police, and at the same time the Tietê Rowing Club in that city barred four African-Brazilian athletes from membership. On 7 July 1978, Afro-Brazilian groups held a large protest rally, something very exceptional in that repressive context, on the steps of São Paulo's Municipal Theater.

Back in Brazil for the first time since my exile in 1968, I was among the two thousand people who came out for the demonstration, to denounce the police brutality that has always harassed African-Brazilian communities. In an intensely emotional moment, we read in unison an open letter denouncing racism and committing ourselves to resuming the fight for African people's freedom and physical and spiritual integrity.

In the aftermath of this incident, we founded the United Black

Movement Against Racism and Racial Discrimination (MNU). At the time, it seemed to have considerable potential as a national movement. I was elected to represent the organization outside Brazil and helped to consolidate it inside the country in 1978 and 1979, travelling to different cities and states for that purpose. Rather than preaching integration, the MNU asserted the African-Brazilian majority's right to take part in the country's destiny without renouncing our African cultural and national identity. In the course of the 1970s and 1980s, countless other Afro-Brazilian organizations were created with much the same general position.

For a number of reasons, including some of its militants' identification with ideological tendencies of European origin, and their consequent attempt to use the organization to serve the interests of certain political parties, the MNU did not grow significantly, and today it exists actively in only a few cities.[32]

The new generation of black organizations continued a practice traditional to Afro-Brazilian movements: the participation of women in its ranks and leadership, and discussion of their specific concerns. Among the most outstanding early examples of this participation were Professors Beatriz Nascimento, Lélia Gonzalez, and Helena Theodoro, who continued in the tradition of Arinda Serafim, Marina Gonçalves, and Guiomar Ferreira de Mattos of the Black Experimental Theater, Luiza Mahin of the *Malê* insurrections in nineteenth century Bahia, and Aqualtune of Palmares.

Dictatorship, Persecution and Exile

Things became very difficult after the United States-sponsored military coup of 1964, but as I see it the worst change was in 1968, when the regime became more hardline. Until then, people were able to do some things, at least in the cultural arena. I founded the Black Arts Museum in May 1968.

A group of African Brazilians also organized a round table discussion, sponsored by the journal *Brazilian Notebooks*, on the topic "80 Years of Abolition." The São Paulo magazine *Reality* put out an issue on racism, but under hidden pressures the result was very poor.

The most serious articles, by Florestan Fernandes and Fernando Góes, were cut by the Censorship Bureau. We had better luck with the journal *Brazilian Civilization*, which put out a special issue on theater, including an article I contributed on black theater (Nascimento, 1968).

Along with my Afro-Brazilian militancy, I had also been active in the Superior Institute for Brazilian Studies, ISEB, a progressive think tank founded during the Kubitschek and Goulart administrations. After the military coup, ISEB was extinguished and its members persecuted. As a result of both activities, I was named in several Military Police Investigations (IPMs). In 1968, invited on a grant from the Fairfield Foundation on African Affairs, I went to visit New York for two months. My visit coincided with the hardline turn in the military regime, and I realized that going back to Brazil was no longer an intelligent option.

Exile in the United States

As I said before, I was always an exile in my own country. If I have a homeland, it is Africa. Brazilian society tried to refuse me my African roots, to cut them off, pull them up by force. I had to put out roots from the top down, by conscious effort, sending them out in the air like some plants do. Coming to the United States did not create my exile. Indeed, here I was able to express myself much more effectively, continuing the work I had been doing in other contexts.

One big difference is that here in the United States, the merit of my work was recognized. This is something I cannot deny. I was fifty-four when I left Brazil, yet I had always been an outsider there. For example, the only time I was invited to speak at a Brazilian university was on 13 May 1968, at the 11 August Academic Center, at the University of São Paulo Law School. The Law School's director refused to allow the event to be held in the main hall, forcing us into clandestinity from the start. So I spoke on the patio, threatened by the arrival of professors who would put a stop to this nonsense and get rid of this band of Negroes. My topic was "Negritude." On the basis of this incident, a group of African students created an organization at the Law School, which probably didn't last long.

When I arrived in the States at the end of 1968, I had just begun to do artwork in my little Copacabana apartment. A Columbia University department bought one of my paintings for a thousand dollars. This was a real pleasure. Not so much for the money itself, but for the recognition.

Real recognition came from New York City's African-American community. My first exhibit was held at a small gallery in Harlem. Amiri Baraka, whom I had met with at Spirit House in Newark (accompanied by African-American social scientist Angela Gilliam), agreed to write a preface for the catalogue. He went to see my work at the house of the Bagley family, who had generously offered me a place to stay in Manhattan. The preface never came through, but the support and solidarity of my African brothers and sisters in the United States was always there. The writer John O. Killens was the first to buy a canvas of mine, the face of a *filha de santo*[33] with rivers of ceremonial blood.

When my second exhibit was being held at the Crypt Gallery in Columbia University, there was a demonstration by African-American students, with widespread damage to university property, including the gallery. To my surprise, when I went in the next day, amidst the chaos and rubble of what had once been the gallery's furniture and other objects, my paintings were still in place, intact! The only difference was that, on some of the artworks which expressed my people's oppressive living conditions, the students had put up signs saying "Justice!" It was as if the exhibit was part of the protest demonstration.

During this time, my relationship with the African community in the United States grew and broadened. I made several visits to the New Lafayette Theater and had meetings with dramatist Ed Bullins and with the poet Marvin X. At the New Lafayette I saw some plays that were unforgettable, partly due to the dynamic nature of the sets and the audience. They were unconventional sets that gave the impression of natural disorder, but actually they obeyed a criterion of arrangement and use of space that made for extraordinarily flexible and beautiful staging.

Barbara Ann Teer spoke to me passionately and intelligently of her project of building a National Black Theater. An energetic woman with revolutionary impulse, she left a very deep impression in my spirit. But of all the visits and meetings I had, one stands out from the others: the visit I made to the Black Panthers' headquarters in Oakland, California. Since Chairman Huey P. Newton was in prison, a meeting was set up with Panther leader Bobby Seale. When I got there, in the company of an aging white woman, a writer, I was afraid there would be tension. But Bobby Seale was very gracious. When he found out about my political exile, he manifested solidarity and offered his help and support. Working Pan-African solidarity strengthened my confidence in the future of the Africans who were rising up all over this part of the world. When I visited Harvard University, this same sentiment led me to join the vigil around the presidential building, which had been taken over by African students protesting against the university's investments in South Africa. But the Black Panthers' military apparatus demonstrated a dignity and consciousness that would be impressive even to the least impressionable of individuals.

Soon after this, the Yale School of Drama invited me to be Visiting Lecturer. This illustrates what I was saying about recognition of my work. No school of theater in Brazil had ever taken notice of me, almost certainly never would, and if one did, it would avoid me like the plague. At Yale, I encountered a lone African-American student, Pamela Jones.

In 1970, through Professor Karl Scheibe, the Center for the Humanities at Wesleyan University, Middletown, Connecticut, invited me for a year as Visiting Fellow. Next came the State University of New York at Buffalo, which offered me a position as Associate Professor at the Puerto Rican Studies and Research Center, created and directed by a magnetic and dynamic personality called Francisco Pabón. In two years I was promoted to Full Professor with tenure, teaching African Culture in the New World and African experience in South and Central America.

I was invited constantly to speak, exhibit, participate in panels, seminars, and conferences. Thus, I have spoken to the audiences of the Studio Museum in Harlem; Yale, Harvard, Howard, Princeton, and Tulane Universities; U.C.L.A. and the Inner City Cultural Center of Los Angeles; the Center for Positive Thought, the Black Dance Workshop, the Museum of African and African-American Arts and Antiquities, and the Langston Hughes Center in Buffalo; the All-African People's Revolutionary Party Conferences in Washington, D.C. on African Liberation Day; and many other events and places, always denouncing Brazilian racism against more than seventy million Africans who are oppressed in my country, unable to speak and express their values effectively.

Of course, I have suffered discrimination in the United States. I went to the Human Rights Commission in New York City with a case against a woman who wouldn't rent me an apartment because of my color. Of course, white United States Americans participate in the oppression of Africans and other peoples the world over. But here in the United States, the protest movement reached a level that has forced the ruling classes to respect or fear the African community. Also, the political regime sustaining democratic rights and freedom provides cracks in the system, opportunities to work constructively for the African cause. These opportunities were won at the cost of much blood and many African lives. In Brazil, however, African blood has been spilled for centuries with virtually no result. This is the difference.

By way of illustration, it is useful to point out that Africans have been in Brazil since 1500 or very shortly thereafter, while in the United States they arrived quite a bit later. Slavery in Brazil was abolished in 1888, almost three decades after abolition in the United States. Africans constituted two thirds or more of the population in colonial Brazil, and their descendants are still a majority today. Yet, despite the violent oppression suffered by Africans in the United States, here they fought and won, at great cost, victories as yet unattained by Africans in Brazil.

On the level of power and decision-making in the country's national institutions, the African-American community in the United

States is far more advanced. One example I witnessed personally is that of the Congressional Black Caucus, which twice invited me to speak on the situation of Africans in my country. The first opportunity was in 1980, at the invitation of Representative Walter Fauntroy of Washington D.C. and the National Alliance of Postal and Federal Employees. I was honored to be introduced to the audience by former Attorney General Ramsey Clark, whose generous recognition of my work in the cause of justice for African Brazilians was particularly gratifying. In the first report ever heard on the subject by those dozens of Black Caucus members, I summed up briefly the historical and contemporary situation of Africans in Brazil, a people who are daily humiliated, destitute, and oppressed.

The second time I addressed the Caucus was in 1983. At that time I represented Rio de Janeiro State and the Democratic Labor Party (PDT) as the first African member of the Brazilian National Congress dedicating his political work to the Afro-Brazilian cause. At the initiative of Representative Mervin Dymally, through the competent offices of the late Professor Archie Singham, I went to Washington in September 1985 to participate in the Black Caucus Legislative Weekend conference on "International Dimensions: the Reality of an Interdependent World."

The United States Congress boasts an organization like the Black Caucus, made up of African-American legislators who represent a minority population of about fifteen percent. In Brazil, by contrast, Africans are a majority with virtually no Congressional representation at all. This fact, in itself, is a poignant statement of the nature of Brazilian race relations.

The crowning gratification of my experience in the United States is the joy that came to me in the person of my wife, companion, and collaborator Elisa Larkin Nascimento.

Art and the Orishas

A sensational thing happened to me in the United States. Blocked by the English language, I found that I had inside me a different form of communication: I could paint, and in artwork I would be able to say things no words could convey. The sensation I experience in painting is hard to describe. The most appropriate way is to say that the Orishas come into me, and I paint my canvases in communion with them. I do not do any conventional painting, or ceremonial painting *per se*. Nor is it a question of arbitrary invention, and certainly not of monotonously repetitious "folklore," since I am opposed to what Eurocentric critics label "primitive" or "naïve" art.

My art is born in the ceremonial drawings and songs of Candomblé. They are its basis, its foundation. My painting expresses a profound experience of *living* Afro-Brazilian culture. I apprehend certain visions, fantasies, revelations contained in Candomblé symbols.

Religions of European origin generally worship static, inaccessible, distant, essentially dead gods. African religion is different. The Orishas (deities) come out of their cosmic habitats and "mount" a human medium's body. They dance, eat, drink, make love. Candomblé is pure vitality, never an "opiate of the proletariat." Its gods are dynamic, they embody a deep sense of freedom. They are historical divinities, involved in the dynamics of African liberation.

In my painting, I try to distinguish between those symbols and myths that exist only as tradition and those that fulfill the needs of our time and can open up perspectives for the future. I don't advocate simply that we recall our past. My Orishas are not immobilized in time or space. They are powers of the present. They emerge in daily life and in secular matters. My Orishas receive the names of living people and take on the defense of the heroes and martyrs still offered by the African people as sacrifices to the search for freedom.

To mention Ogun is to evoke the idea-force opposing African peoples' submission anywhere in the world. Deity of iron and of war, and by extension of all metals and technology, Ogun embodies the principle of armed vengeance and breaks through the cosmic barriers of this world and beyond. Ossaim, the leaf-deity, presides over the reign of nature. She manages not only the herbs, plants and roots used by traditional African pharmacology and medicine, but also the raw materials that nourish developed nations' economies and hopefully someday our own. Yemanjá, sea goddess and mother of all the other Orishas, presides over the species' fertility and procreation. She combats the birth control imposed upon our people by anti-African interests. She is also the mistress of droughts and fishing seasons. Shango, god of fire, storms, lightning, and justice, keeps watch over human rights and freedom. His symbol, the double-headed axe, represents the deity's warlike disposition in carrying out his ritual obligations. Oshun is the love and creativity that should inspire life in all its moments. Goddess of love and patroness of the arts, she is also my mother and guide. Ora-iê-iê-ô! Ifá reveals the past, present, and future; he furnishes us with knowledge of history, enables us to make plans and projects. Omolu, the physician, healer of the poor, moves between life and death. Eshu, whom the Christians mistakenly identify with the devil, is master of the crossroads of life, the paths of the universe. An ambivalent god, he symbolizes the contradictions and dynamics inherent in human existence, propelling life's perpetual movement. Eshu is the most polemical and controversial Orisha, since he incorporates many levels of ceremonial roles, and many different powers. He is the polymorphous master of *axé* (ah-*sheh*), the spiritual life-force, the mystical power of the Orishas.

I should make it clear that my artistic "revelations" do not include authentic mystic trance. I am not an initiate, and I have never entered trance, except on stage, when I played the leading role in Joaquim Ribeiro's *Aruanda*. I was never more than an apprentice of Candomblé. I was very close to *Iyalorixá*[34] Mãe Senhora, head of the Ilé Axé Opô Afonjá community, one of the oldest Candomblé houses in Bahia. I went there to learn, but I was not initiated. Several religious leaders urged me to go through the process of initiation, but I knew the weight of the initiate's responsibility. It demands total dedication, submission to discipline, hierarchy. The mystic life of Candomblé is not as rigid as that of other religions, but everything is carefully regulated by ceremonial responsibility. I didn't have the temperament or disposition to take on that kind of regimen. I decided I could do more service in lay life, which was also the advice Mãe Senhora gave me.

In the Rio de Janeiro suburbs and metropolitan area, which resembles the African townships surrounding Johannesburg, I became quite involved with a number of *terreiros*, communities or houses of Afro-Brazilian worship, I recall that when Albert Camus visited Rio, I took him to participate in a Candomblé ceremony. He registered that episode in his diary, but I think he did not comprehend the message of the Orishas.

Mysticism and spirituality are present for me in the enthusiasm of the struggle. Recently, in a more serene way, they are there in the care I take with my painting. One thing does not negate the other; they all converge. The several dimensions complement each other. In the crossroads, the flux of life, contradictions gain meaning and our picture takes shape.

Africans in the United States are more organized and currently[35] more combative than African Brazilians, although our movement is growing fast. But they do not have the cultural background we do. For a number of historical reasons, they lost the threads of tradition in its explicit expression. But there is an active, sometimes dramatic search for those threads, which gives my paintings an important role. Often, when United States African Americans stand in front of my canvases for the first time, they don't understand what they are seeing. But they *feel* the painting. They make an effort to comprehend, they ask questions, get interested, study. More than once, I've seen people weeping at my exhibits. This phenomenon shows that African roots, apparently destroyed by the European religious culture imposed on African Americans in the States, are still alive. One has only to touch them the right way and they respond, alert and positive.[36]

I get many invitations to exhibit. Showing my paintings in the African-American community is what gives me most pleasure, because it is a question of fraternity, brotherhood. But I've also exhibited in less African places, like the extremely white universities of Yale, Harvard, and Tulane.

One time, at the Yale University gallery, I visited an exhibit of Afro-Brazilian pieces that had come from Brazil's police archives and psychiatric institutions (mostly from Rio de Janeiro and Bahia). This is how Brazilian society sees African creativity: a thing of criminals or psychotics. That exhibit represented centuries of my people's conflict with the police, who sacked and robbed the *terreiros*, putting their sacred art and icons in curiosity collections.

As a result of the civil rights and Black Power struggles, things are different here in the United States. My paintings are bought by people of modest means as well as upper class individuals and institutions. But my purpose in painting is absolutely cultural. When, on the buyer's insistence, I end up selling a canvas, I suffer. I have enough money to live on. What I don't have yet is the peace of spirit that can only come with my people's total freedom.

Pan-African Encounters

Not only in the course of my exile, but as a result of it, I have had the opportunity to participate in several international encounters of the African world. The case of the First World Festival of Negro Arts (Dakar, 1966), sponsored by UNESCO, is a good example. The Festival took place during Brazil's military regime. In any event, African Brazilians almost without exception did not have the means to travel abroad independently. So the Brazilian delegation was controlled by the government, whose intention was to present Africa with the Brazilian face of "racial democracy." Independent African organizations not representing that ideological line were excluded. The Black Experimental Theater and I myself, of course, were the first to be cut out. At the time, I wrote an open letter of protest, which was published by Présence Africaine (Nascimento, 1966). But I could not get to Dakar. This kind of ideological veto was why I could actively participate in African world affairs only after I left Brazil.

Nevertheless, while I was there I did what I could. During the early part of the 1960s, I was the MPLA's representative in Brazil. This would have been a more gratifying experience if not for the Brazilian military regime's brutal torture of Lima Azevedo, my Angolan colleague. In 1975, while briefly visiting Brazil, I organized a public commemoration of Mozambique's independence in Rio de

Janeiro. It was almost a clandestine affair, because Brazil supported Portugal in all the liberation wars, and politically pro-African positions were considered subversive.

There was also an incident in the 1960s, when a UNESCO meeting on African culture was held in Rio de Janeiro. A group of Brazilian Africans were denied the opportunity to speak to the conference. We demonstrated against the Foreign Relations Ministry, Itamaraty, which had determined this exclusion. Marietta Campos (later Damas) was active in this event, and Aimé Césaire spoke for us at the plenary session.

It is a tribute to the great Pan-Africanist C.L.R. James that he, as senior organizer of the Sixth Pan-African Congress, took the position that there should be a strong and numerous Brazilian delegation at that event. Aware of the fact that we represent the largest African population in the world outside of Nigeria, James was prepared to dedicate a full day of deliberations to African experience in Brazil. He conveyed his hopes to me at a meeting in Washington D.C. arranged by Roosevelt Brown. Later, in 1973, I participated in the Planning Meeting for the Congress, held in Jamaica. Along with our Australian sister Bobby Sykes and African-Cuban writer Carlos Moore, I was able to meet with Marcus Garvey's widow, Amy Jacques Garvey. In the face of strong internal pressures criticizing and attempting to sabotage aspects of the Congress preparatory process, Mrs. Garvey gave us great encouragement and support.

At the Congress in Dar-es-Salaam, I was the only Brazilian delegate. Again in the company of Carlos Moore, I met with President Julius Nyerere and spoke at length with him about the situation of Africans the world over. While supporting the correct-line ideological stance of the Congress, Nyerere nevertheless was sympathetic with the plight of Africans in Brazil, which he said justified the work I was doing.

Unfortunately, C.L.R. James' vision of the Congress did not come true. It turned out to be a meeting of governments, and with the exception of some Caribbean states, we of the Diaspora do not represent governments. Aside from that factor, there was the language problem: no facilities existed for translating Portuguese or

Spanish. Finally, there was the prevailing Marxist political line, which reproduced the same arguments the Brazilian left had always employed to deny our movement legitimacy and support. All these factors made it very difficult for me to transmit the Afro-Brazilian message. But I held my ground, and with the well-intentioned help of a French translator who did not speak Portuguese, I made my presentation (Nascimento 1989).

In 1976, I participated in the first plenary assembly of the African Writers' Union in Dakar, organized by the inexhaustible creative force of Wole Soyinka's Ogun spirit. In Dakar, I was able to meet with Africa's great thinker and scientist Cheikh Anta Diop, leaving with him a small oil painting of Oshun. I also spent a year as Visiting Professor at Ife University in Nigeria, living in the sacred city and ancestral home of my people, nourished by the immediate spiritual contact with the Orishas, deities of my ancestors' religious culture.

I had the occasion in Nigeria, in 1977, to confront the official Brazilian government delegation of handpicked white or semi-white "intellectuals" at the Colloquium of the Second World Festival of Black and African Arts and Cultures in Lagos. The Brazilian government did its best to silence me, using diplomatic pressure against the Nigerian government, the Festival's Presidency and its Colloquium director, Ugandan exile Pio Zirimu.

The agents of the military regime were unable to achieve their goal. They successfully lobbied to have my paper officially rejected, over the objections (some have alleged, over the dead body) of Dr. Zirimu, who had requested it. However, they were unable to prevent the Nigerian press from publishing the paper or prevent me from registering at the Colloquium as an observer. During its proceedings, the Brazilians used parliamentary and police tactics to try to keep me from addressing the plenary. Despite all this, and thanks to the solidarity of my African colleagues, among them Ola Balogun and Wole Soyinka of Nigeria, and Maulana Karenga, Ron Walters, and Molefi Asante of the United States, I made my statement on racism in Brazil. The story is told in my book *"Racial Democracy" in Brazil: Myth or Reality?* (1977).[37]

The First Congress of Black Culture in the Americas was held in August 1977 in Cali, Colombia, on the initiative of African-Colombian physician and writer Manuel Zapata Olivella and his Peruvian colleague José Campos Davila. I presided over the Working Group on Ethnicity and Miscegenation. This was a nongovernmental meeting and, largely for that reason, a productive first encounter of Africans in this part of the Diaspora. Three leading participants were Eleanor Traylor and the late Larry Neal of the United States, and Nigeria's Wole Soyinka. The Brazilian government could not be content without demonstrating its repressive apparatus. Under the usual mask of bureaucratic subterfuge, it prevented the Brazilian delegation of some forty members from travelling to Cali.

The Second Congress of Black Culture in the Americas took place in Panama in 1980, and I was elected General Coordinator of the Third Congress, which was held in São Paulo in 1982. But that is another story.[38]

In 1983, the Regional Conference for Latin America in support of Namibia's fight for freedom was held in San José, Costa Rica. On this occasion, in the company of my wife Elisa and African-Brazilian Professor Lélia Gonzalez, I was able to visit Puerto Limón, the first home of Marcus Garvey's UNIA, and Bluefields, the African community of West Indian origin on Nicaragua's east coast.

As a Member of the Brazilian National Congress and of the House Foreign Relations Committee, I was invited in 1985 to visit Israel as part of a delegation of Brazilians. In several encounters with Israeli authorities, despite being there at the expense of their government, I did not hesitate to raise questions obviously considered by them and my Brazilian colleagues to be somewhere between the scandalous and the taboo. Everyone was indeed quite uncomfortable when I declared to the Foreign Cabinet Member and Foreign Ministry officials that I was concerned about the involvement of Israel, a state founded on the basis of antiracism, with apartheid South Africa and particularly with that country's nuclear program. They did not, however, deny that involvement. I also expressed my concern with the complaints I had received from Prince Asiel Ben-

Israel, at the Memorial Zumbi pilgrimage to Serra da Barriga in 1983, about the Israeli policy regarding the African Hebrew community that had settled in Dimona. Under Israeli Constitution, any Jew is considered a citizen of Israel. But these African Hebrews had not been granted citizenship, under pretexts that masked a political refusal to apply the constitutional principle to them.

As a Pan-Africanist, I considered it a high honor to be invited in 1988 by the W.E.B. DuBois Center for Pan-African Culture in Accra to give the inaugural lecture of its annual W.E.B. DuBois Memorial Lecture Series. My wife Elisa and I met with Jerry Rawlings, Ghana's dynamic, lucid and effective revolutionary head of state, whose Pan-African consciousness honors Ghana's tradition. Our son Osiris Kwesi, born in 1985, now enriched our travels. Indeed, it was his godfather, Kofi Awoonor, then Ghana's Ambassador to Brazil, who mediated the invitation prompting our visit.

I spent a month in Angola, in 1989, as a consultant for UNESCO. Here, the offices of Angola's Ambassador to UNESCO, the writer Domingos Van-Dunem, were a driving force in Eshu's tradition of clearing paths. In Luanda, I met with President José Eduardo dos Santos at a moment when he deftly handled the problems involved in the return home of Namibian freedom fighters. One of the most impressive aspects of this visit was to witness the work of the National Language Institute, responsible for literacy campaigns and development of the use of African languages in modern Angola. I did my best to encourage and assist in the implementation of the idea of creating a National Theater as well.

Since 1988, I have taken part in the creation of the Institute of Black People created at the initiative of Burkina Faso's government, represented by State Secretary of Culture Mme. Salambere Alimata, with UNESCO's support.

Perhaps the crowning event in these Pan-African peregrinations was my presence at Windhoek on Namibia's Independence Day, 21 March 1990. It was the culmination of a long, hard struggle in which I had tried to do my part, participating in United Nations-sponsored symposia in New York and in San José and organizing a national symposium in Brazil, sponsored by IPEAFRO. It was an unnameably exhilarating experience to share Namibia's day of freedom. Particularly , it was a joy to share it with my longtime colleague and brother Andimba Toivo-ya-Toivo, Secretary General of SWAPO and Namibia's Minister of Mines and Energy.

Perspectives

My experience in the United States showed me that national borders are not really important. I was in the United States and Africa for thirteen years, visiting Brazil the few times conditions there allowed it during that period. I have been to the Caribbean, Europe, and Africa, and I find that African people's problems are essentially the same. Of course, there are historical differences and contrasts. To a great extent, Africans in the United States absorbed, or were absorbed into, the cold and individualist Anglo-Saxon mentality. So I was very happy to see Rio de Janeiro and my friends again when I was there in 1974, 1975, and 1978. It was renewing and inspiring to feel the warmly human atmosphere and witness Africans at a stage of awakening and organization. I met with young African Brazilians who left me with the certainty that the struggle would continue. At the same time, deep down, my relationship with Brazil is paradoxical, full of revolt, tangled in a web of contradictory feelings. With that Brazilian communicability and warmth of spirit come the white paternalist hypocrisy, false camaraderie and boldfaced lies of racial democracy, which leave me with the bitter knowledge that Brazil can never constitute a true home for me. It can make me no better offer than a slightly more pleasant exile.

I felt really at home in Africa: Tanzania, Guinea Bissau, Angola, Ghana, Senegal, Nigeria, Uganda. Guinea Bissau was one of the most moving visits, if the shortest. In early 1976, I saw some of the first fruits of a nation's fight against the same Portuguese that tyrannize Africans in Brazil. The open, friendly spirit of a people still suffering the astonishing impoverishment visited upon them by colonialism and its aftermath, but embarking upon the consolidation of their hard-won freedom, was a moving and unforgettable phenomenon. I recalled the torture of Lima Azevedo, my MPLA colleague in Brazil, and drew a deep breath of Bissau's air of freedom.

In Uganda, I visited the source of the Nile. The river that had fed so many ancient African civilizations flooded my soul. Bathing in them as in a primordial baptism, I felt born anew. I waded into those waters with sixty years on my back and came out fresh as if at sixteen, ready to start all over again. Similar renewal of spirit came in Nigeria, where I visited Candomblé's sacred places: the ancient shrine of Oshun, where the golden fish jumped into the hands of the priest-king and founded the mythical center of her worship in Oshogbo. Although I was told that Oshun is no longer identified with art and creativity in Nigeria, her city Oshogbo is the country's most outstanding arts center, home of Twins Seven Seven and other great artists. In Ile-Ife, I saw the Ogun festival at the shrine of the cosmic warrior, shatterer of borders and barriers. I visited Oyo, historic and mythical city of Shango as well. These are African-Brazilian people's spiritual centers, our places of pilgrimage. We need no Meccas or Jerusalems. Our home in Africa is ready to receive us with our own pilgrimage points.

This is not to suggest a mass return of African Brazilians to Africa. Such an idea is not only unrealistically romantic and utopian; it would be suicide. The same is true for the idea of creating an autonomous black state in Brazil. The entire nation was built by Africans, and we are not about to hand it over to others at this late date.

Literal return to the traditional communal agricultural life of our ancestors would demand an impossible worldwide revolution transforming all values. Industrial society is a hard reality, and we must find realistic solutions for it. Rather than a return to Africa, the goal for African Brazilians must be to build an African Brazil, institutionally speaking, since in fact it has always existed. First, we must break with the mulatto myth of Africans passing for whites, success through "integration," the race mixture that always ends up white. In the United States, whoever has a drop of African blood is considered African, even if his skin is light, hair straight, nose and lips fine like a European's. In Brazil, the opposite is true. Many of those who have a drop of European blood want to be classed as *clarinho* and pass as whites.

The prospect of liberation for African Brazilians means going through an experience of cultural independence and autonomy. Without this, we can't talk about "equality of rights," because "equality" without identity and autonomy is just depersonalization, the source of weakness and dependence. We must urgently take up the work of organizing for social demands, political power, assertion of our cultural identity: the path of Afro-Brazilian freedom and dignity.

In Brazil, such proposals immediately trigger cries of "reverse racism!" But there are honest white people who understand this need and are not threatened by the idea. Florestan Fernandes is an example of a Brazilian far ahead of his time in this respect.

In postdictatorship Brazil, it will be time to start thinking about holding the Second National Afro-Brazilian Congress, with a clear commitment to the international African movement in the tradition of Marcus Garvey, Patrice Lumumba, Shaka, Kwame Nkrumah, Malcolm X, and Zumbi of Palmares. Frantz Fanon, Nzinga, George Padmore, W. E. B. DuBois, Aimé Césaire, C. L. R. James, Wole Soyinka, Amilcar Cabral: these are a few of the names our people need to know and honor. They are our teachers in life and struggle.

And my exile continues . . . .

Editor's Epilogue: Quilombismo, the Zumbi Memorial, and the Brazilian Congress*

Returning to visit Brazil during the process of political liberalization in the late seventies and early eighties, Abdias Nascimento found an Afro-Brazilian movement much more assertive of its African identity. Many African cultural groups had been formed, since ostensibly

* The edited interviews end here. The following Epilogue, written by the editor, highlights a few of Nascimento's achievements in Brazil since his return from exile.

political organizations would not be tolerated by the military regime. But their practice was essentially political: the search for Afro-Brazilian identity, self-determination, and freedom.

In 1980, Nascimento helped begin a historic Afro-Brazilian movement. Organizations from all over the country joined to create the Zumbi Memorial. The goal was to recover, for the African-Brazilian community, the lands of the Republic of Palmares and to build a dynamic center of African Liberation Culture in Palmares' territory. The group's first pilgrimage to Serra da Barriga, in 1980, was a movingly momentous experience for all involved.

Afro-Brazilian groups had already called for institution of National Black Consciousness Day on 20 November, the anniversary of Zumbi's death in battle, in 1696, defending his people. Since 1980, the Zumbi Memorial has sponsored pilgrimages to Serra da Barriga on that date. These pilgrimages have become an annual national and international event. National Black Consciousness Day is clearly a victory of Afro-Brazilian movements. Not even the major television networks, notorious for their ignorance and stereotyping of Africans, are able to ignore this event. Each year, Africans in Brazil organize seminars, demonstrations and conventions on this date.

More significantly, the Serra da Barriga has been declared a National Monument and disappropriated by the federal government. The land is now awaiting transference to the Zumbi Memorial, through the Palmares Foundation,[39] for the project's implementation.

Not coincidentally, perhaps, 1980 was also the year Abdias do Nascimento published the book *O Quilombismo*. Its title essay was based on his communication to the Second Congress of African Culture in the Americas (Panama, 1980) and the book contains other papers he presented at African world gatherings.[40] His major thesis in *O Quilombismo* is that Africans in Brazil must develop their own liberation ideology, based on their own historical experience, not in order to separate themselves from the rest of Brazil, but to prepare to lead the nation, as its majority population, in a democratic context.

Nascimento contends that African Brazilians created the first free republic in the Americas (long before Haiti). Palmares' saga of a hundred years' resistance to colonial siege by the Portuguese and the Dutch, from 1595 to 1696, is an example and a symbol to Pan-Africanists the world over. Palmares was the highest expression of the Afro-Brazilian experience in building free communities called *quilombos* (hence Quilombismo). Nascimento builds his model of Afro-Brazilian resistance and social change from this historical experience.

Socially, the model of Palmares is that of a pluricultural, multi-ethnic nation based on mutual respect and conviviality among the different groups making up the Brazilian population, especially its three major components: Africans, Native Americans, and Europeans. A prerequisite for this proposition is the teaching of African, African-American, and Native American history from the Afrocentric and Native American perspectives. This measure is necessary not only in the interests of historical truth, but also in order to rebuild these colonized peoples' psyche, self-determination, and protagonism.

Quilombismo teaches the democratic exercise of power in a stable political system. Economically, the Palmares model employs rational production techniques (e.g., diversified agriculture instead of monoculture for export) in an economy whose means of production are collectively owned and rationally administered to the community's benefit. Quilombist economics maintain a harmonious relationship with the fauna, flora, mineral wealth, and the environment as a whole.

Quilombismo proposes the organization of a Brazilian state based on these principles, and not a separate African state in Brazil.

The differences between Quilombismo and European-derived socialism are evident. The latter makes no attempt to address the question of plurality of cultures or harmonious social relations among distinct ethnic, religious, or other groups. Much less does it discuss the need to recover and reconstruct the cultural identity, human dignity, and protagonism of peoples subjected to the holocaust of European colonialism.

Perhaps the most important innovation of Quilombismo derives from this pluricultural dimension. European socialist models do not deal organically with the matter of ecology, which has been added as an emergency measure at the tail end of centuries of European leftist political thought. On the other hand, the ecological perspective is part and parcel of African and Native American traditional cultures.

Quilombismo understands that for nearly two millennia the Europeans, like two year olds, have destroyed in the name of profit whatever comes before them, ignoring their actions' future implications. African and Native American peoples have known the need for harmony with nature from time immemorial. They include in their plans and projects not only the ancestors and the living, but also the generations yet unborn. African and Native American traditions respect nature, the cosmos, and the ecossystem. They understand that nature's forces are larger than we are. If we do not treat her with care, she will someday destroy us.

Quilombismo is not only Afro-Brazilian, but pertains to all the Americas and to Africa as well. The historical experience of *quilombos* is a phenomenon common to all Africans, known by such different names as *cumbes*, *cimarrones*, *palenques*, maroon societies, or African anticolonial traditional society. Quilombismo stands therefore as a general model for Africans the world over.

In Brazil, reception of the book *O Quilombismo* in 1980 was predictably cold. Some African groups and individuals were inspired and moved by the idea. Other segments of the Afro-Brazilian movement were too influenced by the various currents of European-derived leftist thought and political commitments to openly acclaim it. As for conservative and leftist Brazilian intellectuals (both Eurocentric), they cried "reverse racism" and "nonsense!"

What really outraged these circles was Quilombismo's assertion of the African foundation of Western civilization and the pre-Columbian African presence in the Americas. Such notions are inconceivable in Brazil, and the works of Cheikh Anta Diop (1974, 1978) and Ivan Van Sertima (1976) have yet to circulate there, whether in translation or not. Quilombismo is indeed a proposal for the future and, like most innovative ideas, is ahead of its time.[41]

In 1981, leaving exile behind and coming to live in Brazil, Nascimento founded the Afro-Brazilian Studies and Research Institute (IPEAFRO), at first in São Paulo at the Pontifical Catholic University (PUC), an institution identified with the Liberation Theology and progressive political thought. Unfortunately, PUC was financially unable to sustain the Institute. It was moved to Rio de Janeiro as an independent organization. There, it continued publishing *Afrodiaspora* journal and offering courses at the State University of Rio de Janeiro (UERJ) on African and Afro-Brazilian culture, aimed largely at primary and secondary public school teachers. In 1985, IPEAFRO sponsored a national symposium on Namibia and published, for the first time in Brazil, a full-length book in Portuguese documenting the Namibian people's fight for freedom (*Afrodiaspora*, No. 5).

In a shared exile, Nascimento had strengthened his relationship with Leonel Brizola, Brazil's strongest and most consistent progressive national leader.[42] Co-founder from its earliest moments in exile of the Democratic Labor Party (PDT), Nascimento was instrumental in making the African struggle one of the Party's first statutory priorities. He and Sebastião Rodrigues Alves came together once again, with other Africans, to create an Afro-Brazilian Secretariat within the party in 1981. This was an unprecedented occurrence in Brazilian politics, except when the same pair had created a Black Affairs Department in the early PTB, historical predecessor of the PDT.[43] Likewise, Governor Brizola's public commitment to the Afro-Brazilian cause is unprecedented among political leaders in the nation's history.[44]

Abdias do Nascimento ran for Congressional office, and in 1983 took office as the first African-Brazilian Congressman to raise the question of African human and civil rights in the Brazilian parliament. His speeches and bills of law from this period are published in six volumes entitled *Fighting Racism* (Nascimento, 1983-87). Among his major proposals and bills of law were the definition of race-based discrimination as a severely punished crime (rather than a misdemeanor, as it was classed by the Afonso Arinos law); suspension of diplomatic relations with South Africa; recognition of

SWAPO as the Namibian people's legitimate representative; compensatory action (akin to affirmative action), creating opportunities for African Brazilians in employment, housing, and education; privileges for Portuguese-speaking African immigrants equal to those granted Portuguese immigrants; and declaration of National Black Consciousness Day (20 November) as a national holiday.

In the 1990 elections, Nascimento was elected to the Senate on the PDT's ticket, along with Doutel de Andrade and Darcy Ribeiro, two of the most outstanding intellectuals and public figures in Brazilian history.[45]

In March 1991, Leonel Brizola took office for his second elected term in the Rio de Janeiro State executive. Governor Brizola created the State Secretariat for the Defense and Promotion of Black Populations and appointed Abdias do Nascimento Secretary of State. This was the first time in Brazilian history that a state government instituted an instrument of action in favor of Africans on the highest level of administrative power.

At Nascimento's inauguration ceremony, held 10 April 1991 at Rio de Janeiro's Guanabara Palace (seat of the State Government and former home of the slaveowning Imperial Family), a crowd unprecedented for this kind of event marked its political importance. Also present were Ghana's Ambassador Michael Hamenoo and the Minister Plenipotentiary of the Nigerian Embassy, Olu Olusanmokun. The Afro-Brazilian cultural presence was marked by presentations of Mestre Tourinho group's presentation of *capoeira*, a martial art of Central African origin, which has evolved in Brazil as a major African art form, and by African-Brazilian lyrical singer Aída Batista's mini-recital. As an appendix to this chapter, we have included a translation of Nascimento's history-making speech on this occasion, inaugurating the latest phase of his continued activity on behalf of the African-Brazilian people and their cause.

APPENDIX

Text of the speech given by Professor Abdias do Nascimento, Secretary Extraordinary for the Defense and Promotion of Black Peoples, Government of Rio de Janeiro State, Brazil, at the ceremony in which he took office (Guanabara Palace, Rio de Janeiro, 10 April 1991).

YOUR EXELLENCIES
GOVERNOR LEONEL BRIZOLA,
VICE-GOVERNOR NILO BATISTA,
AMBASSADOR MICHAEL HAMENOO OF THE REPUBLIC OF GHANA,
MINISTER PLENIPOTENTIARY OLU OLUSANMOKUN OF THE REPUBLIC OF NIGERIA,
CONSULAR REPRESENTATIVES,
STATE SECRETARIES,
MAYORS,
HONORABLE REPRESENTATIVES OF THE CONGRESS,
HONORABLE STATE ASSEMBLY REPRESENTATIVES,
OTHER AUTHORITIES PRESENT,
MY AFRICAN-BRAZILIAN BROTHERS AND SISTERS—I SALUTE IN PARTICULAR THOSE WHO HAVE COME FROM OTHER STATES,
LADIES AND GENTLEMEN:

As we gather here, we are conscious of participating in a historical moment of great and profound significance. The institution of the Extraordinary Secretariat for Defense and Promotion of Black Peoples of the Government of Rio de Janeiro State represents a step toward winning the just participation of citizens of African origin in Brazilian society which no one in our nation before has dared to take.

In the first place, we pause to pay homage to our African and African-Brazilian ancestors, exemplified in the persons of fighters like Queens Nzinga and Yaa Asantewaa, Zumbi of Palmares, Luiz Gama, and Luiza Mahin. *Axé Babá!*

More than a century ago, during the time of the Empire, when Africans were still enslaved in Brazil, the Honorable African-Brazilian Congressman António Rebouças (father of the famous engineer André Rebouças), who represented the State of Bahia in the House of Representatives from 1830 to 1873, criticized Dom Pedro II, Emperor of Brazil, stating that the Royal Cabinet of Ministers lacked legitimacy, because it contained no representatives of the African population in Brazil. Someone argued from the floor that this fact was due to the absence of African Brazilians qualified for such a position. Rebouças replied then and there: "Here I am, and nobody has appointed me!"

Indeed. They do not see us. From the outset, African Brazilians have suffered this condition of invisibility, so poignantly portrayed by the African North American writer Ralph Ellison in his novel *Invisible Man*. I believe that today will be registered in history as the day that African Brazilians became visible. Here we are, in the heart of the Palace, participating in the State Secretariat of a Governor who, with his vision of a statesman, has finally seen us, and understood the larger meaning of Congressman António Rebouças' secular protest.

A question is in the air: why a Secretariat for the Defense and Promotion of Black Peoples?

In order to consider the reasons for this Secretariat's institution, we must first understand this: who are the black populations? In Brazil, a veritable web of mystifications has been created around this subject. Let us be clear about this: Blackness is not a question of skin color. The color of our skin, in all its varied and sundry shades, functions only as a badge of our African origin, the root of our identity. *Mulato*, *cafuso*, *negro*, *escurinho*, *moreno*: all the famous euphemisms converge toward this identity, which the ruling elites in Brazil have always tried to disclaim. Therefore, when we are denied a job or shown the service entrance, it is not only our skin color that provokes the discrimination, but above all the African identity announced by the color of our skin.

For this very reason, when we fight for our rights, we fight alongside those who, all over the world, suffer the same discrimination, and whose grandfathers are our own: The victims of the greatest holocaust ever to occur in the history of mankind, the chattel slavery of Africans, which counted more than two hundred and twenty million victims.

Above and beyond the identity of family and history, we have in common with the peoples of the African world our civilization and culture of origin, constructed from the time of ancient Nubia and Egypt to the Medieval states of Africa, persisting and developing, despite colonialism's perversions, to contemporary times.

Symbolizing this identity of culture, history, and struggle, it is an immense pleasure to have with us today Ambassador Michael Hamenoo, of the Republic of Ghana. The late President Kwame Nkrumah, leader of Ghanaian independence and untiring soldier of Pan-Africanism, stands among Africa's greatest statesmen. Ghana's presence here, in the person of Ambassador Hamenoo, along with the presence of Nigeria through Minister Plenipotentiary Olu Olusanmokun, marks the solidarity and fraternity among our country and the nations and peoples of Africa.

The affirmation of African origin in no way implies a rejection of our Brazilian national identity, for the simple reason that Brazilian national identity is also African. It merely occurs that, recalling the case of many pallid African Brazilians who internalize anti-African prejudice, the ruling classes refuse to put on their own face. The minority elite, when defining African participation in the context of the Brazilian Nation, generally refers to black people's "contribution" or "infiltration" in a totality to which, implicitly, they do not belong. Brazilian intellectuals speak of "reminiscences" or the "survival of traces" of an African culture supposedly alien to Brazilian culture. On the other hand, when these same elites speak of Brazilian nationality, they say we are a Western country, of Latin civilization, in sum: a European nation.

Africans in Brazil no longer accept these definitions. We are not infiltrators, nor do we contribute to a nation that belongs to others. No! This nation is ours as well, it was built by our forefathers, and we will not give it up.

The question of Africans' participation in Brazil is first and foremost a question of *citizenship*. The abolition of slavery did little or nothing to return the citizenship that the regime of chattel slavery stole from us along with our very humanity. On the contrary, the living conditions imposed on African Brazilians after the "Golden Law" of abolition stripped us of our citizenship for the second time. And since the Eurocentric elites could not tolerate the idea of a nation composed in its majority of blacks, they arranged for the arrival of immigrants recruited in Europe.

These new citizens did not take long to gain their full participation in the modern economy and the command of the nation. After dislocating the exslaves from the formation of the industrial and agricultural working class, they rose, in the short interval of half a century, to all levels of executive, legislative, judicial, military, and economic power. While this was happening, the Africans, who had worked singlehandedly for three hundred years to build the nation, remained excluded from the country's economic, political, social, and cultural development. They were kept continually "in their place" by that veiled, hypocritical, and outrageously effective discrimination that comprises the fabric of Brazil's so-called racial democracy.

For these and other reasons, the history of Africans in Brazil, similar to that of Native Americans, became a history of genocide, the destruction of an entire people by means of direct assassination, extreme poverty, homelessness, unemployment, hunger, and lack of health care, and particularly through the denial, destruction, and distortion of their original identity and culture.

Who is responsible for this unhappy situation? The African and Native American peoples? Definitely not. The responsibility belongs to the Brazilian elites or ruling classes: those who placed and maintained themselves in power at the cost of the destitution, marginalization, and genocide of Africans, Native Americans, and the poor, not to mention the systematic destruction of the environment, ecossystem, and natural resources of this huge land.

Therefore, the same Brazilian society, through its public power structures, is responsible for repairing this situation of profound injustice. At precisely this highly sensitive point of our existence as a civilized nation and people, there is a clear need for a specific instance of power designed to channel the voice and aspirations of these disinherited millions: the Extraordinary Secretariat for the Defense and Promotion of Black Populations.

This Secretariat follows the example of the entire Afro-Brazilian community, as history has witnessed, and plants its *axé*[1] on the person of the African-Brazilian woman. As even the official statistics of the Brazilian History and Geography Institute (IBGE) demonstrate, she is the most oppressed among the oppressed. She earns the lowest wages, when she earns anything at all for her work, and she has practically no access to higher education or to upper-echelon positions. Moreover, this same African-Brazilian woman witnesses the daily killing of her children, for the great majority of victims of the internationally infamous extermination of minors in this country are black people. She laments the impunity of her children's murderers. She suffers her own unemployment and that of her companion, undergoes with him the violence of the home's invasion by police, and supports the family in his absence. And to all this, we must add the aggression embodied in the campaigns of mass sterilization waged against her, to complete the picture of our community's oppression.

But on the other hand, she also personifies the resistance, courage, and fighting spirit of our people, for the African-Brazilian woman has never ceased to struggle. In the *quilombos*, in the *terreiros* of Afro-Brazilian religion, in the Catholic and Protestant churches, on the hills and *favelas*, in the schools of samba, she always held a position of leadership in the heroic collective resistance of Africans in Brazil.

For many years, the Afro-Brazilian movement has been stating that the racial question is first and foremost a national question. As long as the nation does not restore the full citizenship of this huge portion of its population, Brazil will remain fragmented, like a family who lost or exiled forever more than half its members.

The truth is that Brazil as a nation has only to gain by bringing all its components to the fore. Africans taught the European colonizer techniques of metallurgy and agriculture. Afro-Brazilian cultures still have great lessons of philosophy and worldview to offer Brazil. One of them is in the environmental perspective, for African cosmology is characterized at its core by the harmonious relationship between man and the forces of nature, based upon the principles of mutual respect and support. The national environmental movement will be incomplete as long as it is not committed firmly to sounding the drums of Afro-Brazilian culture's ecological message so they echo to all corners of the country.

Responding to the call of History and the clamor of the organized Afro-Brazilian community, this Secretariat will seek to assure the reparations demanded not only by an unjust past, but by a future in which the dignity, humanity, and full citizenship of African Brazilians are fully respected.

Governor Brizola, the African-Brazilian community congratulates you because, among leading national politicians, you are unique in understanding this need in its true dimension. Indeed, how long a road we have walked to arrive at this inauguration of this Secretariat! From the time of our political exile and the organization of our party, while still overseas, when we inscribed the commitment to the cause of the black peoples as the fourth national priority in the Party's political program, we have been making historical progress.

The Democratic Labor Party (PDT) was the first political party to institute a statutory body, the Secretariat of the Black Movement, where African-Brazilians themselves are the protagonists of their own concerns. In 1983, for the first time in Brazil's history, Your Excellency appointed three African-Brazilian Secretaries of State: a woman, Dr. Edialeda Salgado do Nascimento, and her two colleagues, Col. Nazareth Cerqueira and Carlos Alberto de Oliveira, Caó.

During that same period, as the first African-Brazilian Federal Congressman committed to advancing his people's cause, and the only one in that legislature, this speaker introduced several bills of law in the National Congress. They defined racial discrimination as a crime against humanity, with corresponding sentences; established the principle of compensatory action in favor of groups historically victimized by discrimination; cut off diplomatic and economic relations with South Africa. Another initiative was to propose the recognition of SWAPO as the legitimate representative of the Namibian people in their armed struggle for independence. Today, a democratically elected SWAPO exercises power in the Africa's newest sovereign nation, the Republic of Namibia.

In the Constituent Assembly of 1988, we gained four African-Brazilian congressmen and we finally won promulgation in the Constitution of the article defining racial discrimination as a crime without recourse to bail. Several other constitutional measures related to the attempt at reparation of the injustices suffered by the Afro-Brazilian community were also included.[2] As part of the governmental structure of several states, councils for Afro-Brazilian affairs were created under different names.

Now, Mr. Governor, with the election by the PDT of two African-Brazilian Governors—Alceu Collares of Rio Grande do Sul and Albuíno Azeredo of Espírito Santo—and with the creation of this Secretariat, we have arrived at a new stage in this historical process. For us, this represents a victory won collectively by African Brazilians, but it also represents a grave responsibility.

The Secretariat is born fully conscious of the difficulties it will face, particularly in reference to the comprehension of the cited ruling elites. They deem themselves the sole repository of truth, good, and beauty, while to them the African represents falsehood, evil, and ugliness. Thus, we must maintain a patient didactical action to influence individual and collective attitudes and behavior. We will collaborate with the Secretariat of Education, directed by our longtime ally, Professor Maria Yedda Linhares, and with the Integrated Centers for Public Education (CIEPs), public schools of all levels, and the University of the State of Rio de Janeiro (UERJ), in order to assure access to education, ensuring young African Brazilians' training and educational development. We also must work to free school curricula and textbooks of negative stereotypes of Africa and Africans, propitiating an educational experience reflecting the true dimensions of the culture, history, and civilizations built by

African people and their contribution to universal science, technology, arts, philosophy, and knowledge.

All this will be done without allowing the Secretariat to become a ghetto, for its structure will be inspired by the expectation of a program of close reciprocal cooperation with other units and secretariats of the State Government. We intend not to duplicate administrative departments, but to make effective specific policies geared to the only population brought by force from its homeland and kept in captivity throughout almost four centuries.

Merely by example, we will cite a few of the possible areas of the Secretariat's action.

Along with the Secretariat of Justice, working with Dr. Nilo Batista (a longtime ally of our cause), we would like to elaborate and implement programs of legal assistance to victims of anti-African discrimination in all of its multiple expressions. We hope to be able to help expedite the investigation and punishment of those responsible for the violence against African-Brazilian children and families. Also, there is a basic need to create new forms of action to improve programs for prisoners and exconvicts, who are mostly African-Brazilian.

We hope to collaborate, as well, with the Secretariats of Military and Civilian Police, in the effort to develop antiracist programs aimed at improving relations and mutual understanding between the police and the black community.

In the area of housing, the Secretariat will try to articulate new ways of defending the interests of the great majority of the homeless, who are African Brazilians. There is also a great opportunity for this administration to play a vanguard role in the enforcement of the Constitutional measure that guarantees to the communities reminiscent of *quilombos* the ownership of their land.

With respect to the environment, and specifically to the United Nations Conference on the Environment to take place in Rio de Janeiro, ECO-92, the Secretariat hopes to be able to collaborate with Secretary Roberto D'Avila to make the effective participation of the African-Brazilian community with specific and self-defined projects.

The Brazilian Constitution provides that the State will protect, among others, the manifestations of Afro-Brazilian culture. We have every reason to trust that the Secretary of Culture, Professor Edmundo Moniz, will accept our collaboration so that, instead of perpetuating the stereotypes that reduce and restrict Afro-Brazilian culture only to samba, soccer, and so-called folklore, it will be considered, in its most profound dimensions, among the institutions and activities of official Culture.

Faithful to its perspective of broad African solidarity, the Secretariat intends to encourage and strengthen those sectors of civilian society engaged in developing the ties of this solidarity in all the world. There are several examples. In the near future, a World Conference on the Genocide of African Peoples will be held in Toronto, Canada, and the Seventh Pan-African Congress, to be held in Nigeria, is now in the organizational phase. There are arrangements being made to bring to Brazil the great South African leader Nelson Mandela, as well as a delegation of members of the Constitutional Committee of the African National Congress (ANC) of South Africa interested in learning more about the transition to democracy in Brazil.

The response and contribution of civilian society to the Secretariat's initiatives will be equally important to its work. For this reason, we will create a Council for the Defense and Promotion of Black Peoples, with members representing all sectors of organized civilian society, including African-Brazilian and non-African-Brazilian personalities.

Mr. Governor, without hesitation I can assure Your Excellency that the Afro-Brazilian community will react correspondingly to your decision to reflect the African presence at the highest level of decision-making and execution in the democratic and popular institutions of the Rio de Janeiro State Government. Only the unwavering conscience of a true statesman could sustain a gesture of such great civic courage in the swampy terrain where our country's politics withers with lack of greatness. But under your leadership, as each day passes, the Democratic Labor Party, our PDT, finds new spaces of freedom and protagonism for our people. It broadens our democratic consciousness and channels collective dreams and aspirations for change of the structures of domination and usurpation of power perpetuated by insensitive and genocidal ruling elites. The days of these elites are numbered. The people—the African-Brazilian people included—will pull up that weed by its roots, taking its destiny in its own hands.

Axé!

2

PAN-AFRICANISM, NEGRITUDE AND THE AFRICAN EXPERIENCE IN BRAZIL

(Miami and Dakar, 1987)

The present text is a fusion of Abdias do Nascimento's contributions at two international African meetings: the conference on *Negritude, Ethnicity and Afro Cultures in the Americas*, held at Florida International University, Miami (26-28 February 1987); and the Symposium on the theme *Pan-Africanism and the African World*, held in Dakar, Senegal (15-20 December 1987), as part of the organizational process for the Festival of Pan-African Cultures (Fespac). They were co-authored, translated, and edited by Elisa Larkin Nascimento.

Introduction

I am asked in this paper, by the organizers of the present conference on *Negritude and Afro Cultures in the Americas*, to address two themes: "The African Presence in Brazil" and "Negritude: the Black World's Humanizing Response to the Racialization of Human Relations." For the Fespac Symposium on *Pan-Africanism and the African World*, I am asked to offer considerations on the theme "Pan-Africanism, Negritude, and the African Experience in Brazil."

Evidently, the topics are so broad as to invite one not to engage in detailed academic discussion, but rather to reflect on questions of historical and immediate importance to the destiny of the African world. Indeed, the events for which these texts are solicited constitute excellent opportunities for African scholars and thinkers to remove themselves from the minutia of current research engagements in order to discuss the broader concerns which, as African scholars and thinkers, we have a responsibility to consider in the interests of our people. For creating these opportunities, I would like to commend the organizers of this conference on Negritude, in particular my friend and colleague Carlos Moore and Florida International University. Congratulations are in order to Senegal's President Abdou Diouf and his government, for having supported the Fespac event without imposing state criteria on its proceedings.

We will go a little beyond the themes indicated, dealing in the first section with issues raised by so-called Latin America's participation in Pan-African world affairs. We will briefly examine the specific case of African experience in Brazil in the second section, then devote a third section to the miscegenation ideology prevailing there and in the region as a whole. In a fourth section, we look very superficially at contemporary Afro-Brazilian resistance. And finally, we will engage in some Afro-Brazilian considerations on Pan-Africanism and Negritude.

Pan-Africanism and "Latin" America

A conference of this nature on the general topic *Negritude, Ethnicity and Afro Cultures in the Americas* is today a timely initiative. One of the most outstanding issues at this point in African history is the reemergence of peoples of African descent in Spanish and Portuguese-speaking South and Central America as actors on the stage of Pan-African world affairs.

I say "reemergence" because these peoples have never in fact been absent from that stage. The early history of anticolonial resistance shows that Africans in this region waged one of the first, most heroic, and longest lasting battles for freedom known to the African world. Brazil's Republic of Palmares and its great leader Zumbi, defeated in 1696 after a century of anticolonial resistance, symbolize this early Pan-African history in the Americas (Nascimento, 1989). Further witnesses are the *palenques*, *cimarrones*, and *cumbes* of the Spanish-speaking Caribbean and South and Central America, boasting heroes like Baoruco, Diego de Guzmán, Lemba, King Bayano, and Benkos Bioho throughout the colonial period (Larkin Nascimento, 1980).

As Ivan Van Sertima (1976) has shown, earlier yet (and long before the dispersion from the Continent caused by European chattel enslavement), Africans were present in this part of the Americas, where they exchanged, perpetuated, and developed aspects of classical ancient African civilizations in a Native American context.

Yet in this century's Pan-African events, the voice of the region's African Americans was hardly heard, and there are still problems to be overcome in asserting our presence.

The first difficulty we confront is the language barrier. International events carried on in French and English (and sometimes Arabic) exclude those millions of Africans who speak Spanish and Portuguese, or limit seriously their ability to participate fully. For this reason we support, as a long-term goal, the establishment of an international African language, probably Ki-Swahili, to be taught our children the world over. I supported this proposition at the Encounter on African World Alternatives in Dakar in 1976, and it has been advocated generally since the Rome conference of African writers.

Besides linguistic isolation, our communities' miserable poverty and lack of means to travel abroad also obstructed our presence at Pan-African encounters until very recently. On the other hand, certain aspects of the specific nature of white supremacism in South and Central America, which we will examine in this text, made the very existence of our communities generally unknown to Africans in other regions.

The concept of Diaspora itself is usually assumed to encompass Africans in the United States and the Caribbean, and also in Europe. This assumption goes to such lengths that in the United States, I have been repeatedly surprised, when invited to speak about Brazil, to find that my contribution is classed under the topic "Caribbean Culture."

I recall insisting, at working sessions of the Encounter on African Alternatives in Dakar, 1976, that members of the United States delegation take care not to reproduce the habit of their country's ruling class and monopolize the hemisphere by referring to themselves exclusively as "African Americans." And I also remember the concerted efforts of the late C. L. R. James, during the organizing process of the Sixth Pan-African Congress held in Dar-es-Salaam in 1974, to assure a solid and significant representation from Spanish and Portuguese-speaking South America and particularly from Brazil, the country with the second largest African population in the world. Ultimately, however, the "small people's delegation from Brazil" (Campbell, 1975:152), whose participation he was instrumental in assuring, consisted of only one member: the present author.

It was not coincidental, I believe, that the first South American representative at a Pan-African Congress was Brazilian, for aside from its huge African population, Brazil constitutes a key country in the African world due to its demographic, historical, geo-political, and economic importance (Larkin Nascimento, 1980).

I would like to take the opportunity, at this historic conference, to render special tribute to C. L. R. James, one of our living legacies of commitment and struggle. One indication of the correctness of his concern with Spanish and Portuguese-dominated South America has been the realization of three Congresses of African Culture in the Americas, initiated by Africans from Colombia (Manuel Zapata Olivella) and Peru (José Campos Davila). The first was held in Cali, Colombia, in 1977; the second in Panama in 1980, and the third in São Paulo, Brazil, in 1982 (Larkin Nascimento, 1980). All three of these events made very explicit their insertion in the African world context, by giving the floor to African delegates from the Continent, issuing motions and performing deeds of solidarity with the Southern African fight against colonialism, and repeatedly demonstrating their deep concern with African affairs.

Evidently, linguistic isolation and lack of financial means are barriers to be overcome, but they do not by themselves constitute the root cause of the noninclusion of this important segment in the African worldwide community. Rather, the major historical agent of our absence has been the force and fury of the racial democracy or miscegenation ideology in South and Central America. This insidious form of white supremacism is masked by ostensible (or ostentatious) racial tolerance and a hypocritical encouragement of race mixture, [1] whose goal is not to create a "new, universal color, " but to eliminate the African presence through dilution over generations until the population becomes entirely *Latin*, meaning white and culturally European. "Marrying white" becomes a social compulsion in which one seeks to better one's children's status by ensuring their lighter skin color. "Marrying black, " on the other hand, is a major error. Sociological studies (Ianni, 1972) have shown that modern Brazilians, for example, prefer to avoid intermarriage, leaving race mixture to extrafamiliar relationships. The question of identity, crucial to any black community, is a thousand times more problematical in these societies.

White supremacist oppression in South and Central America is reflected in the general habit of referring to the area as "Latin" America, in a show of insensibility or ignorance of the great majority of the region's people, who are not Latin at all, but African and/or Native American. The phrase expresses the European ruling classes' imposition of their cultural and ethnic identity on the region's very definition. Yet reference to "Latin America" has been legitimized in progressive and Third World circles. Obviously African "progressive" Puerto Ricans, Dominicans, Peruvians or Colombians will say: "Oh no, I'm not black, I'm Latin (or Puerto Rican, or Colombian, and so on)."

In popular usage, the term "Latin" has come to convey the mixed ethnic nature of the region's populations. Once again, employment of a European-identifying term to signify racial amalgamation, where the European element is a small minority, reflects the bias against non-Europeans. More importantly, the emphasis on this supposedly unique Latin propensity to race mixture paints a rosy picture of conviviality and nonprejudice.

Conventional eulogies of *mestizaje* or *morenidade*, the process of race mixture, ignore both the sociohistorical origin of that mixture and the fact that, mixed as their ethnic origin may be, the identity of these populations is forcibly defined as Latin, while their Native American and/or African heritage is repressed or despised.

Still, conventional academic works on race relations and slave systems in these countries have placed them on the map as examples of racial harmony. This false pride in the supposedly nonracist nature of these societies led to the suppression of African people's identity and, more importantly, their consciousness of racial oppression.

African Presence in Brazil: A Case of Historical Distortion

Basically, the same ideological impositions are suffered by Africans in Colombia, Ecuador, Costa Rica, Peru, the Dominican Republic,

Puerto Rico and other nations of the region. Their forms and minutia may differ from one context to another, but the essentially white supremacist nature of these social structures is common to all.

Here, however, I am asked to discuss specifically the African presence in Brazil. My initial observation would be that to speak of African *presence* is to understate the case from the outset, for history shows that Brazil is demographically and culturally an African country.

Africans arrived in Brazil soon after the territory's so-called "discovery" by Pedro Alvares Cabral in 1500. By 1535, the African slave traffic was a normal, organized activity. This date is simultaneous with the establishment of colonial Brazil itself, i.e. the subjugation and murder of its native people and the sacking of its resources by bands of greedy Portuguese bent on milking the land to its last escudo.[2] It was this enterprise that laid the country's economic and infrastructural foundations, and African know-how, technology, and labor made it possible. Africans were brought in chains to Brazil and they did not help others build the country, they built it themselves. Given the more advanced state of metallurgy and agricultural technologies in Africa at the time, it was often the enslaved Africans who taught their masters techniques useful to this enterprise.

From the beginning, the agroindustrial policy of monoculture for export condemned the nation to a process of dependency and foreign debt culminating in today's infamous standing as world champion of insolvency. Sugar was the colony's first industry, feeding the European craving for newly-discovered sweets. In today's states of Bahia and Pernambuco, sugar plantations sprang into action so fast that by 1587, Bahia alone had forty-seven mills. Africans, the majority population all over the colony, were clustered in this area for about two centuries, while the sugar industry dominated the economy. Later, cotton was king, and concentration of the slave population moved north to Maranhão. Discovery of diamonds and gold in the eighteenth century, in today's Minas Gerais State, moved slavery's focal point south. This process repeated itself in the first half of the nineteenth century, with falling productivity in the mines and the beginning of the coffee cycle. Plantations of this object of European vice were found in Rio de Janeiro and São Paulo, and the African population gathered there in higher concentrations.

It is virtually impossible to pinpoint the number of Africans who arrived in Brazil. This fact is due not only to the vagueness and unreliability of statistics, when available, but particularly to Finance Minister Ruy Barbosa's infamous decree of 13 May 1891, which ordered the destruction, by fire, of all historical documents and archives related to slavery and the slave trade. Estimates are extremely precarious, but at least sixteen million Africans were imported alive. Of these, approximately 38 percent went to Rio de Janeiro, from where some were sent to Minas Gerais and Goiás. Twenty-five percent went to Bahia, 13 percent to Pernambuco, 12 percent to São Paulo State, 7 percent to Maranhão and 5 percent to Pará (Azevedo, 1975:16).

If statistics on the total number of Africans to arrive in Brazil are unworthy of credit, even worse are those that pretend to locate their places of origin in Africa. Ethnologists of European origin and persuasion confuse ports of embarkation with ports or areas of origin, names of places in Africa with those of sovereigns, and so on. This branch of Eurocentric scholarship was dedicated in Brazil largely to the proposition that the enslaved Africans it designated Sudanese were "culturally more advanced" and generally more docile than those inferior ones they labeled Bantu (Lopes, 1988).

What we do know about the enslaved Africans is that they never stopped fighting for their freedom. The list of *quilombos* is long and incomplete (Nascimento, 1989; Moura, 1972). Their perennial consciousness and untiring struggle inspired my theory of Quilombismo, a form of Afro-Brazilian social and political organization based on our specific history (Nascimento, 1990).[3]

Constant rebellions and uprisings like those of the Hausa or Muslim Malês, the Tailors' revolt, the Balaio and countless others, were the true and conventionally unrecognized historical agent of slavery's abolition. Brazil was the last country in all the Americas to abolish slavery, with a decree signed on 13 May 1888.

Next year, 1988, the nation commemorates abolition's centennial.

Africans in Brazil have little to commemorate. We can only say that one hundred years of civic lies and official hypocrisy do not deserve celebration. The black movement has long since rejected May 13th as a day of celebration for our community. In the late 1970s, National Black Consciousness Day was instituted on November 20th, the anniversary of elected King Zumbi's death in defense of Palmares.[4] Since 1980, the Zumbi Memorial, a federation of Afro-Brazilian organizations, has sponsored each year, on that day, a pilgrimage to the site of Palmares at the Serra da Barriga in Alagoas State.

Conventional histories generally omit the African-Brazilian heroes of the abolitionist cause. Among them the giant is Luiz Gama, along with his mother Luiza Mahin. Poet and precursor of Negritude, Luiz Gama's exceptionally lucid African consciousness was his main weapon, wielded in various forms. He was a poet, an attorney, an orator, a writer, and a militant of the abolitionist cause. His legacy to the contemporary African community in Brazil is one of inspiration and example (Larkin Nascimento, 1985).

Luiza Mahin was another example of African resistance and consciousness, whose image and inspiration live in the minds of our community in spite of the almost complete lack of documented information about her life. We do know that she was a leader of resistance movements in Bahia linked to the nineteenth century Muslim-led *Malê* revolts.

Abolition of slavery brought few real benefits to Africans in Brazil. Now labeled free, most were left to the streets without work, education, health care, housing, or land. Others stayed with former masters on the latters' imposed conditions. Black women were doubly victimized by this process, in which they became at once the last on the social scales and the mainstay of their families and community.

In a process of social engineering based on the most crass assumptions of racial Darwinism, the European elite in Brazil promoted mass immigration of white people in order to "improve the nation's racial stock." The ruling class was in panic over the Africanness of this newly-declared citizenry and hurried immediately to deny it suffrage by instituting in the 1891 Constitution, for the first time, the literacy requirement for voting. This done, it went about subsidizing European immigration, to saturate the labor market, leaving Africans unemployed and destitute. Simultaneously, the ruling elite inculcated in the national consciousness a social compulsion to "marry white." The idea was to eliminate the African presence entirely, hopefully by the end of this century. This campaign and its white supremacist rationale are examined in depth in Thomas Skidmore's classic *Black into White* (1974).

The architects of the immigration for whitening campaign entertained their hopes in vain. When we say that Brazil is demographically an African country, we refer to the historical and contemporary failure of these policies designed to wipe the "black stain" from the population. According to available statistics, in 1600 there were 20, 000 Africans in Brazil, twice as many as there were Europeans. Native Americans counted 35, 000 (Vianna Filho, 1949:45). In 1798, the proportion remained constant for Africans and Europeans, while the "discovery" of more Native Brazilians brought their count to 250, 000 (Azevedo, 1973:87). By 1822, the artifice of counting *pardos*[5] separately from *pretos* (dark-skinned Africans) was already being used, in the attempt to diminish the official number of Africans. The sum of the two categories (2, 456, 000) is almost two and a half times the number of whites listed (1, 043, 000). In 1872, the count was: whites, 3, 787, 289; *pretos* and *pardos*, 6, 143, 279 (Nascimento, 1968:19, 31).

In spite of European immigration, Africans remained a numerical majority (even according to official statistics) through 1890, when they represented 56 percent of the population. At this point, the white population began to increase relatively. By 1940, according to the Brazilian government, whites represented 63.47 percent of the Brazilian people. Their proportion declined until 1980, when there were 54.77 percent whites and 44.34 percent Africans (*preto* plus *pardo*) in the country's populace. These data are from the IBGE (Brazilian Institute of Statistics and Geography) of Rio de Janeiro, Brazil's official census bureau.

This rough statistical outline must be qualified by the fact, widely cited by demographers and statisticians, that racial ideology in Brazil distorts them highly in favor of the white category. Mixed-race people obviously African, questioned by the census taker, almost invariably declare themselves white or *pardo*, and in the resulting statistics "... the Black group loses a great deal, the *pardo* group gains much more than it loses, and the white group gains a lot and loses nothing" (Mortara, 1970:458). If we add to this the fact that Africans are disproportionately represented among those groups that the Census does not reach (isolated rural communities, poverty pockets, and so on), it becomes more than clear the Africans represent much more than 44.34 percent of the Brazilian population. There is more than enough reason to state that African Brazilians make up a majority of the country's population.

In this distortion of statistics, we come upon a cornerstone of Latin racism: the compulsion to identify with European values, aesthetics, and criteria of personal beauty, creating negative psychological complexes which are nothing new to students of Frantz Fanon or Albert Memmi. What distinguishes the Latin situation is that, rather than being seen as one of white supremacism's many faces or as a legacy left by colonialism, this compulsion to whiteness is presented as proof positive of Latin antiracism! Thus, we are treated to the following declaration by a member of the Brazilian military dictatorship's delegation to the Second World Festival of Black and African Arts and Culture (Festac '77), held in Lagos (Diegues Junior, 1977):

> the predominance of the white portion [of the Brazilian population] is evident, since in Brazil, even those of mixed race who have a small or large amount of black or Indian blood, but without one of these groups' physical traits, are considered white.[6] Which demonstrates the absence of any discrimination of racial nature, in terms of the person's ethnic origin.

This author assumes unchallengeably, as do most Brazilians, that Africans and Native Americans yearn to be honored with the exalting title "white." Condescension to this desire, a magnanimous gesture, is a certain sign of the Brazilian elite's nonracism. It never seems to occur to these thinkers that the extolling of whiteness as a virtue is the essence of white supremacism. Nor do they recognize the absurdity of accepting as valid the statistical conclusion of whites' "predominance" in the population, despite the distortions they themselves so enthusiastically expose.

With authors like Nina Rodrigues and Oliveira Vianna in the forefront, this kind of "scientific reasoning" has furnished major justifications for postabolition racial discrimination in Brazil (Nascimento, 1989). However, African-Brazilian sociologist Guerreiro Ramos (1957:175) identified the true nature of these sophistries:

> To ensure exploitation, the ruling minority had recourse not only to force and violence but also to a system of pseudo-justifications, stereotypes and processes of psychological domestication. Dogma such as the excellence of whiteness and the aesthetic degradation of blackness formed one of the psychological pillars of exploitation.

Another branch of Eurocentric scholarship in Brazil spent enormous energies on the proposition that Brazilian society entertained a certain *prejudice of mark*, or color prejudice, described as "purely aesthetic" because it discriminates on the basis of phenotype as opposed to racial origin (Nogueira, 1959). This aesthetic bias, the argument goes, has nothing to do with racism, a phenomenon associated exclusively with societies employing the "rigid descent" rule of ethnic identification in a system of legalized segregation. As Ghanaian scholar Anani Dzidzienyo (1984:13) has observed, "even this Brazilian [system], which provides a much more complex range of definitions between blackness and whiteness, is based upon prejudice directed against nonwhites." Yet in the name of "science," this school of Brazilian writers dissociates the rejection of black people's physical features from their African origin and invents a purely gratuitous aesthetic aversion, proclaiming Brazilian prejudice "more benign" or "less serious" than United States racism. To them, the suggestion that this "aesthetic" aversion to blackness is a function and product of white supremacism can only come from heretics or reverse racists.

These ideas are popularized to an extent probably unprecedented for academic theories. In a discussion with almost any Brazilian, race mixture will be extolled as a positive value *sui generis* and as an irrefutable proof of nonracism. In many cases, "Marxist" class analysis will have led the person to idealize the ultimate amalgamation of races in a universal *café-au-lait* mass as the automatic solution to the race problem and the road to unity of the proletariat. Long discourse will follow on the fact that in the United States (where racism really exists), one must discern whether someone has one thirty-secondth part of African blood in order then to refuse them a place on the bus or train. The argument usually culminates in the Brazilian, almost always a mulatto of more or less obvious African descent, exclaiming: "If this were the United States, even I would be considered black!"

The "aesthetic prejudice" theory and its popular corollaries fly in the face of statistics on race discrimination in Brazil. We define as Africans the 44.34 percent of Brazilians who represent, in the IBGE's 1980 census, the sum of two categories: *preto* and *pardo*. Only 5.89 percent classify themselves as *pretos*. But statistics on employment and education show that the 38.45 percent who call themselves *pardos* suffer the same kinds of discrimination. Among men classified as *pretos*, for example, 46.7 percent have one year of schooling or less, while about half that percentage (24.3 percent) applies to the education of whites. And *pardos*? Their situation is slightly worse than that of *pretos*: 48.2 percent with one year's schooling or less.

On the other hand, 5.6 percent of white men had twelve years of education or more, while only 0.5 percent of *preto* men and 0.9 percent of *pardo* men had as many years of schooling. In other words, whites have six times more chance to complete twelve years or more of education.

In terms of income, the situation is much the same. Among white men, 17.8 percent earn one minimum wage or less, [7] while among *pretos* the percentage is 33 percent, and among *pardos*, 32.5 percent. White men earning more than ten minimum wages are 6.5 percent of the total, while only 0.4 percent of *pretos* and 1.1 percent of *pardos* earn that much.

Among women, double discrimination is evident: 14.6 percent of white women earn one minimum wage or less, while 28.5 percent (twice as many) among *pretas* (black women) and 19.8 percent among *pardas* (brown women) are in the lowest income group. These data reflect the only significant advantage held by mixed-bloods. The vast majority of *pretas* are still exploited today as domestic servants at less than poverty wages. Some mulatto women have a greater chance of escaping this trap. On the other hand, they do not do much better than *pretas* on the high end of the income scale: 0.8 percent of white women earn more than ten minimum wages, while 0.03 percent of *pretas* and 0.09 percent of *pardas* are in that bracket.

These statistics, as a whole, render useless the "mulatto escape hatch" theory in which some sociologists (Degler, 1971) posit that higher social status conferred upon mixed-bloods creates an outlet through which potential protest is neutralized by the possibility of social ascension through miscegenation.

In contrast to the image of racial democracy, these data show a clear racial hierarchy in terms of income and educational opportunity. At the top are white men; next, white women; third, black men; and lastly, black women. Between 1980 and 1982, this situation grew worse.[8]

Nevertheless, Africans who raise the question of racism in public as a political issue are still dismissed with the allegation, "That's not race discrimination, it's a class question. Here in Brazil we have poor whites and poor blacks but not racism." This in a country where, even according to distorted official statistics, [9] about 50 percent of whites as opposed to more than 75 percent of blacks live on or below the poverty line.

Contemporary Afro-Brazilian Resistance

The most sinister effect of this racial ideology is that the victims themselves become convinced that racism does not exist. Thus, the black movement expends enormous energies trying to "prove" to its own people that their situation is due to race. Continuously, we must answer the question "Does racism really exist in Brazil?, " turning our energies away from the real questions of our struggle. Indeed, if Brazilian racism is effective from the statistical point of view, keeping Africans well "in their place" socioeconomically, its real achievement lies in this capacity to curb the growth of African consciousness and the community's protagonism on its own behalf. This is what we mean when we say that Brazilian white supremacism is more pernicious than South African.

This is not to say that Afro-Brazilian resistance abated after abolition. On the contrary, the present century has witnessed from the start an active vanguard of black consciousness. Most often, this consciousness is expressed in nonpolitical forms such as Catholic religious brotherhoods, African religious organizations, mutual aid societies, recreational clubs, samba schools, and so on. Even at the turn of this century and into the teens, there existed a proliferation of these organizations with the name "Quilombo" or "Palmares, " in direct reference to the military struggle carried out by our ancestors. An active black press also existed, with foreseeable problems and lack of continuity due to the community's lack of funds.

In the 1930s, the Brazilian Black Front, led by José Correia Leite and others, sponsored mass demonstrations against discrimination in São Paulo State, where Jim Crow policies were common. The focus on African identity and cultural values was introduced by the Black Experimental Theater (TEN), founded by this author in Rio de Janeiro in 1944. The TEN organized the National Black Convention (São Paulo and Rio de Janeiro, 1945 and 1946) and the First Congress of Brazilian Blacks (Rio de Janeiro, 1950), among many other similar events.

The National Black Convention of São Paulo, in 1945, was

responsible for presenting to the National Constituent Assembly, [10] a series of antidiscrimination measures which, predictably, were rejected under the allegation that no discrimination existed in Brazil. Characteristic of Brazilian power relations and black alienation is the fact that among more than three hundred members of that Assembly, only one was African: Claudino José da Silva of the Brazilian Communist Party. He voted against the African-Brazilian community's proposal.

During the military dictatorship of the sixties and seventies, the mere discussion of the racial question was considered "subversive" by the National Security Law. Nevertheless, the black movement grew, particularly during the seventies. Black organizations, in various forms and branches of activity, appeared all over the country. In 1978, a major demonstration against racism was held in São Paulo. As the process of redemocratization progressed, these organizations also grew and developed.[11]

During the 1982 Congressional, state, and local elections, several African Brazilians ran for legislative office. While few of these were successful (the present author was the only African-Brazilian Representative to the Federal Congress), the political weight of the movement did increase. In Rio de Janeiro, three Africans were appointed to first-line administrative posts in Leonel Brizola's state government. In São Paulo, the state government created its Council for Black Community Development and Participation. In 1985, with the inauguration of the first post-1964 civilian federal government of President Tancredo Neves (whose untimely death caused Vice-President José Sarney to take office before Neves was even sworn in), an Afro-Brazilian Advisory Council was created in the Ministry of Culture.

Currently, in 1988, two historical moments are converging to create a unique crossroads in Afro-Brazilian experience. First, the Brazilian Congress elected in 1986, like its predecessor in 1945, is a Constituent Assembly in a postdictatorship era and is writing a new Constitution for the nation. Promulgation of this Constitution will coincide with the second landmark: the centennial of slavery's belated abolition in Brazil.

While only four African-Brazilian representatives[12] were elected to the current Constituent Assembly, the process of drafting the document has illustrated the extent to which the Afro-Brazilian movement, organized in almost every state, is making its political weight felt.

As we wrote this text in 1987, the Constituent Assembly had not yet finished its work. Draft measures were being considered by several committees and subcommittees, which consolidated, edited, and revised the drafts. These texts were consolidated and presented by the subcommittees to the Systematization Committee, which further edited, revised, and consolidated them as the final texts to be considered by the plenary Assembly.

Among the articles included in the draft document submitted to the Systematization Committee, were the following proposals, submitted by representatives of the African-Brazilian community to the respective Committees and Subcommittees:

> *Article 86.* Everyone, man and woman, is equal before the law, which will punish as a crime without recourse to bail any discrimination offending human rights or rights established [in this Constitution]. It is considered a form of discrimination to underrate, stereotype, or degrade ethnic, racial, or color groups, or persons belonging to such groups, in words, images, or representations in any communications media.

> *Article 87.* Application by the State of compensatory measures designed to implement the constitutional principle of equality before the law with respect to groups or persons victimized by documented discrimination does not constitute privilege or discrimination. Compensatory measures are those designed to give preference to certain citizens or groups of citizens, in order to guarantee their equal participation in and access to employment, education, health care, and other social rights.

> *Article 88.* Education will emphasize juridical equality among the sexes, affirm the multicultural and pluriethnic characteris-

tics of the Brazilian people, and condemn racism and all forms of discrimination.

Article 106. At all educational levels, the government will reformulate the teaching of Brazilian history, with the goal of contemplating on an equal basis the contributions of different ethnic groups to the Brazilian people's multicultural and pluriethnic formation. The law will provide for fixation of commemorative dates important to the different national ethnic segments.

Article 89. Brazil will not maintain diplomatic relations or sign treaties, agreements or pacts with countries which adopt official policies of race discrimination, nor permit in its territory the activities of these countries' corporations.

Article 216 §5: Sites of remnants of the former *quilombos*, as well as all documents pertaining to them, are declared historical monuments.

Transitory Dispositions: Definitive ownership is conferred to the remnants of *quilombo* communities occupying their lands, the State being committed to emit the respective titles.

These were not the only draft dispositions presented by the Afro-Brazilian movement to the Constituent Assembly for consideration by its subcommittees. Nevertheless, the debate of these propositions and the approval of some of them by the subcommittees represented a considerable advance in Afro-Brazilian political struggle.

It was not likely for the Constituent Assembly to approve the measures cited, since the process of voting in the plenary was to alter the draft text almost in its entirety. Conservative forces dominated in the plenary to a greater extent than the subcommittees and committees, or the Systematization Committee itself, which was to draft the working text to be submitted to the vote.

Indeed, the final outcome confirmed these doubts. The definition of racism as a crime without recourse to bail, considered a major victory for the Afro-Brazilian community, was the only measure of general impact incorporated into the new Constitution. Also, the cited provisions on the *quilombos* were left intact. But draft Articles 87 and 89 were omitted entirely, and the other articles transcribed were edited considerably. Their language was diluted into almost metaphoric terms and in most cases transferred to other articles with the result of minimizing their impact. The items on the use of media to transmit stereotyped or degrading images and the revision of school curricula were omitted. The affirmation of the pluricultural and multiethnic nature of Brazil's history and people was reduced to "protection by the State of Afro-Brazilian and indigenous culture" and severed from the context of education.

African Brazilians have no illusions. The new Constitution probably will not solve the emergent problems facing the African community in Brazil. But the movement's victory is clear, even if only to the extent that these questions have been addressed and debated seriously on the national level.

The Afro-Brazilian movement has asserted for years that the so-called black problem is not the African community's concern but a national one. Until the present author raised Afro-Brazilian issues in the House of Deputies, the national ruling elite ignored these questions almost entirely, dismissing them as the invention of racist agitators intent on importing non-Brazilian problems from other regions of the world. This situation has changed radically, and today the Afro-Brazilian movement not only won certain victories in the Constitutional process but has gained much ground in the discussion and consideration of these questions as national issues.

During the 1982-86 legislative term, when I participated in the Congress as the first and only African-Brazilian legislator working specifically to defend the human and civil rights of the black community, the first steps in this advance were palpable. While other African-Brazilian legislators have existed, they do not identify themselves as black, much less carry the banner of the Afro-Brazilian cause.

The idea of raising the question of racism as an issue before the

Brazilian Congress was patently absurd to a ruling elite convinced of the racial democracy theory's absolute truth. Reaction by the House of Deputies to my first speeches and bills of law, for the most part, was governed by the traditional Brazilian elitist attitude of irony or disdain: "Imagine the Brazilian Congress wasting time and energy on this nonsense!"

During the course of the term, however, it became clear that many colleagues were rethinking the question. I presented several bills of law, including, among others, one considering racism a crime against humanity with severe penalties, another establishing programs for integration of blacks in the labor force, housing, and education through quota systems and compensatory action, and another one establishing November 20, National Black Consciousness Day, as a national holiday (Nascimento, 1983-86). Most of these were approved in the various committees of the House of Deputies, but did not come to the plenary vote for bureaucratic reasons. One was approved in committee and by the House plenary but rejected by the more conservative Senate.

At any rate, the influence of these bills of law can be seen in the fact that several of the draft articles presented to the Constituent Assembly on the Afro-Brazilian question use language taken directly from them.

Another indication of the prevalence of this new recognition of Afro-Brazilian concerns as national ones is the position of leftist forces like the Communist Party and its several splinter groups, and some socialist parties as well. Traditionally, they have been more reluctant to discuss the question of racism than other political forces. The imperative "unity of the working class" and other slogans sufficed to render them entirely insensitive to the specific problems of African Brazilians. Today, these parties are sympathetic and actively seek to recruit and develop African-Brazilian militants within their ranks.

Our goal is to consolidate the autonomy of the Afro-Brazilian movement, rejecting its cooptation by any political party. Nevertheless, the growing sympathy of leftist circles and liberal "progressive" thinkers reflects our movement's effectiveness in recent years, in terms of gaining support for our cause in the society in general and in political circles in particular.

The second historical landmark of 1988, the Centennial of Slavery's Abolition, brought about another cause for reflection, by the nation as a whole, on the state of the African-Brazilian community after one hundred years of so-called freedom. Debates, seminars, and many other activities were scheduled, and in almost every university, high school, and community group the question of racism was discussed. The black movement was at the forefront of these activities, organized in hundreds of groups founded specifically as black consciousness organizations.

It is worth noting, in the context of this proliferation of African organizations, that almost all Christian churches, both Catholic and Protestant, have black consciousness groups, and that most universities have some kind of Afro-Brazilian student organization.

The centennial activities were channeled partly through the National Commission for the Centennial of the Abolition of Slavery, created by the Ministry of Culture through its Advisory Council on Afro-Brazilian Community Affairs.[13] This commission took suggestions and supported activities presented and carried out by the African-Brazilian community. In a national meeting held in Salvador, Bahia, the community's position was stated very clearly. While recognizing the relative historical importance of the abolition date, May 13, Africans gathered at this meeting resolved that it deserves no celebration. Rather, it provides an occasion for reflection upon and denunciation of the injustice and oppression which still weighs upon the African-Brazilian people.

This position is consistent with the same attitude announced by the black movement in several demonstrations in recent years, in which May 13 has been symbolically buried as a protest against abolition's falseness. That date has been designated National Day of Denunciation of Racism in Brazil, while November 20, National Black Consciousness Day, has been successfully instated as the true day of celebrating the African fight for freedom in Brazil.

Afro-Brazilian Perspectives on Pan-Africanism and Negritude

As a protagonist and/or witness to almost all this century's major African events in Brazil, I can attest to the Negritude movement's importance for African Brazilians. To us in Brazil, the term *Negritude* (which, in Portuguese, means "blackness") not only refers to the historical movement of that name but encapsulates the essence of our struggle and that of Africans worldwide. It indicates the fight for our people's dignity and the courageous statement of our human protagonism in the face of those who deny it.

After centuries of dehumanization and systematic humiliation, it is natural that Africans worldwide sometimes disagree over the details of the identity we are working to recapture. Beyond these disputes, however, lies that essence we call Negritude, among other names: the humanness, in its unique forms, of our people and their civilizations. In this sense, Negritude for us transcends the definitions conceived by the formal movement's founders, Léon Damas, Aimé Césaire, and Leopold Senghor.

Rather than restrict the concept of Negritude, African Brazilians tend to identify it with what leaders like Maulana Karenga (1978) and Molefi Asante (1980) have defined as Afro-American Nationalism or Afrocentricity. In the words of another of our outstanding minds in the United States, John Henrik Clarke (1977:1):

> There is no way to separate Pan-Africanism from nationalism. Nationalism is the catalytic agent that sets Pan-Africanism in motion, the cohesive force that drives it forward and establishes its reason to exist.

To us, then, Negritude and Pan-Africanism are linked into one historical force that represents African consciousness: from Zumbi and Benkos Bioho to Queen Nzinga and Ottobah Cuguano; from Martin Delaney and Edward Wilmot Blyden to Garvey, DuBois, Nkrumah, Malcolm, and Lumumba; from Cheikh Anta Diop to Karenga and Asante; from Agostinho Neto and Eduardo Mondlane to Ivan Van Sertima and Steve Biko.

Eventual disagreements with the founders of the Negritude literary movement should not lead us to reject Negritude itself, for its historical importance is undeniable. In the same way, whatever our disappointments with the results or organizational processes of any of the six Pan-African Congresses, it would be a mistake to discard the notion as politically defunct or of little contemporary utility. The role of both these movements in mobilizing the process of African independence is a fact, and their repercussions in African communities outside the Continent, including Brazil, are undeniable. In deference to our own history, we must seek to glean the positive and poignant cores of these ideas, incorporating them in an ever more dynamic concept of African world liberation.

Aimé Césaire identified three elements of Negritude: identity, fidelity, and solidarity. This solidarity is universal and antiracist, repudiating hatred and aggression among all peoples. However, independently of this dialogue with others, African liberation is intrinsically a humanist proposal because it contributes to the liberation of humanity as a whole, whose qualitative existence is defective as long as Africans or any other people are deprived of their identity, human dignity, and historical, cultural, and social protagonism. We need not waste much energy or space contesting the Brazilian habit of condemning Negritude and Pan-Africanism with the tired and tattered cliché of reverse racism.

There is a simple axiom of psychological health and human relations: Only if I love myself may I truly love and interact with others. Yet Africans are daily exhorted, taught, and brainwashed not to love themselves, internalizing white supremacist ideas of history, aesthetics, religion, and sociology with which they are daily bombarded by the mass media. This problem is perhaps more acute in Diaspora communities, but Africa is by no means immune. Her foreign reserves are still used to import cosmetics, wigs, skin creams, foodstuffs, beverages, clothing, and so on, sustaining the urge to whiteness created by European propaganda. This urge, one of neocolonialism's major mainstays, is no longer a monopoly of monied elites but penetrates ever more to the African masses (Munanga, 1986).

Wole Soyinka's famous observation is correct. The tiger has no need to proclaim his tigritude. But this is because there has been no worldwide campaign, orchestrated and enforced by the rich and powerful, to remove him from the forest, demote him to the status of cockroach, and forcibly impinge upon his cubs that new identity. In the Afro-Brazilian context, the tiger's pounce in Soyinka's metaphor is what we mean by Negritude. It could also be called Black Consciousness, Afrocentricity, Kawaida, or Quilombismo. All these terms denote the same search for liberation on the basis of our own history, identity, and self-definition. In Brazil, there is no doubt that this need is felt by the masses of African people who have expressed it through countless movements like "Black Mad, " "Black Rio, " "Soul, " "Rastafari, " and others.

The major difference between Brazil and most other African communities in the Americas is that, as the majority democratic force, a unified Afro-Brazilian community, in defining and determining its own destiny, is implicitly responsible for the nation's affairs as a whole. Thus, Quilombismo, an Afro-Brazilian theory of social and political organization, is also a proposal for global organization of Brazilian statehood, based on our own history and values (Nascimento; 1980, 1990). This statement simply takes to its logical conclusion the idea that racism is not a dilemma of the black community alone but of society as a whole in a multiracial state, and of humanity as a whole in the world context.

It is worthwhile to underline the universal value of Negritude in the cultural and literary sense. There exists a tendency to dismiss it as simply a reaction, a defense strategy against white supremacism, without whose previous existence Negritude could not itself exist legitimately. This is to deny the legitimacy of the African world itself, for all peoples have their unique expressions of universal values. Love, hate, life, death, human relations, family unity and breakdown, all these themes are dealt with in languages, manners and styles specific to the culture from which the literature or other manifestation arises. To deal with them abstractly is to engage in philosophy, and philosophies are also culturally specific. If one can speak of Oriental, Western Judaeo-Christian, or Native American culture and philosophy without raising protests of "reverse racism," why must this occur when we speak of an African culture and philosophy distinct from, say, that of the Arab world? Negritude, in our definition, is one expression of this specificity, repressed for centuries from the world's consciousness and our own. The argument that no such specific culture exists, only ethnic tribes and customs, has long since been put to rest by authorities from Frobenius to Diop (1978), and so many others (Asante and Asante, 1990).

As Wole Soyinka has observed (in Asante and Asante, 1990:16), African languages express this concept of a larger African cultural unity in terms like the Yoruba *enia dudu*, the Ga *meedidzii*, and the Hausa *baike mutane*. However ideologically correct it may seem to some, one cannot simply program this reality out of existence, for "the fact remains that in usage and consciousness, our societies have recognized this particularist reality of our ethnic consciousness, one that has not, in *our* histories, bred racism."

This is not to say that we accept one or two men's definitions of our culture and philosophy as correct; nor does any other people. All civilizations engage in healthy debate over the concepts and priorities of their collective art, thought, and social, economic, and political practice. The difference is that we Africans have been led to believe that we have none and that to entertain any such pretension is to indict ourselves for the crime of reverse racism. Negritude's great contribution has been to help throw off that yoke.

To disagree with the Negritude movement's founders and spokesmen is in no way incoherent with a due recognition of its inherent value and positive role in our civilization. We cannot accept, for example, exaltation of the French language as a unifying element among African peoples. One of my last memories of Léon Damas, just before his death, is of a long argument we had over this question at his apartment in Washington, D.C. I defended universal adoption of an African language, preferably Swahili, as a vehicle for our mutual understanding. Obviously, this is a long term goal but certainly preferable to expending our energies upon a choice among the languages colonialism imposed on us.

Likewise, we must be careful in our definition of Césaire's first principle, identity, not to incorporate uncritically qualities attributed to us by Eurocentrism. Depiction of Africans as a people who do not invent or explore is belied by our own history as architects of the first scientific civilization, that of ancient Egypt, and as travellers of the Americas and the world, long before Diogo Cão, Colombus, and their accomplices (Diop, 1974; Van Sertima, 1976, 1985, 1985).

Yet we must also maintain some historical and human perspective when raising these questions. That the Negritude writers, fiery young men studying in Paris, were able to turn the very stereotypes used against Africans into positive values and throw them back in the face of their depreciators was an aggressive form of self-defense, a sort of ideological boomerang. Senghor (1965:99) characterizes it as "a weapon of defense and attack and inspiration, rather than a tool of construction."

In Brazil, the figure of the *malandro*, akin to the hustler or the bad dude, with his street wisdom and ability to dupe the man, is often flouted in the face of white society in the same spirit. The Orisha Exu, misrepresented by the Catholics as the devil, is represented as a *malandro* in the Umbanda religion. Called Exu Pelintra, he opens the doors to survival and victory for the black community.

In certain critiques of Negritude, we find some of our colleagues judging by European yardsticks the values we consider in our reflections on self-apprehension. Too often, objections to Senghor's polemical argument that emotion is African focus on its supposedly racist tenor, when it is clear that its author is dealing not with genetics or biological chemistry, but with civilization and cultural values. To reject emotion as a pejorative quality is to accept unquestioningly a European value judgment not necessarily applicable to our peoples' experience. Whether it is in fact, for us, a "mode of knowledge" or a "higher state of consciousness" (Senghor, 1965:33-35) is the question that should concern us, and it is not to be dismissed, I think, as patently absurd or unworthy of discussion. Emotion has its own reason, and our indignation at the oppression of our people is a case in point.

We must also be careful in articulating the advocation of a single "universalist civilization, " incorporating African values fused with others, as the ultimate goal of antiracism. In the first place, this goal seems contradictory to Negritude's own most essential contribution. Rather than eliminate the differences among human beings and cultures, so enriching to our existence on earth, by amalgamating them in one great cultural "melting pot, " the goal should be to end transformation of these differences into inequalities or rationale for oppression. It should be to respect and demand respect for ourselves as human beings with a specific history and identity, and to live in peace with others, respecting their specific identities in turn.

This, indeed, is one of the basic principles of Quilombismo, which is founded upon two main aspects of our experience as African Brazilians. One is the history of the antiracist liberation struggle contained in the collective saga of hundreds of *quilombos* organized by Africans during their sojourn in colonial Brazil. This experience is crystallized symbolically in the episodes of Palmares and Zumbi. It points to a decentralized socialist form of political and economic organization, complemented by multiracial and pluricultural social organization respecting the cultural values of all ethnic components and their specific identities. The second major aspect of Quilombismo is the dynamic preservation, practice, and development of the philosophical, spiritual, and communitarian values embodied in Afro-Brazilian religions.

The combination of these two currents of thought and practice is the essence of Quilombismo (or Afro-Brazilian Nationalism, or Negritude if you wish) in Brazil. The Pan-African dimension of this practice has been demonstrated by the Afro-Brazilian movements' constant concern with African liberation struggles and issues, particularly in South Africa and Namibia, and in their continued contact and exchange with the African world in general. Symbolic of this practice has been the presence of Africans from all areas of the African world at the annual pilgrimages sponsored by the Memorial Zumbi to Serra da Barriga, site of Palmares, on 20 November, National Black Consciousness Day.[14]

It seems to me that the hazy concept of "universalist civilization" promoted by certain spokesmen of Negritude runs the risk of endorsing certain distorted forms of abstractions similar to itself. Perhaps this was the case with Brazilian theories that became so seductive to certain leaders of the Negritude movement.

Brazilian mystifications about race mixture, cultural syncretism, and social democracy culminated in the postulation of a supposedly "universalist civilization" dubbed Luso-Tropicalism, the invention of Gilberto Freyre (1959). It seems that the mirage of this happy civilization said to have been created by the Portuguese led leaders like Leopold Senghor, as President of Senegal, to welcome and honor certain spokesmen of racial democracy at international cultural events. Apparently, these Africans were unaware of the fact that such people build their careers and prestige at the cost of rationalizing the continued exploitation and marginalization of African Brazilians.

As we discussed earlier in this paper, perhaps the most effective element of Brazilian white supremacism is its very self denial, and the myth that race mixture led inexorably to nonracist social relations is the pillar of that strategy. Gilberto Freyre (1969:34) is the master of this reasoning:

> The cross-breeding so widely practiced here corrected the social distance which otherwise would have remained enormous between plantation mansion and slave quarters. What the large-landholding, slaveowning monoculture produced in the way of aristocratization, dividing Brazilian society into classes of masters and slaves, with a piddling and insignificant middle section of freedmen sandwiched between the two antagonistic extremes, was in great part neutralized by miscegenation's social effects. Indian and African women, at first, then mulatto women, the yallers, octoroons and so on, becoming the white master's domestics, concubines and even legitimate wives, played a powerful role in Brazil's social democratization.

Freyre is a prolific creator of mirages, coining phrases like *metaracial brunettism* and similar euphemisms, in his attempt to depict Brazilian racial harmony in the rosiest hues possible. Metaphorically, he goes to the extreme of harnessing Africans to the sinking ship of colonialist illusions (1976:8), by characterizing black Africans, "despite being slaves, as *co-colonizers* of Brazil, with considerable acculturating influence over the Amerindian, who was less culturally developed than the African Negro."

The advocacy of a notion so preposterous as the idea that a people conquered, hunted, captured, and kidnapped from their home in chains of bondage should be considered "colonizers" of the nation that held them captive shows to what lengths the Brazilian ruling class will go to convince itself of its own nonracism.

In this same text, which was distributed by the official Brazilian delegation at the Colloquium of the Second World Festival of Black and African Arts and Culture, held in Lagos, Freyre (1976:19) contrasts his *metaracial brunettism*, symbolizing for him the ultimate eradication of racism through cross-breeding, against what he considers two patently racist ideologies: Aryanism and Negritude. Ironically, the very theory that so fascinates certain proponents of Negritude condemns their movement as racist.

Freyre is not the only writer espousing these ideas in the African world. I have elsewhere (Nascimento, 1989: 61-70, 144) recounted the depressing spectacle of Pierre Verger pontificating at faculty seminars at the University of Ife, Nigeria, [15] on the "acceptable social status" enjoyed by contemporary African Brazilians and on the marvels of Brazilian slave society, where the masters' sons were "sexually initiated" in the fields with docile, sweet, and foxy adolescent African girls.

Such hypotheses ignore the white supremacist cornerstones of miscegenation in colonial society. Sexual abuse of African women in slavery is a form of the same rape and pillage inherent in war, with the added dimension of dehumanization supplied by white supremacism. Mulatto populations are the logical product of this violence in any slave society, and their existence is more likely to prove racism's presence, justifying this collective form of abuse, than its absence.

Stereotypes involving African women's sexuality are part and parcel of this phenomenon and represent its continuation from colonial times. Scholars like Teófilo de Queiroz (1975) and David Brookshaw (1983) agree that Jorge Amado is a master at nourishing and developing these stereotypes, applying them to Afro-Brazilian religion in particular. Doris Turner (1977:48-49) shows how, in Amado's novel *Jubiabá*, African religion in Brazil, the Candomblé, is portrayed in terms of buttocks, thighs, breasts and "foaming sex." The African protagonist, Antonio Balduíno, is described as "pure as an animal, his only law his instincts." Turner concludes:

> The aggregate of images used to create the vision of *Jubiabá*'s Candomblé manifests implicitly a denial of the Afro-Brazilian religion as religion, rendering it a wild emotional manifestation of primitive sensuality and eroticism.

Classical protagonist of this obsessive "mystical" sexuality, the Brazilian mulatto woman is the victim of one of the most perverse and pervasive systems of racist stereotyping yet invented by white supremacism. Portrayed universally as prostitute, concubine, "loose woman, " object of any man's pleasure, she almost never appears as wife, mother, worker, intellectual, or leader of her community. It is tragically ironic that Jorge Amado, foremost agent of the propagation of this image of the African-Brazilian woman and her worship, has gained international fame as an "antiracist" and a defender of Afro-Brazilian religion.

In Brazil, Jorge Amado is veritably a sacred cow. I once commented briefly, in an interview to a Bahian newspaper, on his treatment of black women in Candomblé, and the reaction was astounding. I was repudiated, branded a racist, a "professional proponent of Negritude" (this is an extremely pejorative epithet; by Bahian standards close to a curse), and generally maligned in myriad public statements, newspaper editorials, and even a motion unanimously passed by the all-white State Legislative Assembly of Bahia. Never has the press dedicated so much space to my statements on African culture in Brazil!

The question of political representation in Bahia is symbolic of the situation in the nation as a whole. In this "antiracist" state, an African majority of close to ninety percent is governed by an all-white democratic minority. As a member of the Brazilian National Congress from 1983 to 1987, I was the only African Brazilian representing the black community. To this day, white elected officials continue to claim that they represent "everybody, regardless of race."

Responding to its motion passed against me on the occasion of the episode involving Amado, I had the opportunity (Nascimento, 1983-86, Vol. 2:68) to ask the members of the Bahian Legislative Assembly:

> Where are the specific benefits these "representatives" of black people bring to the Afro-Bahian community? Candomblé houses are still in the same situation, deprived of ownership of their land, helplessly witnessing its invasion, appropriation and destruction by real estate speculators, even in sacred areas, where sacrosanct trees are cut, gasoline stations are installed in shrines, and business establishments are built. Where are the motions of this Legislative Assembly when, aside from economic and cultural violence, the violence of police repression also descends on the Black community?

With all his prestige, Jorge Amado has done no more to change these concrete situations than his political allies in the State Assembly. It was the Afro-Brazilian movement and religious community in Bahia, and their allies, organized in groups of various different kinds of action, who won some significant victories in the last few months from the democratically elected state administration of Governor Waldir Pires.

Among these victories are the declaration of the Ilé Iyá Nassô Oká, oldest Candomblé house in the country, as a State Monument to be preserved against real estate speculation, and the disappropriation of the gasoline station installed in its Oshun shrine.

Far from supporting its initiatives, Jorge Amado has consistently positioned himself against the black movement and its organizations, under the pretext that they practice reverse racism. If any "white" member of the Bahian elite should be world-renowned for solidarity with the Afro-Brazilian religions and their community, Governor Waldir Pires would deserve this recognition rather than Jorge Amado.

Thus, I would like to end on a note of appeal to our brothers and sisters in the rest of the African world. Heed Aimé Césaire's call for solidarity with respect to the Africans in Brazil! African Brazilians have made every effort to put this principle into practice. Yet, while there have been exceptions, as when Présence Africaine published my "Open Letter" on Brazil's participation in the First World Festival of Negro Arts (Nascimento, 1966), Negritude's general record is sadly deficient.

Throughout the 1950s and 1960s, Negritude was at the center of the debate around racism and black struggle in Brazil. A small group of African-Brazilian intellectuals, this speaker among them, ardently defended the movement against conservative white paternalists and leftist academics, to whom Negritude represented the ultimate pejorative indicating reverse racism.

Nevertheless, aware that diplomatic prestige and credibility in Brazilian government circles were the domain of the anti-Negritude elite, Senegalese diplomats began to endorse that elite's Eurocentric positions on the "Negro problem in Brazil." The proceedings of the First World Festival of Negro Arts, held in Dakar in 1966, became a classic illustration of this process. Among the official Brazilian delegates was Edison Carneiro, an ethnologist whose position on African culture was the antithesis of Negritude:

> The work of what we call Brazil's civilization was precisely the destruction of the specific cultures of black and Indian peoples, [which were] liquidated by the white man.... In my opinion, and perhaps we disagree on this, this seems to me to be extraordinary and good, because it signifies the possibility of the Brazilian people's unity, against their exploiters, of course.... So the fact of blacks having broken these ties with Africa, *even through very often brutal processes*, seems to me a

valid acquisition of the Brazilian people.[16] [Emphasis added.]

Another classic example was Clarival do Prado Valladares, a Bahian aristocrat who personified the Brazilian "etiquette of race relations" described by Anani Dzidzienyo (1971). According to this code, African Brazilians, incapable of critical, intellectual, cultural, or political discourse, must be represented by white paternalists in forums like the all-white Federal Council on Culture.

Valladares was one of these paternalists, and incidentally a member of the Federal Council on Culture.[17] Senegal had courted him at least since 1966, when he was placed on the jury of the First World Festival of Negro Art in Dakar. A classic expression of the irony of this situation is that, after adjudicating the Dakar Festival, Valladares returned to Brazil and promptly published an article entitled "African Backwardness or Chronicle of the First World Festival of Negro Arts, " in which he makes the following statement (1966:4):

> Whites did not hunt blacks in Africa, but bought them peacefully from black tyrants... Thus, it is not surprising that the best understanding and analysis of Africa is not to be found among Africans .... in historical terms, there seems to exist a certain inferiority complex that is African. This is why there is no historical text running parallel to those of Western nations.

A decade later, Valladares was made General Coordinator of the Brazilian Government's delegation to the Second World Festival of Black and African Arts and Culture, held in Lagos in 1977.

This is an extreme case, perhaps, and more subtle positions are all the more dangerous. But the fact remains that white "spokesmen" have more often represented Afro-Brazilian culture at international gatherings sponsored by African governments, and by intergovernmental organizations like UNESCO, than its own protagonists.

The infatuation of Negritude's state leadership with the Eurocentric Brazilian intelligentsia led ultimately to the creation by

Senegal's government of an Afro-Latin American Studies Association in 1974, with the very advocates of the miscegenation ideology whom we have mentioned as its principal protagonists. Gilberto Freyre and Pierre Verger were the Association's honorary Presidents; Clarival do Prado Valladares was a co-founder and officer; and Jorge Amado was among the Association's invited co-founders.

In sum, too often have African leaders been duped by the seductive slogans and pretty mirages designed by the Brazilian ruling class to obfuscate and perpetuate African Brazilians' domination, and too often have they allowed racial democracy to succeed in presenting, as "spokesmen" for the black community, precisely those who provide white supremacism's intellectual sustenance in Brazil.

One of the major functions of meetings like the present one is to raise our consciousness of the realities Africans experience in other parts of the world. In this spirit, I would like to call this plenary's attention to the danger of literary and academic niceties in the context of Brazilian white supremacism. The seductive qualities of its articulation in theories of race mixture and "universalist" cultural amalgamation are particularly pernicious. Race mixture as a social compulsion or as a state policy, in the name of whitening the population, is entirely the opposite of spontaneous interaction among equals of different ethnic origin. Racial purity has never existed among human beings, nor do we promote such an idea. But the encounter of different peoples should occur in a context of mutual love and respect.

Cheikh Anta Diop once commented (1978), in an interview published by the Brazilian magazine *Singular e Plural*:

> I believe that biological miscegenation, cultural miscegenation, elevated to the status of a political doctrine applied to a nation, is an error that can well lead to the most lamentable results.... the fusion of Brazilian ethnic elements will happen not on the anthropological level or the biological, but at the level of the heart and at the mental level of sensitivity.

Similar dangers lie in the "religious syncretism" preached by the proponents of *racial democracy* in Brazil. This syncretism has maintained African religious values in a subservient state, reduced to the level of folklore or superstition, while Christian values are elevated to the status of state religion. As Africans, our concern must be to rescue, preserve, and creatively reconstruct our specific spiritual values, rather than "fuse" them with others in a context of inequality. In a recent public statement, several of the most renowned African religious leaders in Bahia rejected the concept of syncretism, sustaining the integrity of African religions and their specific value systems, regardless of some of their adherents' parallel practice of Catholicism as well.

The Brazilian context is a living example of the need to develop an Afrocentric perspective, avoiding pitfalls like the racial democracy ideology that use apparently antiracist discourse to perpetuate a system of white supremacist domination. Only a truly Afrocentric analysis allows us to perceive the hidden implications of this kind of discourse. The Afrocentric perspective also avoids recourse to "universalist" solutions which end up diluting or doing away with our specific and legitimate identities. It discloses the need to develop and mutually revere cultural and ethnic differences among peoples, respect their specific identities, and end the transformation of these differences into motives for inequality, discrimination, or oppression.

Conclusion

In closing, I want to pay tribute to Aimé Césaire for his practice of solidarity. In the middle sixties, at a UNESCO-sponsored event on African culture held in Rio de Janeiro at the Ministry of Foreign Relations, the usual white "representatives" of Afro-Brazilian culture pontificated, while interested African Brazilians were barred from speaking. At the request of the present author and of Marietta Campos, a courageous black woman with a militant consciousness, who later married Léon Damas, Césaire protested to the plenary against the exclusion policy. And we know that, when protest is articulated, a new value implicitly is being created. In this case, Césaire was fashioning, in practice, Negritude's intrinsic value as simultaneous expression of Africans' specific identity, humanity, and struggle for liberation in all corners of the world.

As we leave the present meeting, we will all take with us, I am sure, the inspiration to follow Césaire's example, putting into practice at all times the defense and development of his three elements of Negritude: identity, fidelity, and solidarity with the African people throughout the world.

Axé!

3

AFRICANS IN SOUTH AND CENTRAL AMERICA

Members of the Pan-African World

(Accra, 1988)

Text of the inaugural lectures in the W. E. B. DuBois Memorial Annual Lecture Series, W. E. B. DuBois Memorial Center for Pan-African Culture, Accra, Ghana, 6-8 September 1988. The lecture was delivered in Portuguese by Abdias do Nascimento and simultaneously translated in English by Elisa Larkin Nascimento, who co-authored, edited, and translated the text.

Introductory Remarks: Scholarship, Pan-Africanism, and South and Central America

It is indeed an honor to be addressing you today, and personally a moment of great significance for us to tread the soil of the land where Yaa Asantewaa, Casely Hayford, George Padmore, and so many of Africa's great ancestors are at rest; the land where Kwame Nkrumah reaped the first fruits of African independence, restoring to life the nation of our forefathers, the pride and glory of Ghana. Among Nkrumah's great symbolic gestures as a statesman was to bring home one of Africa's first sons, W. E. B. DuBois, inviting him to live in Ghana and to carry out his *Encyclopedia Africana* project here.

At the outset, congratulations are in order to the W. E. B. DuBois Memorial Center for Pan-African Culture, for its initiative in inaugurating this lecture series, which undoubtedly shall continue in the future to provide a much-needed forum for discussion and treatment of African world problems, goals, and alternatives. That an African from South America speaks to you today, initiating this continuum of worldwide African debate, is in itself a history making fact. The Center's extension of this invitation to an African Brazilian is a timely revival and reassertion of DuBois' and Nkrumah's spirit in an era when Pan-Africanism, at least in the political sense, has found itself on the defensive.

The independence of African nations ushered in a new age of African world relations, affected by the reality of state power in

Africa and the Caribbean on the one hand, and on the other by neocolonial domination in Africa and the Diaspora.[1] Confronting the enormous task of administration, African governments concentrated their attention on internal problems of state building, the call for unity among African nations on the Continent, and questions of survival and development as states within the international community and diplomatic world. African communities in the Diaspora found themselves obliged to take stands on African affairs, supporting one or another ideological tendency in African states, liberation movements, and even civil wars. These and other considerations brought about problems for Pan-Africanism reflected in the African world gatherings of the postindependence period. Space limitations prevent us from analyzing them extensively or in detail. Suffice it to say here that, with the state machinery of African nations in play, organizing, and financing such meetings, Africans of the Diaspora sometimes saw their dilemma as African communities within states dominated by Eurocentric power structures understated, distorted, or even ignored. This was a bitter pill to swallow, considering the vital role Diaspora Africans had played in the worldwide anticolonial and African consciousness movements that contributed ultimately to the end of colonialism and to the winning of nationhood for the former African colonies.

It is an historical fact that the initiative in the Pan-African movement's founding and development came largely from the Diaspora. Antecedents to this century's Pan-African Congresses appear, for example, in the early religious and community organizations of Africans in the United States, and in the eighteenth- and nineteenth-century initiatives of that community's members and the West Indians associated with it, such as Paul Cuffee, Bishop Henry McNeil Turner, Prince Hall, Edward Wilmot Blyden, Joseph Cinque, Martin R. Delaney, Frederick Douglass, and many others. The Pan-African Conference and Congresses themselves were organized initially by Trinidad's barrister Sylvester Williams, and then by the African-American titan W. E. B. DuBois of the United States. In his *Autobiography* (1957), Kwame Nkrumah relates how Marcus Garvey's ideas, as well as Nkrumah's own relationships with

West Indians and African Americans like George Padmore and DuBois, influenced his intellectual and political growth as a young man. All these are examples of the Pan-African impulse coming out of the Diaspora.

If we accept John Henrik Clarke's definition of Pan-Africanism (1977:1) as "a collective effort to preserve and reconstruct Africans' nationhood, culture and humanity" in any part of the world, its first antecedents appear much earlier than those cited, and they appear in South and Central America.[2] Ivan Van Sertima's work (1976) confirms and brings together ideas raised earlier in this vein by experts in various fields. The facts he gleaned point to African presence and activity in ancient Mexico and Peru, where Africans kept alive and developed many aspects of their culture and nationhood in the context of Native American cultures they encountered centuries before the slave trade. Clyde Ahmad Winters (1985) has suggested that the same sort of African contact took place around 1300 A.D. in Brazil.

Although these movements of Africans in the Americas demonstrate the effort to preserve African culture in new lands, they are not characterized by a fundamental aspect associated with Pan-Africanism: self-defense against white supremacist domination and dehumanization in their two most outstanding expressions, European colonialism and the chattel slavery of Africans. In the fight to defend African peoples and nations against these systems, South and Central America had an early and prodigious participation. Brazil is one of the foremost examples, as home of the Republic of Palmares (1595-1696). Palmares was an African community of 30, 000 people, an enormous population for the period. We do not refer glibly to Palmares as the first free nation of the Americas after the European invasion, for it resisted colonial wars of aggression waged by the Portuguese, Dutch, and Brazilian colonial forces for over a century. Brazilian Native Americans and anticolonialist whites joined Africans in the building of Palmares, a fact that makes it a symbol of truly multiracial collaboration and conviviality.

Brazilian history is filled with similar experiences, classed generally with maroon societies of different natures in all the Americas and called *quilombos*, from the Kimbundu word ***kilombo***, denoting a concept traditionally linked to anticolonial resistance in that African linguistic region (B. Nascimento, 1986).[3]

This kind of African resistance was common to all the Americas. The examples are countless, and taken together they constitute a continuous and resilient link in the chain of Pan-African resistance around the world. Yet the region's long history of belonging in the African world did not prevent the more recent and formal expressions of Pan-Africanism, articulated ultimately in the Pan-African Congress movement, from excluding this contingent of the African world. It had no representation in any of the Pan-African Congresses until 1974. Then, as the sole South American delegate to the Sixth Pan-African Congress, this speaker was made into a living testimony to the marginal place the region once again merited.[4]

Millions of Spanish- and Portuguese-speaking Africans from Argentina to Mexico had been overlooked in the articulation of Pan-African events. The very concept of "Diaspora" was limited in the minds of many, and certainly in the practice of international gatherings, to Africa, the United States, and the West Indies, and to Africans from these areas living in Europe.

Since 1974, we have witnessed an era in which Africans from South and Central America have increasingly claimed their rightful place at the conference tables of the African world. This is perhaps the most important single contemporary development in Pan-African affairs.

The W. E. B. DuBois Center, by inviting a representative of South American Africans to inaugurate this lecture series, confirms and strengthens this trend, in a gesture of the same spirit and symbolic force as Prime Minister Nkrumah's invitation to DuBois. And in the same spirit, special mention of Ghana's current ambassador to Brazil, Kofi Awoonor, is in order. His extraordinary presence in Brazil as a man of culture, as a writer, historian, and critic, and as a Pan-Africanist, has been of great value to the African-Brazilian community.[5]

It seems an appropriate paradox that Kofi Awoonor was absent from our first encounter with him. During the January 1976 Conference on African World Alternatives and first plenary meeting of the Union of African Writers, held in Dakar, we signed a petition calling for his release from prison. Imprisonment, particularly for political reasons, is really a form of exile. Hence, the first encounter between two exiled Pan-Africanists was marked by a kind of exile from each other. Barely seven years later, we met again, this time in person, each having put an end to his respective exile. Abdias had returned home to Brazil, where Kofi had arrived as Ghana's Ambassador. Later, he became godfather to Osiris Kwesi, our first-born son and travelling companion here in Ghana.

Humbled by the weight of the responsibility that accompanies the honor conferred to us by the invitation to deliver the inaugural W. E. B. DuBois Memorial Lectures, we need to set forth certain parameters of the ideas and information we intend to present in these lectures.

First, we do not entertain pretensions of academic excellence, being less concerned with scholarly niceties than with the spirit, commitment, and utility of our work in the context of African world affairs. This does not mean we are unconcerned with fidelity to truth and fact. On the contrary, conventional scholarship, in the case of African experience in South and Central America and the Spanish-speaking Caribbean, is responsible more for distortion of truth and twisting of fact than for their clarification or illumination. This is true for reasons related to those causing the region's isolation in the African world context.

One is the language barrier. Africans in South and Central America and the Spanish-speaking Caribbean suffer the consequences of our colonial powers' inferior status in relation to the dominant ones, England and France. Once the Spanish Armada was defeated and the wind taken out of the sails of Portugal's maritime fleet, these two countries took on a semicolonial status with respect to their industrially developed European neighbors. As French and English became the languages of industrial and scientific progress, the Portuguese and the Spanish, and even more so their colonial subjects and exsubjects, became dependent upon translation for diffusion of their ideas and information in mainstream intellectual and political circles, not to mention the world of science and literature.

The Pan-African movement was no exception. Its meetings were carried on in English and French. Spanish and Portuguese were included as official languages of an African world event for the first time, to our knowledge, at the preparatory meetings for the Festival of Pan-African Culture (Fespac), held in Dakar as recently as 1987.

Divisions and difficulties arising from the imposition of European languages on our peoples are no novelty. Here is one more instance in which this imposition creates obstacles to our unity and communication. While there is a dearth of material in English, for example, on the African experience in South and Central America and the Spanish-speaking Caribbean, it is very difficult to find publishers interested in translations. Only the more prestigious among conventional scholars, either Eurocentric Latins or European researchers, are published in the mainstream languages, whether in translation or in the original.

This academic bias has been largely responsible for wide diffusion of the racial democracy myth (Nascimento; 1977, 1989) and its tantalizing corollaries eulogizing miscegenation and so-called cultural assimilation. Authors who support these theories are published in the mainstream languages, for theirs has always been endorsed as the supposedly objective academic view. On the other hand, the racial democracy and miscegenation theories inspire a peculiar fascination on the part of European scholars, who cannot resist the temptation to delve ever further into their details and subtleties, perhaps unwittingly contributing to dissemination and aggrandizement of one of the most monstrous falsehoods ever devised by the apologists of oppression anywhere.

We do not hesitate to identify the force and fury of the miscegenation or racial democracy ideology in South and Central America and the Spanish-speaking Caribbean as the major historical agent of the region's isolation in African world affairs. Unfortunately, the seductive qualities of the academic theories sustaining this ideology have not failed to attract African scholars, who have tended in the main, until very recently, to accept the distorted data coming out of conventional works on the region, as well as some of their conclusions. Even Africans engaged in the forefront of the Pan-African movement were sometimes duped by such theories. A classic example appeared in the draft *Programme* written in the early 1940s for the United League for Defense of the Negro Race, one of the groups involved in the organizational prelude to the Fifth Pan-African Congress. The League directed its appeal (cited in Geiss, 1974:311) to "all Africans and African-Americans (except for some in Latin American states because racial prejudice was rigorously suppressed there)."

This sort of ignorance of anti-African oppression in our region was not remedied by the independence process. African governments organizing international events like the First and Second Festivals of Black and African Arts and Culture (Dakar, 1966 and Lagos, 1977) welcomed dubious "representatives" of African communities, at least in Brazil's case, giving the floor to white Eurocentric "spokesmen" for Afro-Brazilian culture, while African-Brazilian artists and intellectuals themselves were excluded, served as pawns, or were relegated to nonofficial status (Nascimento; 1966, 1977, 1981).[6] This tendency of certain Africans to be seduced by the theories of the mentally white spokesmen of racial democracy is caused in part by the appeal of academicism, overvaluing pseudoscientific discourse at the expense and to the detriment of social and historical truth, not to mention political and ideological coherence.

Related to these considerations is the fact that the conventional parameters of academic work are intrinsically Eurocentric in their conception and application. Their validity for any African community is questionable at best. So-called "scholarly neutrality" is generally a mask for Eurocentric bias, just as so-called "universalism" has been a mask for the imposition of European critical values upon the literature and artwork of the world's other peoples. Moreover, as quantum physics has proved that no object can be studied without undergoing some transformation as a result of the observer's interference, so we believe, especially in the case of dominated peoples, that no observer can be entirely neutral in his studies and conclusions. These, in turn, will inevitably be used to affect in some way the observed people's experience of domination. The scholar or observer must take a position: He or she either contributes to prolonging domination or contributes to the process of liberation.

In our own case, the choice is clear. In the case of this speaker, all my life's work (creative, scholarly, and political) has been dedicated to advancing my people's cause. My coauthor's adult life has been dedicated to the fight against racism and imperialism. These lectures are no exception. Rather than engaging in "objective" analyses or "unbiased" scholarship, they express our commitment to the search for an Afrocentric approach to African world reality and its study. While the European perspective may be partially legitimate for Europeans, we contend that it leads to the propagation of untruths, and we reject its violent imposition upon all the world's peoples. An Afrocentric philosophy does not discard outright all postulates of European origin. However, it does reserve to Africans the right to define which of those postulates might be valid for them and the right to design and develop alternative principles based upon their own experience, methodologies, and forms of knowledge.[7]

The material covered in these lectures will deal with emergent questions of Pan-Africanism, focusing on the South and Central American region, particularly on Brazil, and their relationship to the rest of the African world. We pretend neither to be exhaustive nor to delve into the minutia and detail of the points raised. Rather, we will discuss issues we consider to be of historical and immediate importance to the African world.

In the first section of the text, we intend to deal with some general questions raised by the banner of Pan-Africanism, questions that remain live issues affecting the African world, especially South and Central America and the Spanish-speaking Caribbean. In a second section, we will present a brief introduction to four basic dimensions of the African experience in the region: the history of Pan-African resistance; the suppression of the African demographic presence and the reality of anti-African discrimination; the miscegenation illusion or ideology; and the so-called syncretism between African and European religious cultures. This section is an overview, deficient with regard to particular national experiences but intended to give a general picture. And third, we will look at Brazil as a key country in African world affairs. In the last section, we will address some questions arising from the nature of the South and Central American region's insertion in that world.

General Considerations on the Pan-African Cause

Tanzania's President Julius Nyerere pinpointed (1974:18-19) the basis for growth and development of Pan-African consciousness among the world's people of African origin when he wrote that

> men and women of Africa, and of African descent, have had one thing in common—an experience of discrimination and humiliation imposed upon them because of their African origins. Their colour was made into both a badge and a cause of their poverty, their humiliation and their oppression.

It hardly seems worth dwelling upon this point, which strikes one as self-evident. Yet there has been a concerted effort on the part of anti-Pan-Africanists the world over, and particularly in South and Central America and the Spanish-speaking Caribbean, to deny its truth. These detractors sometimes adhere to the class analysis or economic determinism theory which states that discrimination against black people is not based on African origin but merely reflects inferior economic status. Both this theory and that of innate African inferiority as the "natural order of things" lead to a common conclusion: Africans and their descendants have no business fighting against racism or uniting themselves for that purpose. The innate inferiority theory is now so demoralized as to deserve little comment. The class analysis argument, on the other hand, merits our attention because it has been propounded by leading African statesmen and thinkers and is still influential among students and youth.

This theory's main tenet is that economic factors are the sole cause and determiner of historical trends and human motivation. Lest we erroneously attribute this idea to Marxist thought, we shall take the cue from Kwame Nkrumah (1964:1), who quotes from the pen of Frederich Engels:

> According to the materialist conception of history, the *ultimately* determining element in history is the production and reproduction of real life. More than this neither Marx or I have ever asserted. Hence, if somebody twists this into saying that the economic element is the *only* determining one, he transforms that proposition into a meaningless, abstract, senseless phrase. . . . We cannot exempt many of the more recent "Marxists" from this reproach, for the most amazing rubbish has been produced in this quarter, too.

The term *real life* does not signify merely economic value, for the goal of the classless society is to reduce or eliminate preoccupation with mechanical reproduction of economic values, freeing all citizens to pursue, unfettered by class distinctions, the higher values of life: cultural, intellectual, artistic, or leisure.

With their footing in the economic determinist base, the proponents of the "class only" position go on to posit that European mercantile slavery was a system instituted and motivated solely by economic considerations, i.e., the need for labor in the colonies. Racism, in their view, is merely a tool wrought of social and religious substance to serve, consolidate, and support the prevailing economic system, be it colonial, neo-colonial, or transnational monopoly capitalism. In this view, Africans need only to fight against the exploitative economic system, for with the victory of socialism and classless society, racism will be eliminated. To fight against anti-African racism is to divert attention from the real issues, divide the working class, and defeat the true struggle against capitalist and imperialist economic forces.

Economics alone do not fully explain the motors of expansion and conquest. Domination involves the reproduction of economic, political, religious, philosophical, linguistic, social, cultural, epistemological, and scientific norms and notions. In a word, it involves imposition upon conquered peoples of a dominant civilization, way of life, and worldview. To single out the economic factor as determinative reflects the European habit of pigeonholing the world and its manifestations into separate and unblended categories, one of the distinguished marks of conventional academicism. Currently, just as more advanced thinkers in Western medicine are questioning the value of increasing specialization and emphasizing the advantages of general practice, progressive academic circles are moving toward a multidisciplinary approach to social and scientific research. Exclusivist orientations like economic determinism are increasingly discredited.

In any case, white supremacist ideology is not the creation of mercantilist or capitalist economic systems. It is deeply rooted in ancient Judaeo-Christian cultural tradition. From the first book of the Old Testament, Ham is condemned: "the meanest of slaves shall he be to his brethren" (Genesis IX:18-27). Ham was identified with Africa and her descendants. In their exposition of this myth, Talmudic scholars of the sixth century wrote the following passage (cited in Ben-Jochannan, 1971:21) a full millennium before Europeans had occasion to justify chattel slavery of Africans:

> Canaan's children shall be born ugly and black! Moreover, because you twisted your head around to see my nakedness, your grandchildren's hair shall be twisted into kinks, and their eyes red; again because your lips jested at my nakedness, they shall go naked, and their male members shall be shamefully elongated! Men of this race are called Negroes, and their forefather Canaan commanded them to love theft and fornication, to be banded together in hatred of their masters and never to tell the truth.

Anti-African discriminatory practices, including racial segregation, existed as part and parcel of the Greek and Roman empires of antiquity, which enforced them against conquered Africans in their Egyptian home. The difference is that the dominating classes of that era depended upon Africans for technological, scientific, and cultural know-how. As Cheikh Anta Diop's life work showed, the Greeks drank humbly at the fountain of Egyptian knowledge. Evidently, therefore, racism could not take the same forms it has in the modern world order, a product of the violent interruption by Europe of Africa's economic, scientific, and technological development.

Another proposition often invoked by proponents of the "class only" position, as well as anti-African historians, is that slavery was practiced by Africans, who themselves participated in the European trade in enslaved Africans. Therefore, the argument goes, Africans cannot legitimately claim that enslavement of Africans by Europeans was unique or fundamentally racist in character.

This view ignores the unprecedented nature of European chattel slavery of Africans, based upon the idea that they were not human, but animals or objects, their natural destiny being servitude. No other system of slavery practiced in Africa was founded upon the assumption of the slaves' innate inferiority, much less upon absolute denial of their humanity. Slavery, as practiced in precolonial Africa, was most often a consequence of war, with captives taken into servitude. This servitude was not an immutable or "natural" condition, and the slave could elevate his social standing within the captor society. He did not lose his status as human being.

Related to the minimization of the racist nature of chattel slavery of Africans is a tendency among certain social scientists to minimize the consequence and import of white supremacism by likening it to the general preference a people holds for its own culture in relation to that of other peoples. Anthropologists have called this tendency ethnocentrism, and there are those who like to shrug off Eurocentrism and the doctrine of white supremacy as one more manifestation of this universal human trait. Implicitly, they wonder why Africans and other dominated peoples make such ado about this particular case. They are quick, indeed, to cite the ethnocentrism of African peoples, emphasizing its tribal nature, once again placing the onus of oppression on the oppressed.

A kind of corollary to this line of academic research and reasoning is another which likes to investigate the minutiae of what it calls the "clash of cultures, " in which two peoples displaying ethnocentrism confront one another and problems arise which are studied from the angles of ethnology, anthropology, sociology, and "comparative social systems."

The central fallacy of such theories is that they neglect the overall context of domination. Ethnocentrism among African groups cannot legitimately be compared with the violent dehumanization and attempted destruction of African civilizations over centuries by the entire structure of European colonialism. Neither can feelings of cultural superiority among African groups be compared with those of Europeans taught over nearly a millennium that civilization is a Western invention, while Africa has been barbarous, savage, and stagnant throughout human history. Similarly, the term *clash*, which evokes an image of like bodies colliding, is patently useless in the colonial context. While African cultures proved strong and resilient in their resistance to colonial imposition, the sheer weight of European missionary, educational, mass media, scientific, commercial, economic, and political systems, backed by the superior force of arms, renders the *clash* concept inoperative.

Similar considerations are appropriate to other concepts, like assimilation, miscegenation, and religious syncretism, generally applied to the African experience in South and Central America and the Spanish-speaking Caribbean, which will be mentioned in the course of these lectures. What we are trying to say here is that academic discourse, couched in the language of "scientific objectivity, " repeatedly has furnished us with dangerously misleading terms of reference, unfortunately not without influence among African youth and intellectuals.

Convergence of academic theories like these with the pseudo-Marxist position on class struggle brings us to the need for an Afrocentric perspective. While some Africans may identify with ruling classes and exploit their fellow Africans, this fact does not justify denial of the need to rebuild African identity and consciousness after centuries of colonial domination. This problem differs in nature and particularly in extent between Diaspora communities and independent African nations. For Diaspora communities within European-dominated multiracial states, race is the foremost social contradiction in their experience. It must be addressed first, in the general move toward social change and resolution of class distinctions. This need derives not only from the danger that new power structures might perpetuate race distinctions, but also from the principle that only with a sense of selfhood and protagonism can an individual or group be an effective actor in social movements with interests greater than its own.

Economically speaking, African consciousness is a basic need for the liberation of African peoples in all the world. Cultivation of European tastes imposed by white supremacism leads to consumption of foreign reserves in the acquisition of often inferior imported products which could effectively be substituted by African ones. Hunger in Africa could be greatly reduced if, instead of depending on foreign aid, Africans investigated and exploited African resources, including energy and vegetable protein sources, in alternative ways oriented by African-centered values (Ayensu, 1976; Asante, 1988). These are only some aspects of the economic need for Afrocentric thought.

There are those who argue that a movement for African identity implies lack of solidarity with other oppressed or dominated peoples. To them, only one point of reference is legitimate: the "Third World" or "oppressed peoples" in general. This position is based on a false premise, for nothing prevents me and my people, with a grounding in identity and solidarity among ourselves, from supporting the just demands and struggles of other peoples. Indeed, we will render a more effective support to them if our own sense of self-worth is mature and developed. As Maulana Karenga has pointed out (1977:110-111):

> the liberation of Black people brings the whole of humanity closer to liberation; ... human experience is as a whole is deformed and denied full development as long as Blacks or any other part of humanity is enslaved, oppressed or exploited.

On the other hand, Third Worldism can be misleading by obscuring the differences in power and pretense among so-called Third World nations. Brazil's relations with Africa will be discussed later in this context.

Another false form of solidarity is the idea that we must strive to create a "universal" or "raceless" society and culture valid for all peoples. This is a particularly attractive mirage, especially familiar to African Brazilians, to whom it is held out incessantly as the correct goal of human relations. It usually takes one of two forms: either we are to pursue the universal culture of "scientific socialism" in revolutionary society, or we are to create, through progressive miscegenation, a new *café-au-lait* humanity whose monolithic ethnicity and cultural amalgamation would eradicate all forms of racism and racial distinctions. The Brazilian intellectual left traditionally marries both these goals in one ideological utopia.

"Scientific socialism" is a notion grounded in European philosophies developed in utter disregard of the most revolutionary movements that surrounded its forefathers: African maroon societies in the Americas, notably in Haiti and Brazil (the Republic of Palmares), and anticolonial resistance in Africa (from Samory Touré to Chaka and Yaa Asantewaa). Marxist historians consistently neglect to class these movements as revolutionary, although they challenged the colonial mercantile economic structure, and therefore the world capitalist order, at their very foundations. We need not belabor the history of African relations with the Eurocentric left, which has been told by George Padmore, Richard Wright, Wilson Record, and others. It is worthy of note, however, that the Afro-Brazilian experience has been no different, and would provide many anecdotes to illustrate if space permitted (Nascimento, 1989; Larkin Nascimento, 1980).

As for the idea that socialism is to be "scientific, " we are painfully aware of the disservices consistently visited upon Africans in the name of "science." Africans in Brazil and in the world have been the objects of countless and highly respected scientific investigations into the nature of our innate inferiority. Our skulls have been measured, our religions dissected, our art confiscated to Police Museums and psychiatric institutions, our sanity questioned, all in the name of science. So-called Afro-Brazilian Congresses were convened to engage in this scientific activity. In the end, academia has been unable to convince these authors, at least, that science will be responsible for creating a just and reasonable society for our children and grandchildren to live in.

The idea of the universal mulatto race as a solution to racial discrimination attempts to reduce white supremacism to a crude notion of skin criteria. Far more than rejection of a people's epidermic color, racism is a denial of that people's humanity, history, and civilization; a rejection of its ethos, its total being. The proposition of a raceless society generally involves the suppression of African or other dominated people's culture and identity, with the happy alignment of the new colorless race under the exclusive aegis of "universal" European civilization. This, indeed, is the classic Latin American proposal.

Diversity, however, is the most universal condition of human existence, and the richness of human experience derives largely from interaction, intercommunication, and interchange among specific cultures. The truly revolutionary goal is not to eradicate differences among cultures and identities but to cultivate and respect them. It is to see that they not be made the cornerstones of oppression, inequality of opportunity, or economic and social stratification. Even the Marxian goal of a classless society in which the higher values of life could be cultivated is served far better by a vision in which the many cultures and identities of the world's peoples share and exchange living values than by one in which all the world conforms to a "universal" model, however "scientifically" elaborated.

Realization of this goal depends upon the reaffirmation, rehabilitation, and revitalization of cultures suppressed by colonialism and white supremacy. Here is the crux of the need to develop an Afrocentric system of thought to delineate the perspectives of African world experience. Despite denials by those afflicted with a "saline consciousness, " in Wole Soyinka's lucid expression (Asante and Asante 1990:19-21), this supracontinental African identity is a hard reality. The richness of its internal variations denies its existence no more than the variations among European national cultures and their overseas offspring negate the existence of a "Western civilization" whose boundaries have expanded beyond the shores of Europe.

One of the primary needs of Afrocentric research is to develop the concept of "African civilization" in a spirit analogous to that of the "Western civilization" encompassing so many diverse cultures. In the work of Cheikh Anta Diop, Ivan Van Sertima, and their colleagues, we have the cornerstones of such a concept in the exposition of ancient Egyptian civilization and its Nubian and Central African forerunners. Molefi Asante has laid the groundwork for the Afrocentric idea (1980, 1987, 1990); Maulana Karenga has contributed with his translation of *The Husia* (1984) and with his other works. We hope the present lectures will also contribute, by elucidating African peoples' experience in South and Central America and the Spanish-speaking Caribbean from their own perspective.

African Experience in South and Central America

The first fact of African presence in South and Central America and the Spanish-speaking Caribbean is its implicit denial. African-Peruvian poet, activist, and scholar Nicomedes Santa Cruz (1974) has eloquently observed this reality:

> If there is anything that in these parts of America they have always tried to pilfer and maliciously hide (aside from our civil rights), it is our historic presence, decisive in many cases, as well as our enormous and positive contribution in folklore and the arts. A traditional policy of silence, absurd theorization when silencing is no longer possible, or outright usurpation, have been the systematic responses given in Peru to every African contribution. And we, the slaves' descendants, at the margin of "official" culture, receive the feeble adjective of "negroid" for all our manifestations.

Largely for this reason, it is seldom recalled that throughout four centuries, comprising four-fifths of their existence in time, most of the region's colonies and republics had majority African populations. In Peru, the Lima census shows that in 1640 there were 15, 000 Africans in that city alone, representing half its population (Moura,

1977:101). In Chile, between 1540 and 1620, black people numbered far more than whites (Mellafe, 1959:252). As late as the nineteenth century, Argentina's capital Buenos Aires was more than a third black (Rama, 1967:15). Ecuador, in the seventeenth century, had about 90, 000 Africans, nearly a third of the population (Moura, 1977:102). Venezuela, upon independence, had 200, 000 Europeans and 406, 000 Africans (Franco, 1975:418). According to Nicolás Guillén (n.d.:70-75), in Cuba in 1840, "the black population surpassed the white, native and Spanish all together." According to official data, Colombia's Africans formed a majority of 55.6 percent and 63.7 percent in 1778 and 1823 respectively; in 1901, Vergara and Velasco state that they accounted for 80 percent of the nation's population. Gonzalo Aguirre Beltrán tells us that in 1570, the African population in Mexico numbered 20, 569 (Franco, 1975:415). The African population in Brazil has always been a majority and continues so to this day.

During colonial times, thousands of Africans reemigrated, especially from Brazil and Cuba, back to Africa, to countries like today's Benin, Nigeria, Ghana, and Togo. They played important roles of varied nature in the societies into which they returned.[8]

It would be a mistake to envision Africans in pre-independent South and Central America and the Caribbean exclusively as slave populations. There was a large number of maroons, manumitted Africans, Africans who arrived free in the Americas, and slaves or semi-slaves called *negros de ganho* or *ganaderos*, who earned their own money by street peddling, with considerable freedom of movement. "These Negroes are so richly dressed and decorated with gold, that in my opinion, they have more freedom than we have, " complained Archdeacon Alvaro de Castro of Santo Domingo, in his 1542 report to the Council of the Indies (Price, 1973:38-39).

All over Spanish and Portuguese America, the preponderance of Africans caused deep concern to the authorities, and justifiably so. *Cimarrones*, *cumbes*, *palenques*, *quilombos*, and other maroon societies proliferated, in armed confrontation against the colonial order. Other forms of African resistance undermined the economy and forced the Spanish in the Caribbean, for example, to set up a special police force for catching fugitive slaves. Rebellions, wars, urban guerrilla movements, and organized free African communities abounded from the sixteenth century to the eve of the twentieth. These were not isolated rebellions but a collective phenomenon that seriously callenged the entire world economic order. Their importance lies not only in their resistance to colonial structure, however, but also in their legacy of African sociocultural, economic, and political principles. Jean Casimir of Haiti (1980) has pointed out the import of these principles for contemporary African thought.

African culture, in the words of John Henrik Clarke (1973), "became the cohesive force and communication system that set these revolutionary struggles in motion." An example is the Yanguicos community, a Mexican *cimarrón* that combined Bantu military leadership with West African civic organization. Its saga of military confrontation with the technologically superior Spanish forces is a moving page in Pan-African history. So also are those of the *palenques* led by Baoruco and Vega, Diego de Guzmán and his nation in San Juan de la Maguana, Diego de Campo, and Captain Lemba's guerrilla forces in Santo Domingo. In Venezuela, King Miguel the African's *cumbe* was a formidable foe. It established a capital city, organized an army, and by 1555 had a thriving community that successfully attacked the Spanish settlement of Barquisimeto. Miguel's group joined with other *cumbes* to elect a common king, Bayano. United under him, the maroons were undefeatable, obliging the Spanish to settle by treaty. This was a common occurrence throughout South and Central America and the Caribbean. The treaty with King Bayano guaranteed freedom to the Africans and created a legal right of manumission to all slaves who were abused or mistreated (Price, 1973:41).

In a similar example, growing *palenque* populations were united in Cartagena, around 1600, under the African king Benkos Bioho, who consolidated his strength by building a stockaded town and thus founding a settlement that became the famous *palenque* of San Basílio. Again, the Spanish were unable to defeat these Africans and finally settled under treaty in 1772. San Basílio remains intact today, with its own African-derived language and distinct culture (Friedemann, 1979).

Elected political leaders, usually kings, are one of the characteristics common to these maroons. In Mexico and Cuba, Venezuela and Colombia, their strength lay in uniting under this democratic leadership. In Brazil, consistent with this trend, Zumbi was the last in a succession of elected kings who led the united *quilombos* of Palmares.

In such cases as the Surinam Maroon (1715-1863), the Berbice revolt at Guyana (1763), and the Haitian revolution, John Henrik Clarke (1973) has noted a pattern of Yoruba organizational skills combined with Akan military leadership. Cuban historian José Luciano Franco (1975:288) notes the importance of the creole language and the voodoo religion in the Haitian revolution, observing that colonial authorities and slaveowners persecuted voodoo

> not so much because of what this religious belief meant vis-à-vis the official Catholic cult, but more significantly because the majority of its secret ceremonies had an intimate relation with the growing activity of the *cimarrones*, and the slaves' periodic rebelliousness.

As Wole Soyinka has pointed out (1976:54):

> Ogun for his part becomes not merely the god of war but the god of revolution in the most contemporary context—and this is not merely in Africa, but in the Americas to where his worship has spread. As the Roman Catholic props of the Batista regime in Cuba discovered when it was too late, they should have worried less about Karl Marx than about Ogun, the rediscovered deity of revolution.

It is important to recall that *palenques* and other maroons were not merely vehicles of war. They aspired primarily to be peaceful communities living according to their unique traditions. In this sense, they represent the deeper significance of Pan-Africanism as the international diffusion of African civilization and not only as a reactive force combatting oppression.

Richard Price (1973:27-29) has commented on the maroons' cultural integration:

> They could and did look to Africa for deep-level organizational principles, relating to cultural realms as diverse as naming their children on the one hand, or systems of justice on the other.... However "African" in character, no maroon social, political, religious or aesthetic system can be reliably traced to a specific tribal provenience; they reveal, rather, their syncretistic composition. The political system of Palmares, for example, did not derive from a particular central African model, but from several.

Perhaps this is the truest sense in which such cultural systems can be called African, for Africa represents the integration of the different systems existing within her. This aspect of New World experience most intrinsically expresses its Pan-African essence.

Doubt nevertheless has been raised in some circles as to whether a truly Pan-African character has been established for these movements. Even if we use a more rigorous definition than John Henrik Clarke's (1977) and agree with St. Clair Drake (1982:343) that Pan-African struggle involves an "articulated sense of worldwide activity with interrelated responsibilities, " there are grounds for characterizing these episodes of resistance as Pan-African. Documented instances of such articulated consciousness do exist, as in the revolt led by Emiliano Mandacaru in Recife, capital of Pernambuco State, Brazil, in 1824. His troops sang in the city's streets (Nascimento 1989:36):

> As I imitate Christophe
> That immortal noble Haitian
> Hey! imitate his people
> Oh my sovereign people!

Nevertheless, Afrocentric analysis dispenses the need for extensive written documentation of such interrelationship. First, the identification of written documentation exclusively as historical evidence is a European standard inappropriate to peoples whose history is preserved and transmitted principally by oral tradition. Lack of reliable written documentation of the African experience is notoriously a consequence of the fact that the documents available were written by the European colonial authorities. Second, only in this century (and to a lesser extent in the nineteenth) would it be possible, due to advanced communication and transportation technologies, to expect interrelated responsibilities of Pan-Africanism's protagonists to be made explicitly concrete through immediate international contact. When overseas voyages took months to convey news from one part of the world to another, evidently the forms immediate solidarity could take, susceptible to documentation, were more restricted. But to assume our African ancestors were less than aware of the interrelated character of their different local struggles would be sadly to underrate both them and ourselves. Communication did exist, despite the difficulties, and the link to Africa has always been strong, so much so that it has survived nearly five centuries of suppression.

In the perspective of Quilombismo (Nascimento; 1980, 1990), a proposal presented originally at the Second Congress of Black Culture in the Americas (Panama, 1980), the legacy of maroons forms the foundation of an Afro-American sociopolitical theory based on our own historical experience. This idea proposes in essence a decentralized democratic socialism with emphasis on collective land ownership; the multiethnic and multicultural nature of American societies; the need for respect and reconstruction of non-European (African and Native American) history and cultural values; an Afrocentrically articulated ecological stand defending harmony with nature; and a critical concept of development focusing primarily on the need for more just income distribution and for employment, health care, and education opportunities for all. This philosophy is appropriate, with variations taking into account specific circumstances, for the Americas in general and for Africa as well.

In the case of Brazil, the African segment constitutes a majority population. Therefore, Quilombismo addresses not only the African community, but the nation as a whole. It is a proposal of national administration and organization, taking into account the needs of specific populations in a multiracial context. However, even where the African population is a minority, the need for such a perspective is clear. Specific identities deserve to be respected in the articulation of a new, democratic sociopolitical and economic order.

Demographic Manipulation and Suppression of African Populations

Not only the maroon resistance movements, but the very populations from which they emerged, have been minimized in conventional versions of the region's history. In their eagerness to insert themselves into the Western world, Latin American elites strove to identify their nations as European in culture and character.

Perhaps the most effective tool used to this end is the manipulation of demographic statistics. In Brazil and Colombia, for example, race classifications were removed entirely from census data in a hypocritical denial of racial "problems."[9] As if to illustrate to what extent this lack of statistics facilitated distortion of fact, Brazil's Ministry of Foreign Relations announced to the world in the book *Brazil 1966* (Itamaraty, 1966:125) that "the majority of the Brazilian population is made up of whites, the percentage of persons of mixed blood being minute." Official Colombian statistics published from 1810 to 1963 show that introduction and withdrawal of such categories as "mestizo" drastically inflate the "white" population and deflate the "black, zambo and mulatto, " seemingly at the authorities' whim (Larkin Nascimento, 1980:22-24).

The first lesson in Afro-Latin-American studies is the one demographic statistician Giorgio Mortara learned (1970: 458) in relation to Brazil. As a rule, statistical data are highly distorted in such a way that "the black group loses a great deal and gains but little, the brown group gains much more than it loses, and the white group gains a great deal and loses nothing."

This process is greatly responsible for the general lack of awareness of African populations in the region. Peru is a good example. Its African contingent of more than 50, 000 is widely ignored or underestimated. So is the African-Uruguayan population. As Ildefonso Pereda Valdés has stated (Rout, 1976:202):

> racial discrimination is deeply embedded in our society, with much deeper roots than is generally supposed. It is a barrier which denies to black people in Uruguay their full development. Jim Crowism is applied despite guarantees of law and the Constitution.

In nineteenth century Uruguay and Buenos Aires (Argentina), African political organization and protest was voiced by an active black press through newspapers like *La Conservación*, *Nuestra Raza*, and *La Raza Africana o sea el Democrata Negro*. Afro-Uruguayan activism culminated in the formation of a black political party, the Autochthonous Black Party, which called for racial redress and black political consciousness (Pereda Valdés, 1965; Jackson, 1975; Andrews 1979). Paraguayan independence owes a great debt to African soldiers, one it shares with Uruguay, Argentina, Chile, Peru, Venezuela, Mexico, and Colombia. To a great extent, Brazil depended on African soldiers in the war it waged against Paraguay in the nineteenth century, with the support of Uruguay and Argentina.

In Ecuador, the northwestern province of Esmeraldas is virtually an African state. Several towns in the valleys of the Andes, where sugar production demanded the use of slaves, are other African centers. Salinas del Norte, site of a huge salt mine, remains a locus of Africans' exploitation since colonial times.

Educated Mexicans are often the first to deny the existence of African communities in Mexico. Yet Africans were and are an important component of Mexico's people and history (Palmer, 1976). In Veracruz, the black community that inspired Katherine Dunham's Afro-American dance *La Veracruzana* continues to celebrate its African cultural and heritage in various forms (Capitaine, 1975).

An important historical phenomenon is the emigration of West

Indian Africans to Central American counties like Panama, Honduras, Nicaragua, and Costa Rica, where they worked to build the Canal and related railway networks, and where they constitute bilingual or English-speaking enclaves within these Spanish-speaking nations (Bryce-Laporte, 1979; Olien, 1970; Duncan and Meléndez, 1972). These communities are located mainly on the Atlantic coast and in the Canal area. Marcus Garvey's United Negro Improvement Association had its headquarters in Puerto Limón, Costa Rica, where the UNIA building still stands today, along with remnants of the organization's original membership. In Nicaragua, the Bluefields community on the east coast had a self-assertive role and relationship with the Sandinista government, which the present authors were able to witness briefly in 1983. In Panama, the Second Congress of Black Culture in the Americas took place in 1980 under the leadership of the African-Panamanian poet and sociologist Gerardo Maloney.

Major African populations found in Cuba, Puerto Rico, the Dominican Republic, Colombia and Venezuela are better known. At least a quarter of Colombia's population is of African origin, and intense concentration of Africans is found in the fertile valley of the river Cauca. Cali, site of the First Congress of Black Culture in the Americas (August 1977), organized by African-Colombian physician and writer Manuel Zapata Olivella, is located in this valley.

Most impressive in Colombia, however, is the Department of Chocó, on the west coast, with Caribbean and Pacific shores. An African state in Colombia, ninety-eight percent black, Chocó is little known to the world outside and "forgotten and segregated by the rest of the country, " according to African-Colombian writer Jesus Lacides Mosquera (1975:44), a native of Chocó. As for the attitude of the ruling strata, it was expressed by a Colombian politician who remarked to delegates at the Cali Congress: "Colombia has been very generous to Chocó. Chocó is not qualified to be a Department, but Colombia has given Chocó the honor of being a Department."

Chocó's situation is analogous to that of Bahia State, the famous seat of Candomblé, Brazil's African religion. Bahia and its capital, Salvador, with a population of two million, are at least ninety percent African. Popular wisdom says there is no one in Bahia, even among the aristocrats, who does not have at least a distant drop of African blood. Indeed, in their effort to present Bahia (and themselves) as a world example of anti-racism, such aristocrats are sometimes the first to stress this fact. They also cite the prevalence of African culture, from the culinary to the religious.

Yet the African cultural matrix is still seen as exotic and classed as folklore, while European norms and values prevail in Bahian society. Power relations are divided not so subtly. There are no African congressmen from the state. In the local and state governments, professed African Bahians are almost entirely absent as well. Positions of political, social, and economic prestige are occupied almost exclusively by whites who reside in luxury beach-front buildings and control business, banks, universities, police and the justice system, politics, and mainstream culture and art.

Bahia is a portrait in miniature of Brazil's overall society. In the country's armed forces, soldiers and sailors are of African origin in their vast majority, while officers are white: the higher the rank, the more exclusive the color bar. In government, African Brazilians generally serve coffee to exclusively white holders of office.

According to the 1980 census, African-Brazilian children have six times less opportunity than white children to complete twelve years of schooling. Twice as many African adults and three times as many African school-age children, as compared to white, are illiterate in Brazil. Only three percent of college students are black. In São Paulo, Brazil's most developed state, according to research done by the respected Carlos Chagas Foundation, black workers earn from twenty to fifty percent less than whites for the same jobs (when they can get them), and the gap widens as educational requirements increase.

Brazil is the archetype of the Latin model of racist hegemony touted as racial democracy, and it is so not only by virtue of this discriminatory reality. Brazil also furnishes us with the most sophisticated elaboration of the miscegenation ideology of white supremacist domination, whose foremost exponents are men like Gilberto Freyre (1946, 1963, 1969, 1976), Jorge Amado, and Pierre Verger

(1977).

The Miscegenation Illusion: Obfuscation of a Racist Reality

Latin ruling classes evolved a paternalist form of white supremacism, based on the ideal of race mixture, called racial democracy, which is more insidious than aggressive racism. Emphasizing biological and cultural assimilation, it created an illusion of happy intermixture masking its racist content. The question of identity in the black community, crucial to any colonized or dominated group, as students of Albert Memmi or Frantz Fanon will agree, became a dilemma so debilitating as to strip the victims of their collective consciousness of domination.

The region's reputation for nonracism and benevolence toward its African populations is so strong that slavery there is said to have been "ordinarily a mild form of servitude, " in the words of Donald Pierson (1967:45, 76). Pierre Verger expounds this discourse not only in Brazil but in Africa (Verger, 1977). Scores of other writers espouse this idea, according to which race mixture is supposed to have "prevented the problems of racial discrimination." Indeed, "miscegenation and the unawareness of racial prejudice" are taken to be one and the same thing.

Gilberto Freyre is a classic expositor of the miscegenation illusion. He posits that the special nature of Portuguese colonialism in Brazil and Africa resulted in what he calls "Luso-Tropicalism, " a beneficent, nonracist society in which Africans and Europeans are not "two enemy halves" but "two fraternizing halves." These harmonic groups are disappearing through a healthy, happy process of racial fusion.

"Luso-tropicalism" has been taken to such extremes that a Brazilian ambassador, José Sette Câmara, was able with a straight face to make the following statement (Portella, 1974:14) to an African international audience meeting in Zambia in 1974. As he spoke, Portuguese napalm bombs were devastating civilian populations in Angola, Mozambique, and Guinea-Bissau and Cabo Verde's liberation wars. Câmara stated:

> Colonialism in Portugal is different. The absence of racial discrimination, the ease of miscegenation, the disposition of the colonial whites to stay, to grow and prosper with their new lands, exist in the Portuguese colonies as they existed in Brazil. The Africans themselves recognize all these positive peculiarities of Portuguese colonization.

This glorious vision of Portuguese antiracism is contrasted to the United States and South Africa, where the Latins believe there is no miscegenation. Speaking to an African audience at a 1967 Seminar on Apartheid held in Kitwe-Lusaka, Guilherme Figueiredo, the Brazilian writer, diplomat, and later Minister of Education and Culture, emphasized (1975:33-58) his country's "antiracist formation, its miscegenation, " alleging by contrast that blacks in the United States "number 25 million, almost without mixture, almost always pure."

South Africa and the United States are living witnesses to the fact that there is no correlation between race mixture and lack of racism. Apartheid produced a whole caste of "coloreds, " and eighty percent or more of United States Africans are of mixed descent (Coombs, 1978). Miscegenation is an integral part of white supremacist domination, derived historically from the process of sexual violence against African women.[10] Their commercial exploitation continues to be a major basis of Latin miscegenation. Designation of mulatto women as "our most valuable export product" is considered one of Brazilian racial democracy's great generosities toward African women (see *Black Brazilian Women's Manifesto*, issued at National Congress of Women, Rio de Janeiro, 1975, cited in Nascimento, 1989:66).

Elevated to the status of state policy, miscegenation was articulated as a tool of genocide, designed to eliminate the African demographic majorities. In Hispanic America, as early as 1627, Fray Alonso de Sandoval was advocating a halt to the slave traffic in order to begin the whitening process in earnest. Historian José Antonio Saco, of Cuba, exclaimed (Ortiz, 1929:40-45) in 1835: "We have only one remedy: to whiten, to whiten, to whiten, and so to make ourselves respectable." In the latter nineteenth century, horrified at the prospect of citizenship for these African masses after abolition, Latin ruling classes drastically intensified these efforts. Massive subsidized European immigration was combined with the maintenance of Africans in conditions of miserable poverty and with official promotion of "improving the race" through miscegenation.[11] Brazil's delegate to the 1911 Universal Races Congress, held in London, proudly predicted (Skidmore, 1974:66) that, in the course of a century, these policies would result in the "extraction of the Negro race from our midst." As recently as 1982, there was a proposal of collective sterilization of blacks in São Paulo, Brazil's most populous state, on the grounds that they were becoming a majority electoral force (*Afrodiaspora*, No. 3, 1983:120).

Explicit racism having become less fashionable, we have lately been treated to a series of euphemisms like "*mestizaje*, " "mulattization, " "metarace, " and the raceless society (Freyre;1976, 1977; Entralgo n.d.) to substitute the whitening ideal. Such phrase-turning does not alter the anti-African bias of the miscegenation ideology, nor does it modify race relations characterized by segregation, discrimination, and cultural repression.

All over the region there is an enormously disproportionate concentration of African and Native American majorities in the most miserable levels of poverty and destitution. In Brazil, Bolivia, Paraguay, Peru and Ecuador, as in South Africa, nonwhite majorities are dominated by small white minorities. According to Mosquera (1975:34), "ethnic segregation is implicit in the very structure of the Colombian system." Geographical concentrations of Africans, like Chocó in Colombia, Esmeraldas in Ecuador, and Bahia and the northeast region of Brazil, are enclaves of poverty and underdevelopment. This fact is a structural expression of anti-African discrimination (Hasenbalg, 1979). All three Congresses of Black Culture in the Americas extensively denounced this situation:

> Independently of the country or nationality of the different delegates, and independently of their ideological position or their strictly ethnic characteristics, the Congress reflected one

> basic consensus: the recognition of the historical situation of black people's oppression, which today is materialized in the state of socioeconomic destitution in which blacks in the region live as a general rule ... and the persistence of discriminatory practices against black people, which reduces the terms and opportunities of their just participation in all instances of our different social structures. [*Final Report*, Second Congress: 13.]

Rather than divide between whites and all those of African origin, these discriminatory practices enforce a hierarchy based on shades of skin color: the lighter, the more socially acceptable. This system was characterized by the First Congress plenary (*Conclusions and Recommendations*, First Congress, in Nascimento, 1989:18-21) as a *pigmentocracy*:

> This discrimination uses the different tonalities of black people's skin color as a mechanism to see that black people disappear through the ideology of whitening as the search for the ideal man, in order to obtain better living conditions, and uses the same mechanism to destroy the political, economic, religious and family solidarity of black groups.

Nevertheless, Latin Americans on the political right and left still deny the anti-African groundings of this socioeconomic hierarchy of skin color. Racial prejudice, as opposed to racism (which, according to this view, does not exist in Latin America), is claimed to be "... less grave because it discriminates against the Negroid and indigenous phenotype for not yet being diluted into the majority mestizo population, whose ideal of interracial relations is *fusion*" (Ribeiro, 1979:87). Sociologists like Oracy Nogueira (1959) have expounded at length about the distinction between what they call *prejudice of mark*, a purely aesthetic rejection of phenotype based on gradations of skin color, as opposed to *prejudice of origin*, which targets all people with "a drop of African blood." Since the color criterion, or *prejudice of mark*, allows for generational social mobility through miscegenation, it is deemed less than racist and more socially democratic.

Such thinking restricts the analysis to superficial aspects of epidermic nature, obscuring the real basis of the color criterion. It is not merely an aesthetic rejection of somatic features. It is a rejection of the African or Native American origin they reveal. Society discriminates against the African phenotype, not because of gratuitous aesthetic prejudice, but because the phenotype symbolizes a people and their civilization, history, and ethos, which society has deemed inferior. Since the *mark* is the sign of origin, or race, there is no substance to the sociologists' distinction. As for the ideal of fusion, or the social compulsion to whiten, it is a full-fledged expression of white supremacy.

Beside denying its racist content, leftist intellectuals have a habit of extending the idea of racial fusion to that of class unity. They posit that miscegenation must "homogenize" the working class, like milk, in order to avoid formation of dangerous "ethnic enclaves" (Ribeiro, 1979). This is the miscegenation ideology's variation on the theme that black consciousness divides the working class. The Plenary Assembly of the First Congress of Black Culture in the Americas responded to this thesis in the following terms (*Conclusions and Recommendations*, in Nascimento, 1989):

> The attitude adopted by intellectuals of certain political orientations, which denies the existence of racism as an element participating in the creation of social problems, maintaining that the situation is one of rich and poor, oppressed and oppressors only, is a form of racial discrimination.... [We must] discredit the homogeneous political schemes that group together white, black and indigenous lumpen or proletariat, not taking into account the internalization of domination that white groups hold toward nonwhite.

The genius of the nondiscrimination ideology is that, by emphasizing myths of social integration and racial harmony in societies not formally segregated, it obscures the racial grounding of domination.

In the words of Anani Dzidzienyo (1971:14), a Ghanaian scholar dedicated to studying the question, this ideology "achieves *without tension* the same results as do overtly racist societies." This fact does not alter its truly anti-African nature. As African-Brazilian historian Joel Rufino dos Santos has remarked, "the less racial conflict, the more efficient the racism."

Indeed, segregationist racism in the United States seems to be learning this lesson. Since the Civil Rights Acts of 1964 and 1972 (fruits of the United States Afro-American community's organization and resistance), legalized segregation is being replaced by what Molefi Asante (1980:43) has defined as *process racism*, the traditional Latin system. Asante gives the example of Jimmy Carter's Georgia church, which "dispensed with an institutional stand against blacks and adopted a process stand by setting up a screening committee. The idea is to give the impression of running while standing still."

A 1951 Brazilian antidiscrimination law, the so-called Afonso Arinos law, [12] had the same effect. It changed help-wanted ads reading "whites only" to read "persons of good appearance preferred." Employment discrimination continued, documented by independent sources and by the government's own Labor Ministry (Nascimento, 1968; Fernandes, 1972; Hasenbalg, 1979).

Likewise, in the post-Bakke United States, black people suffer exorbitantly disproportionate unemployment rates, the reversal of affirmative action, and a thousand other manifestations of anti-African racism, while liberal society prides itself on its great advances in eradicating racism. In a word, racial democracy has come up North.

The achievement of racist domination *without tension* in Brazil is not, however, an eternal proposition. In the early 1960s, this speaker had occasion to make a prediction (Nascimento, 1968:47) whose fulfillment has already begun. It is also a statement of racial democracy's essence:

> The relative nonexistence in Latin society of violent aggression against blacks, United States, South Africa, Angola or Mozambique-style, is identified with the absence of racial

> discrimination. Those who think this way do not perceive the subtle sociopsychocultural theory that has been intricately building and developing over the course of our history, landing those who participate in it in a surrealist labyrinth. This has retarded, but not eradicated, the spectacular emergence of prejudice and its consequent counterpart, also spectacular, the militant reaction of blacks.

In the last decade, the militant reaction of Africans has come increasingly to mark the region's history. Three Congresses of Black Culture in the Americas (Colombia 1977, Panama 1980, and Brazil 1982) heralded this new militancy, while Afro-American organizations of different natures have proliferated in almost every individual nation in South and Central America and the Caribbean.

In Brazil, this year is the Centennial of the 1888 abolition of slavery.[13] One can observe, on this occasion, that some gains have been made as a result of the Afro-Brazilian community's increased organization and struggle. In Bahia, for example, the Oshun shrine of the elder Candomblé, Ilé Iyá Nassô Oká, had been invaded by a gasoline station. As a result of Afro-Brazilian pressure, Governor Waldir Pires (elected in the first post-1964 gubernatorial race) expropriated the community's land, protecting it from further invasion by real estate speculators.

In related developments, four African Brazilians are now members of the National Congress, currently a Constituent Assembly. Several state and city governments have instituted Afro-Brazilian Affairs Bureaus, and the severe problem of Eurocentric school curricula is beginning to be addressed. The site of Palmares is on its way to being expropriated as a result of Afro-Brazilian national mobilization. In the Ministry of Culture, an Afro-Brazilian Affairs section was set up, currently headed by Carlos Moura.[14] In international forums, Lélia Gonzalez and others have voiced the demands of African-Brazilian women, Joel Rufino has raised Afro-Brazilian academic concerns in the field of history, and other African Brazilians are participating in world meetings.

Yet these gains are only a beginning. The racial democracy

ideology still prevails, and we also witness this year the republication of Oracy Nogueira's major work.

African Culture and "Syncretism"

The miscegenation theory also emphasizes African cultural survivals and syncretism with European culture as proof of nonracism in the South and Central American region. Here again, misinformation has proliferated even among African scholars. Contrary to the popular notion, for example, African cultural expression, especially religion, not only was outlawed during colonial times, but has always suffered harassment and restriction. The Caribbean steel band was born of African drums' prohibition, and Afro-Brazilian religions, in their world-famous home of Bahia, were required until 1976 to register their houses of worship in local police headquarters.

The fact of so-called syncretism is that Eurocentric ruling society was forced to succumb to the reality of African cultural integrity. This was accomplished through Africans' own ingenuity and steadfastness, and also by virtue of certain historical circumstances we have not the space to consider here (see Nascimento 1989:95-175), but never as a result of European ruling society's hypothetical tolerance.

Enslaved Africans were baptized by force, and the slaveowning Catholic Church proselytized with the armed support of the state. Its reaction to African religious worship is exemplified by the Bishop of Espírito Santo State in Brazil, who witnessed in the nineteenth century an African religious ceremony called Cabula, and promptly pronounced a sentence of anathema against it. As recently as the 1970s, the city of São Paulo's former Archbishop denounced the celebration of Ogun and Oxossi as a defilement of the state's religious purity. Even the famous Senhor do Bonfim festival in Bahia was prohibited for most of this century, for the same reason. In 1990, it provoked anti-African statements from the local bishop.

It never escaped the repressive authorities that African religious communities were often seedbeds of resistance. In Brazil, Muslim groups of Hausa origin, notorious for their well-planned insurrections, were effectively destroyed after the first half of the nineteenth century, when Hausa secret societies led a rash of uprisings. Leading exponents of Islam were killed or deported, and virtually nothing was left of their following after the revolts' repression.

Until recently, Afro-Brazilian religious centers, called *terreiros*, were forced to seek refuge from constant police persecution. They were usually located in hidden places of difficult access, like hilltops and forests. Police would ransack the temples and arrest religious authorities and worshippers, confiscating ceremonial artwork, icons, and vestments. These items are still on display in police or psychiatric museums, as relics of African Brazilians' innate criminality or insanity.

The very vitality of African worship in Brazil is a function of its ability to survive repression. Contemporary African-Brazilian thinker Muniz Sodré (Santos, 1976:5) has remarked:

> Black culture in Brazil keeps itself alive, in great part, due to its ability to mask and silence itself. By this we mean that black culture was able to survive, escape extermination (like that which victimized the Muslims of the first half of the nineteenth century), because it hid itself when it wanted to, silencing itself when it had to. Afro-Brazilian cultural history is mainly the history of its own silence, of the circumstances of its repression.

Perhaps more insidious than the allegation of nonrepression of African culture is the much-touted idea of religious syncretism. Here, as in the case of race mixture, the historical origins of cultural amalgamation are glibly ignored. Rather than a symptom of liberalism and generosity on the part of white society, what scholars have called syncretism between Catholicism and African religion was really a cover under which Africans continued clandestinely to practice their own religious worship. Disguising their deities under the trappings of Catholic saints to avoid repression, Africans engaged in traditional forms of worship. While the altar covered with Catholic images catches the outsider's eye, the true religious foundation is African, and it is kept invisible, buried underneath the altar. It is the *axé*,[15] the *terreiro*'s real source of spiritual power and legitimacy.

The appearance of syncretism was an African strategy to confound and avoid repression. But at the International Conference of Orisha Worship held in Bahia in 1983, a group of religious leaders issued a manifesto in which they asserted the integrity of African religions in Brazil. While many of their adherents engage in Catholic worship as well, the belief systems are separate and intact.

Syncretism among different African religious systems in the Americas is a more authentic concept, since here the exchange occurred in a context of relative equality and spontaneity. Mixture among Bantu, Yoruba, and Native American deities and spiritual concepts enriched these religious systems, whose dynamic qualities lead to constant variations (Bastide, 1971, 1978).

More pernicious than outright repression has been reduction of African religious and cultural values to the status of folklore, the picturesque and exotic, denying their deeper philosophical and epistemological essence. Jorge Amado's famous novels are the most popular example. One of racial democracy's foremost exponents, Jorge Amado has gained a reputation as defender and patron of Afro-Brazilian culture. Yet his works are permeated with white supremacist stereotyping of African characters (complete with "animal instincts"), and portrayal of Afro-Brazilian religion and its largely female leadership in primitively erotic terms (Turner, 1977).[16]

In a subtle strategy of cooptation, African religious symbols and deities in Brazil have become the focus of thriving tourist industries and commercialization schemes, whose profits go exclusively to the white moneyed elite. A French student of Afro-Brazilian religions who has made it his business to serve as spokesman of racial democracy in Africa, Pierre Verger (1977) argues among other things that because African deities are worshipped by white Brazilians, the "acceptable social status" of Africans in that country is irrefutable. He also euphorically informs us that "the Yoruba Orisha are recognized as a living reality and highly appreciated in [Brazil's] daily life." To demonstrate this, he cites real estate agencies which

> successfully staked on the popularity and confidence the names of the Orisha inspire among the upper class, [constructing] twenty-three buildings of up to thirty stories, which are placed under the patronage of Yoruba gods and goddesses.

After trafficking Africans' sweat and blood on the slave markets, they now transact with our divinities in real estate enterprise, and this is held up as proof of racial harmony and nonoppression of Africans!

What Verger neglects to mention is that African Brazilians, as a rule, cannot even dream of inhabiting these high-rise buildings. A few who have done so have been viciously assailed by racist aggression. Nor does Verger mention that the Afro-Brazilian religious communities suffer from relentless invasions and encroachments on their sacred lands by real estate speculators who take advantage of the precarious documentation of these properties, a result of the African community's lack of legal support. *Veja*, a major national news magazine, reported in its 10 December 1975 issue:

> Never has the Mayor [of Salvador] outlined legal norms to protect these strongholds of Afro-Brazilian culture, although the Bahian capital has collected fat dividends from the exploitation of tourism fomented by the Orishas' magic. . . . The mayor's office itself, in fact, is frequently accused of trampling with viaducts and avenues certain sites which, though belonging officially to the public domain, for more than a hundred years have sheltered venerated Candomblé *terreiros*. And never has one heard of the application of sanctions against unscrupulous proprietors of plots adjacent to houses of Afro-Brazilian worship, who seize with impunity land belonging to the terreiros.

Prestigious white Bahian "defenders" of Candomblé have done little if anything, in practice, to ameliorate this situation. Yet they capital-ize on the religion's fame and exoticism.

Another good example of the subtlety of processes affecting African culture in the context of syncretism is that of Umbanda. While Candomblé maintained itself for centuries as the bastion and shelter of African religious culture, Umbanda incorporates Catholic and other influences in its spiritual message. It is the fastest growing popular religion in Brazil, partly because it finds stimulus and support in the racial democracy ideology. Umbanda has been increasingly infiltrated by the white middle and upper classes. Concurrently, the command and management of its *terreiros* pass from black hands to white. With the perspective of past experience, one might speculate that Umbanda is likely to share a fate similar to that of the famous samba schools. Originally the samba schools were meaningful African community cultural organizations, but they have been transformed largely into business enterprises by illicit economic interests controlled by whites who commercialize the samba schools for profit.

Recently, in the Catholic Church, the influence of the Liberation Theology has undermined the traditional Christian doctrine that pagan African religious worship is the work of the devil. There is a movement within the Church to respect African religious expressions, and even incorporate them into the mass. A special mass honoring the *quilombos* was written by Bishop José Maria Pires, the only African-Brazilian bishop in the country, along with Bishop Pedro Casaldáliga, one of the Liberation Theology's main exponents in Brazil, and others. The mass was performed in 1981 at the Serra da Barriga, site of Palmares, during the Zumbi Memorial's annual pilgrimage,[17] and was later performed by Milton Nascimento in an impressive *tournée*.

On the other hand, this trend has been offset by the furious expansion in Brazil of Evangelist Protestant churches, a trend which creates a new threat to Afro-Brazilian religions. Reviving the old "work of the devil" slogan, these sects are engaging in a tireless campaign of aggression and slander against African religions in Brazil, with the ultimate goal of destroying them entirely.[18] Beside being solidly financed from abroad, and funded by compulsory donations from their followings, the Evangelists are extremely well organized politically. In the 1990 Congressional elections, they won a significant number of seats in the House of Representatives.

Brazil: Key Country in the African World

The questions examined in the last sections are not without import to the African world as a whole, particularly in the case of Brazil, a key country in the South and Central American region. In this section we look at the reasons for Brazil's singular importance.

Brazil has the largest African population outside the African Continent, and the second largest in the world, after Nigeria. Drastically underestimated official statistics place the Afro-Brazilian population at forty-four percent of the approximately 150 million Brazilians, or about sixty million. A more realistic estimate is seventy percent, or about 105 million Africans in Brazil.

The African-Brazilian people's long history of resistance to European colonial rule makes it a major contributor to Pan-African tradition. Moreover, Brazil is one of the most vital and dynamic centers of African culture in the modern world. Also, it is a key factor politically, economically, geographically, and strategically in South Atlantic affairs.

Brazil has by far the largest territory and population of South and Central America, and the most powerful military of the Americas except the United States. It has the most sophisticated economy and most diverse natural resources. It is no secret that Brazil is close to becoming a nuclear power, whatever the government's public statements. Its military played vital roles in the rightist military coups of Chile, Bolivia, Argentina, and the Dominican Republic.

In the economic sphere, the 1964 military coup ushered in an era of forced industrialization with intense infusion of foreign capital, progressive impoverishment of working people, and extreme repression. Income distribution became more inequitable and the majority of the people's abject poverty worsened, but the "economic miracle" made the country into a major industrial power. Today, Brazil ranks fifth or sixth among nations in world arms production (Brigagão,

1984:47). With insignificant internal markets due to the population's lack of purchasing power, the Brazilian capitalists' only recourse was to expand external markets and investment. This exploitation of foreign economies by Brazilian interests, beyond trade relations and involving the investment of industrial surplus, amounts to imperialism in the classic sense.

As this situation developed, the Brazilian ruling class took pains to identify itself with the Third World, expressing its solidarity with fellow developing nations. Yet, whatever the temptations to class it as a developing nation, Brazil functions as an advanced industrial power with respect to Africa and the rest of South America. By 1972, foreign aid programs to South and Central American nations, in the familiar form of tied loans for purchase of Brazilian products, amounted to US$70 million. This sum has increased consistently.

Brazil's expansionist intentions have been clear since the formulation of General Golberi do Couto e Silva's (1957) "continental interdependence" doctrine. This idea entailed a *loyal bargain* with the United States, in which Brazil would exercise a *near monopoly of dominion* in the South Atlantic region, in return for supporting United States interests there.

Brazil's strategic importance to the South Atlantic region has been clear since the articulation of a proposed Southern Atlantic Treaty Alliance, on the order of NATO, with Brazil, Argentina, Chile, and South Africa as its leading members. The major Buenos Aires daily *La Nación* remarked in 1977:

> Only three countries, which by their cultures and their traditions are part of the Western World, have a geographical situation which enables then to play an important role in the control and protection of the South Atlantic: Argentina, Brazil and South Africa.

Soon after this, a joint Brazilian-Argentine military mission arrived at South Africa's naval base of Simonstown to plan the logistics of their cooperation. South Africa's weakest military force is her navy. South American naval power could complement Pretoria's might, while Brazil and Argentina were interested in diversifying their uranium sources. South Africa has one of the world's largest uranium reserves.

Such are not the only implications for Africa of the Western identity so carefully cultivated by the Latin ruling strata. Immigration policies mentioned in connection with the whitening process had echo in Brazil's welcoming of racist whites expelled from Kenya, the ex-Belgian Congo, Mozambique, and Angola (Rodrigues, 1964: 285). They joined notorious Nazis and Portuguese fascists like António Tomás and Marcelo Caetano, the last President and Prime Minister of Salazarist Portugal.[19] Brazil was also involved intimately in Bolivia's plan for colonization of some of its most fertile lands by refugees, mostly of German stock, from Namibia, Zimbabwe, and South Africa. Bolivia's National Colonization Institute placed US$250 million worth of land at the disposal of an expected 150, 000 whites (Mattelart, 1977). Curiously, this colonization was to take place precisely in the areas where Brazil would engage in frankly expansionist policies of *peaceful penetration* and *Brazilianization of living frontiers* (Brigagão, 1979).

Designed by federal law (Decree No. 7967 of 1945) to "preserve and develop in the population's ethnic composition the more desirable characteristics of its European ancestry, " Brazilian immigration policies have always discouraged the entrance of Africans from abroad. Indeed, one of the proposals this speaker introduced in the House of Representatives was a constitutional provision that Africans from Angola, Mozambique, Guinea Bissau, and Cabo Verde be given the same immigration privileges currently enjoyed by Portuguese citizens, since historical, linguistic, and cultural ties unite us with Africa as with Portugal.

Perhaps the most spectacular consequence for Africa of Brazilian Eurocentrism was the country's firm support of Salazarist Portugal during the independence wars in its colonies. This support capped a long tradition. Brazil's first treaty with Portugal, upon independence in 1822, was one in which it renounced "all policies of alliance with Angolan separatist forces" (Clington, 1975:83).

As if restaging history, one of the military regime's first acts upon seizing power in 1964 was to imprison and torture MPLA representative Lima Azevedo. At the very same moment, the Brazilian diplomatic corps brayed to the world its "unconditional support of the African people's anticolonial struggle." This was an expression of Brazil's classic position, which, according to a 1961 Foreign Ministry communiqué (Rodrigues, 1964:380) resulted on the one hand "from the firm anticolonialist position of our Government, and on the other from the international commitments and ties of extremely special nature that unite Brazil and Portugal."

The upshot of these "extremely special ties" was that Brazil voted against the independence of Angola, Mozambique, Guinea Bissau, and Cabo Verde during the bulk of the decolonization process in the United Nations. Indeed, the 1974 *Report of the U.N. Special Committee on the Independence Process in Southern Rhodesia, South West Africa and the Territories under Portuguese Domination* includes an entire subsection on Luso-Brazilian relations as they affected Portugal's African colonies. Brazil endorsed the most outrageous atrocities of Portuguese warmongering in Africa by voting against or abstaining from United Nations resolutions denouncing them. It went so far as to vote *no* on a proposal that the Red Cross provide reports on Portugal's treatment of prisoners of war. The attitude was one of outright hostility to African independence (see Nascimento, 1989: 177-203).

In the mid-1970s, economic pragmatism began to change this attitude. The African market was irresistible bait for expansionism, and Brazil decided to "play the game of the new African nationalism" (Brigagão, 1979:10). After 1972, Brazil opened thirteen embassies in sub-Saharan Africa, where before then there had been few diplomatic links at all. Staunchly anticommunist Brazilian generals comprising the military junta were the first heads of state outside Africa to recognize Agostinho Neto's Marxist government in Angola, expressing a new foreign policy in which "trade was emphasized over politics, in terms of expansion and new markets" (Brigagão, 1979:14).

In this context, the South Atlantic treaty idea was put on the back burner. Where previously it had cultivated an exclusively

European international image, Brazil now capitalized on its fame as a racial democracy in order to penetrate African markets. In the same vein, Brazil has suddenly begun to publicize its "cultural affinity with Africa, " hitherto an embarrassment to the strictly European-identified diplomatic elite.

Nigeria is probably the biggest partner in the booming Brazilian trade with Africa; Angola and Mozambique follow closely. From 1973 to 1976, Brazilian exports to Nigeria increased thirty times, from US$3.5 million to $90 million. Between 1978 and 1979, exports to Angola rose from US$8 million to $48 million. Brazilian credit lines to Mozambique have financed accelerating imports that increased tenfold, from US$8 to $80 million, between 1976 and 1979. By January 1980, in one month alone they totalled US$4.6 million. Petrobrás, the Brazilian national oil company, has been very visible in this trade, as has Volkswagen of Brazil. Engineering and construction, telecommunications and technical services are also important, as well as armed forces vehicles (Larkin Nascimento, 1980:63-76).

African Brazilians are worlds removed from these commercial ventures in Africa.[20] Postulation of a "black bourgeoisie" in Brazil is largely fictional. In their vast majority, African Brazilians are poor or miserably destitute, even considering some recent gains in social mobility. A nearly all-white business elite reaps the profits out of African commerce. Indeed, it has found a newer, more sophisticated means of extracting surplus value from Afro-Brazilians: marketing. Pelé's radiant face is seen on billboards advertising Brazilian products in Nigeria and other African countries. For now, he is the best-selling symbol of racial democracy.

Angola at least once demonstrated its unwillingness to swallow the racial democracy line, when its national television refused to buy the Brazilian Educational Television series *O Sítio do Pica-Pau Amarelo*. Brazilians consider this show a standard classic of integrated entertainment for children, but its negative stereotyping of black characters and themes was not lost on Angola's government. One hopes that Africa's search for diversity in economic relations and developmental independence from Europe will not obscure its consciousness that its economies are being penetrated by the same Eurocentric Brazilian elite that propagates racist notions and oppresses the African population at home.

While the South Atlantic Treaty Alliance was obscured by economic interests, the civilian government of José Sarney continued the Brazilian tradition of making hypocritically antiracist declarations to the international community, while maintaining relations with apartheid in the face of the United Nations-sponsored boycott. South Africa's Embassy and Consulate actively make their presence felt in Brazil. Every university receives the Embassy's glossy color magazine, *Panorama*, free of charge. Frequent flights of Brazilian and South African airlines carry businessmen and tourists from Rio de Janeiro to Johannesburg and back.

More importantly, South Africa's Anglo-American Company, together with the Bozano Simonsen group of Brazil, controls 72.5 percent of Brazilian industrial gold production. Having acquired various corporations, Anglo-American also controls 72.3 percent of nickel mining, 44.6 percent of niobium mining, 32.7 percent of tungsten mining and 14.4 percent of phosphate mining in Brazil. DeBeers, its South African subsidiary and the largest diamond corporation in the world, is investing in industrial diamond production in Mato Grosso State (Pereira, 1987). It seems South Africa is resorting to business in Brazil as a way to compensate or avoid damage from the worldwide boycott against apartheid. Brazil's government furnishes full cooperation and encouragement to this activity.

President Sarney's Decree No. 91.524, of 9 August 1985, curbed the formerly frequent visits of South African artists and musicians, who were proudly presented to the erudite Brazilian public. It also prohibited participation in athletic competitions and the selling of fuel, arms, and parts to the apartheid state. However, it did not affect economic and commercial interests in which Brazil, in 1986 and 1987, was the deficit partner, importing 30 percent of its orthophosphoric acid and 22 percent of its printing paper from South Africa (Pereira, 1987). Diplomatic ties were left untouched, in a gesture of deafness to the appeals of the organized Afro-Brazilian community.

This situation is one illustration of the importance to Africa of Afro-Brazilian political participation. Positive influences on such policies could alter the face of the nation's relations with Africa. African Brazilians have not failed to act, mobilizing public opinion and calling at every turn for the breaking of relations with the apartheid state and for recognition of Namibia's South-West Africa People's Organization (SWAPO) and the African National Congress (ANC) of South Africa (*Afrodiaspora*, Nos.2, 4, 5). The Afro-Brazilian Studies and Research Institute (IPEAFRO), of Rio de Janeiro, organized the first national symposium on Namibia in 1984, one hundredth anniversary of the Namibian people's struggle against colonialism. A special issue of *Afrodiaspora* was published on Namibia, dedicated to informing the Brazilian public about an issue widely ignored in the country.

As the first African-Brazilian Congressman whose political activity was dedicated to African and Afro-Brazilian affairs, and as a member of the House Foreign Relations Committee, this speaker severely disturbed the peace of the Itamaraty, the Foreign Relations Ministry, by insistently raising the issues of Namibia and apartheid, demanding that Brazil break all relations with South Africa. One result was that, in 1983, for the first time in Brazilian history, the Congressional leaders of all the opposition parties signed a declaration condemning apartheid's illegal occupation of Namibia (*Afrodiaspora*, No.2). Not surprisingly, the Foreign Ministry ignored this and the repeated appeals for recognition of SWAPO and the ANC.

These efforts were not isolated. Through its organizations and spokesmen, the Afro-Brazilian community has consistently supported African liberation movements and attempted to inform and mobilize public opinion. In a country where representatives of African nations are welcomed and surrounded by an all-white diplomatic corps, because blacks have no access to its ranks, we hope that the Pan-African sense of reciprocal responsibility mentioned by St. Clair Drake (1982) will not fail to emerge, inspiring Africans to support our struggle as well.

Pan-Africanism and the Afro-Brazilian Struggle

In other texts,[21] we have mentioned briefly certain shortcomings of African solidarity with the Afro-Brazilian cause. One major illustration of their results is embodied in the proceedings of the First World Festival of Black Art, held in Dakar in 1966. Senegal's diplomatic courting of the Eurocentric Brazilian intellectual elite contributed to the distortion of Afro-Brazilian representation in that event.[22]

But Senegal was not alone in this responsibility. True to the habit of the lace-cuffed gentlemen who run Brazil's Foreign Ministry, the official delegation to the Dakar Festival was brewed in Itamaraty's hermetic laboratories according to a criterion of "national integration" whose effect was to leave out most independent African-Brazilian artists and intellectuals (Nascimento, 1966).

The same sort of criterion held forth at the Second Festival of Black and African Arts and Culture (Festac), held in Lagos in 1977. Having been invited to read a paper at the Colloquium, this speaker was barred,[23] as were other Africans who opposed their governments in Africa and in the Diaspora. The official government-sponsored delegation from Brazil was there, however, to repeat the usual worn-out slogans of racial democracy. It also treated us to a new variation on the curious Brazilian academic tradition of *psychiatric* study of African religions. This time, the distinguished psychiatrist came up with the generous conclusion that these religions are not, after all, instances of psychosis or neurosis (Alakija, 1977).

The Sixth Pan-African Congress (Dar-es-Salaam, 1974) was another instance where delegates from the Diaspora were excluded, specifically the Caribbean Steering Committee, which had been one of the event's main organizers. That group (under the leadership of C. L. R. James), having emphasized the need for nongovernmental focus, also condemned the later exclusion of people's representatives from "Latin America, Cayenne, Puerto Rico, Guadeloupe and Martinique." C. L. R. James, veteran Pan-Africanist, had urged that a full day of deliberations be dedicated to the case of Brazil. Yet despite the Steering Committee's demand (Campbell, 1975:152-153) that "the small Brazilian people's delegation led by Abdias do Nascimento be accorded full status, " I was hamstrung not only by the language barrier but also by the prevailing ideological line of "scientific socialism" that made the Congress deliberations sound like Pan-Africanism's obituary.

In all these events, government control, independently of government ideology, was the cause of distortion and illegitimacy. Nongovernmental meetings have been much more successful. A tribute is in order to the Senegalese government, which financially sponsored the Encounter for African World Alternative Alternatives, held in Dakar in 1976, but did not attempt to control or interfere with the meeting's organization or proceedings. The three Congresses of Black Culture in the Americas were emphatic in asserting their independence from the sponsoring governments and intergovernmental organizations.

Aside from independence in the organizational process, there is also the need to avoid adherence to conventional academicism, which causes similar distortions by limiting participation, in Brazil's case at least, to spokesmen of racial oppression.

Pan-African consciousness calls for sensitivity by Africans on the Continent to the questions of the ignored and usurped history of Africans in the Americas, racist education of our children and the need for Afrocentric consciousness. Independence of African nations has made these problems less immediate, perhaps, on the Continent, but we believe they are still live issues in Africa as well.

Conclusion

African Americans hope to see a future when Africans on the Continent will seek to avoid being confounded by the pretty mirages which obfuscate and perpetuate the domination of Africans in South and Central America. A positive beginning has been made, it seems, in the ongoing preparations for the programmed Festival of Pan-African Culture (Fespac). The organizational process for this event, while not without shortcomings, has shown thus far a concerted effort to remedy the minimization of South and Central America's participation in the Pan-African scenario. Similarly, the Institute of Black People, since its initial meetings in 1985 at Ouagadougou supported by Burkina Faso's government and by UNESCO, has made a similar effort. And the W. E. B. DuBois Center for Pan-African Culture today makes an important contribution to the consolidation of this trend.

In closing, we wish to echo the call made by the Pan-African colloquium gathered two years ago at this Center, on the occasion of the reinterment of the remains of W. E. B. DuBois and Shirley Graham DuBois, for the realization of the Seventh Pan-African Congress as soon as realistically possible and preferably on Ghana's soil. It is a tribute to Ghana's people that their government has supported the creation and activities of the W. E. B. DuBois Memorial Center for Pan-African Culture. We hope this tribute can be carried further, in honor of Padmore, DuBois, Nkrumah, and so many others' dreams and efforts. Perhaps the day will arrive when African nations will join forces in making possible such an effort as the Seventh Pan-African Congress, leaving its organization and proceedings independent and unhampered by state control or interference. We mentioned a previous attempt to write Pan-Africanism's obituary, but we are pleased to witness that, with the W. E. B. DuBois Memorial Center for Pan-African Culture in action, it is still very much alive.

We salute Zumbi, DuBois, Nkrumah, and the Pan-African cause. *Axé*!

BIBLIOGRAPHIC ESSAY

The bulk of the conventional literature available in English on Africans in South and Central America and the Spanish-speaking Caribbean, and specifically in Brazil, examines the nature of slavery and slave societies in the region. Most of the studies then examine postabolition race relations from an academic standpoint—historical, sociological, or anthropological—attempting to reach conclusions relating the nature of these older societies to the contemporary forms of race relations they respectively have bred.

Some relatively recent works in this vein are of particular interest. Leslie B. Rout's *The African Experience in Spanish America: 1502 to the Present Day* is a refreshingly African North American look at the subject. Ann Pescatello's collection *The African in Latin America* provides a survey of African experience in the region up to 1888, while her *Old Roots in New Lands* presents various pieces of research in the tradition of Melville Herskovits. Other works are Robert Brent Toplin's *Slavery and Race Relations in Latin America*, Rolando Mellafe's *Negro Slavery in Latin America*, and Franklin W. Knight's *African Dimensions in Latin American Societies*. The volume *Africa in Latin America*, edited by Manuel Moreno Fraginals and published by UNESCO, brings together essays reflecting Latin American viewpoints on the subject.

These works are also useful because they help to discredit the portrait of the happy African in the friendly slave society that was painted in earlier studies of Latin America. The Catholic Church's supposedly benificent influence and the Latin legal tradition, which generously conferred upon Africans a "moral personality," are two major elements of this view. But the idea that has most transfixed conventional students of the supposedly harmonious conviviality among the races in Latin America, before and after slavery, is that of miscegenation. Their fascination with the origins and implications of the existence of large mestizo and mulatto populations in the region is unending.

Gilberto Freyre's volume *The Masters and the Slaves* undoubtedly is the classic in this tradition. At the time of its publication, this work was considered controversial, indeed revolutionary, because it challenged the conventional wisdom of the epoch, which decreed that the innately inferior African stain tainting the Brazilian ethnic stock condemned the nation to eternal backwardness.

Thomas E. Skidmore's *Black into White* is required reading for the student interested in this Brazilian articulation of white supremacist thought in the late nineteenth and first half of the twentieth centuries. A collection edited by Richard Graham, entitled *The Idea of Race in Latin America, 1870-1940*, extends the discussion also to Mexico and Argentina.

Skidmore documents in detail the debates about race that characterized the making of Brazilian public policy, immigration policy in particular, during the period in question. The scientific notion of the African's innate inferiority was complemented by the idea that interracial breeding would produce an even more undesirable half-breed stock: indolent, unintelligent, and incapable of serious work or creative thought. European immigration was encouraged in order to "improve the race" and eliminate the African stain, hopefully by the end of the present century.

Gilberto Freyre turned these attitudes upside-down and made miscegenation the cornerstone of Brazil's national image as a healthy, robust, nonracist nation. Interestingly, Freyre also described the cruelty of the Brazilian slave regime, sometimes in gory detail. But his major thesis was that intimate sexual relations among the races mitigated this cruelty and laid the foundations for a racially harmonious post-abolition society. This idea was married with the image of the benign Catholic slave system, and the myth of racial democracy was born. Its substance is summed up by Freyre himself in this classic statement (1959:9): "With respect to race relations, the Brazilian situation is probably the nearest approach to paradise to be found anywhere in the world."

Other authors, like Frank Tannenbaum (*Slave and Citizen*), Donald Pierson (*Negroes in Brazil*) and Carl Degler (*Neither Black nor White*), generally contribute to this thesis, varying in the extent of their agreement with the friendly master stereotype and the eulogy of Brazilian nonracism. Tannenbaum, for example, disagrees with Freyre's subjective assertion of easy-going, humanized master-slave relationships and focuses instead on the moral personality argument mentioned above. Degler's "mulatto escape-hatch" theory posits that miscegenation provides an intermediate racial group into which blacks can successfully aspire to enter, thus alleviating and preventing racial tension. Magnus Mörner (*Race Mixture in the History of Latin America, Race and Class in Latin America*) and Harry Hoetink (*Slavery and Race Relations in the Americas*) essentially extend this kind of analysis beyond Brazil, albeit with more subtlety, sophistication, and academic elaboration.

The seminal work of David Brion Davis, entitled *The Problem of Slavery in Western Culture*, successfully challenges the myth of the benevolent Catholic Church in comparison to the role of Protestantism in perpetrating the crime of chattel slavery of African peoples.

Charles Wagley and Marvin Harris (*Minorities in the New World*) look critically at some of the friendly master stereotypes and seek more objective bases of analysis. In his volume *Patterns of Race in the Americas*, Marvin Harris provides an interesting history of the domination of Native American and African populations, seeking to explain the emergence of different social systems by distinguishing between highland economies and lowland plantation systems. Nevertheless, these authors do not differ from the earlier ones in their fascination with the distinction between the "rigid descent rule" (a drop of African blood makes one black) in the United States and the more fluid Latin categories like mestizo, zambo, and mulatto. However objectively materialist the analysis of their origin and functioning, these flexible Latin categories are still interpreted as the mark of more tolerant race relations. These authors consider the miserable socioeconomic status of indigenous and African populations in the Americas, and even the suppression or distortion of their cultural identities, to be the consequences of rigid class hierarchies rather than racial discrimination or white supremacism.

Subsequent works have tended to sharpen the critique of the racial democracy theory by demonstrating the existence of racial discrimination against blacks and mulattoes in Latin societies. Arthur Ramos is a forerunner of this trend. His book *The Negro in Brazil*, published in English in 1939, provides an exceptionally balanced analysis for its day. Ramos was unique among students of Brazilian race relations of his time because he saw Africans as protagonists of their own history and liberation struggles, focusing on Palmares and the Afro-Brazilian tradition of *quilombos*. Ramos also developed a relationship of mutual respect with Afro-Brazilian movements.

In this context, we should mention the classic work that took Ramos' cue and rescued African protagonism from the mire of academic analyses that had reduced a whole people to the status of objects of research rather than subjects of their own history. It is Richard Price's *Maroon Societies*, a collection of essays on African communities that existed throughout the Americas, built from the raw material of human heroism and anticolonial resistance.[1]

Together with Roger Bastide,[2] Florestan Fernandes (*The Negro in Brazilian Society*) contributed to the tradition begun by Ramos, developing sociological research that documented discrimination against blacks and mulattoes. His work generated a series of studies in this vein, generally referred to as the writings of the São Paulo school.[3]

Fernandes and his followers, however, attributed anti-African discrimination essentially to the legacy of slavery, deemphasizing the active contemporary workings of white supremacism and attributing the persistence of the slave heritage to the class structure.

Among non-African-Brazilian authors, it took an African perspective to penetrate the subtle subterfuges of racism in Brazil and identify its active role in the determination of Afro-Brazilian living conditions. Anani Dzidzienyo, of Ghana, took this pioneering step when he published *The Position of Blacks in Brazilian Society*. Some years later, Carlos Hasenbalg, an Argentine sociologist, followed suit in his well-documented dissertation entitled *Race Relations in Post-Abolition Brazil*, published in book form in Portuguese in 1979.

Anani Dzidzienyo's later study, *Afro-Brazilians and Brazilian National Image and Identity*, looks at some of the more subtle issues arising from the peculiar workings of white supremacist domination in Brazil.

Perhaps the most advanced academic critique of the racial democracy theory is to be found in Pierre-Michel Fontaine's collection entitled *Race, Class and Power in Brazil.* For the first time in English, except for the works of Abdias do Nascimento, this volume includes an essay by a militant of the Afro-Brazilian movement, Professor Lélia Gonzalez. Also for the first time in such a work, the contributions of African scholars outnumber those of non-Africans.

Gonzalez' essay reflects an historical moment in which the new Afro-Brazilian movement, emerging from almost three decades of dictatorship and repression, found itself severed from its generational antecedents and exhibited a certain immaturity with respect to its own history. Lélia Gonzalez (1991:2-3) has expressed concern about the repercussion of her own depiction of Afro-Brazilian movements in the essay published in that volume. She writes,

> In the fight against the dictatorship, we cultivated allies on the political left who influenced our own discourse and diverted our attention from Afrocentric analysis. The kinds of statements made in my essay published in the Fontaine collection undoubtedly reflect those influences. Analyses which discredit earlier Afro-Brazilian movements by identifying them with Vargas-style populism are a perfect example. Also, in the enthusiasm of that moment of vanguard activity in building a new generation of African-Brazilian militants, we exaggerated the MNU's importance far out of proportion.

Indeed, the repercussion of the essay in question, combined with the enthusiastic writings of some foreign researchers who erroneously attribute exclusively to that organization (the MNU) the scope suggested by its name, has resulted in the artificial aggrandizement of certain components of the Afro-Brazilian movement, to the detriment of other equally important ones, in current literature on the subject.

The global African-Brazilian point of view has been published in English in the works of Abdias do Nascimento, particularly *"Racial Democracy" in Brazil: Myth or Reality?* and *Brazil: Mixture or Massacre?*, volumes that emerged from his participation in African world events.

Elisa Larkin Nascimento's *Pan-Africanism and South America* is unique in the attempt to set African experience and struggle in South and Central America within the context of African world history. Larkin Nascimento locates Latin forms of racial domination squarely in the ranks of white supremacism.

The latest and among the most original essays by an African studying the origins of racism in the Americas is Jan Carew's *Fulcrums of Change*.

A volume that is fundamental to any study of African experience in the New World is Ivan Van Sertima's *They Came Before Columbus*, which documents the enormous body of evidence pointing to the presence of Africans in the pre-Columbian Americas and to the considerable contributions African civilizations of that time offered to America and its peoples.

The African experience in Cuba merits special attention, especially in light of Cuba's military presence in Angola. Among the works that examine the Cuban experience are Anani Dzidzienyo's *The Position of Blacks in Brazilian and Cuban Society* and John Clytus' *A Black Man in Red Cuba*. Most recently, the African-Cuban dissident Carlos Moore published a radically new and original account in his weighty volume entitled *Castro, the Blacks, and Africa*.

An important dimension of African experience in the Americas is the cultural one. The latest contribution in this field is Abdias do Nascimento's volume of artwork and essays entitled *Orishas: the Living Gods of Africa in Brazil*. Nascimento's play *Sortilege (Black Mystery)* deals not only with the workings of white supremacism, but also with African religious culture in Brazil. Arthur Ramos deals with the Afro-Brazilian religious tradition in his *The Negro in Brazil.*

Two classic works that focus on African culture in the South and Central American and Caribbean region are Roger Bastide's *African Civilizations in the New World* and *The African Religions of Brazil.* Bastide was a French sociologist whose extraordinary contribution to the study of Afro-Brazilian religion was complemented by other activities that placed him at the forefront of Afro-Brazilian studies and at the side of the Afro-Brazilian movement and its leaders in his time.

Another outstanding work on Afro-Brazilian culture is Ruth Landes' *The City of Women*, which focuses on the powerful role of women in religions of African origin.

More recently, Robert Farris Thompson's *A Flash of the Spirit* has made a valuable contribution to the dynamic study of African religious culture in the Americas.

In the area of literature, Richard L. Jackson's *The Black Image in Latin American Literature* is a basic reference. Flora Mancuso Edwards' study entitled *The Theater of the Black Diaspora: a Comparative Study of Black Drama in Brazil, Cuba and the United States* is the basic source on dramatic literature. David Brookshaw's *Raça e Cor na Literatura Brasileira*[4] provides a classic analysis of anti-African stereotypes in Brazilian literature, including the world-famous works of Jorge Amado. Two earlier studies in this area are Raymond S. Sayers' *The Negro in Brazilian Literature* and Gregory Rabassa's *The Negro in Brazilian Fiction.*

Obviously, this bibliographic essay is far from exhaustive. The interested student will find many more sources on the subject. Two existing bibliographies would be of value to such an enterprise. They are Robert M. Levine's *Race and Ethnic Relations in Latin America and the Caribbean* and Dorothy Porter's *Afro-Braziliana: a Working Bibliography.*

NOTES

Notes to Chapter 1

1. We use the expression "African" in the wider sense, referring to Africans and their descendants the world over, and in whatever part of the Diaspora is being mentioned.
2. In Brazil, *Malê* (mah-*leh*) means Hausa and, by extension, Muslim.
3. The National Liberation Alliance (ALN) was responsible for the famous Communist-led *Intentona* rebellion of 1935.
4. Integralism was a Brazilian nationalist political movement which had certain affinities with early manifestations of National Socialism in Europe.
5. Tiradentes, the foremost Brazilian independence hero, was drawn and quartered for conspiracy in the eighteenth century.
6. "Salazarist" refers to a follower of Antonio de Oliveira Salazar, the dictator who controlled a rigidly rightwing police state in Portugal from 1928 to 1968.
7. Felinto Müller and Emílio Romano were infamous police commissioners charged with the persecution of political prisoners and notorious for their merciless hunt, torture, and sometimes murder of leftist leaders. These episodes included the deportation of Olga Benário, a Jewish activist pregnant at the time, to Nazi Germany, where she died in a concentration camp after giving birth to her daughter.
8. This Tribunal was an exceptional court created by the New State dictatorship in order to legally eliminate or neutralize the adversaries of the regime, which had taken power on 1 November 1937.
9. Luis Carlos Prestes was the most important leader of the Brazilian Communist Party for almost seventy years (he died in 1990). He became a national folk hero, symbolizing popular resistance against repression during both the New State dictatorship and the United

States-sponsored 1964 military dictatorship. He was elected Senator in 1945. After 1964, he spent many years in exile in the Soviet Union, returning in the 1980s to participate in the democratization process and struggle for direct presidential elections.

10. See later section entitled "Pan-African Encounters," in this chapter.
11. This is the same Lacerda who later became the reactionary governor of Guanabara state.
12. *Favelas* are shantytowns built on the hills of Rio de Janeiro and other Brazilian cities, with majority African populations.
13. Teatro Experimental do Negro (TEN) is the title in Portuguese.
14. The Republic of Palmares was a conglomerate of African *quilombos* (maroons) with a total population of some 30,000. For more than a century, from 1595 to 1696, Palmares resisted, withstanding twenty-seven wars of colonial aggression waged by the Dutch and the Portuguese. It was located at Serra da Barriga, in the forests of what are now Pernambuco and Alagoas States. Zumbi, Palmares' last elected king, died in battle defending the community.
15. Bibi Ferreira is one of Brazil's most renowned actresses as well as a theater director and producer.
16. O'Neill's original expression is freely adapted in Werneck's translation as "*Estou encagaçado!*"
17. Nelson Rodrigues, Brazil's foremost modern playwright and founder of a new dramatic language in the 1930s, represents for Brazilian theater what Eugene O'Neill represents for United States theater. He was very close to the Black Experimental Theater, and his play *Black Angel* was written especially for TEN.
18. Zbigniew Ziembinski, the famous Polish vanguard theater director and actor, resided and worked in Brazil.
19. *Mineiro* means from Minas Gerais State.
20. Arthur Ramos was a well-known anthropologist, author of seminal works on Afro-Brazilian culture.
21. Alberto Guerreiro Ramos, prominent African-Brazilian sociologist, was perhaps the first Brazilian intellectual to describe the Brazilian system of racism with direct reference to white supremacist ideology (1957). In the late 1960s, he left Brazil for Los Angeles, where he was a professor of public administration at the University of Southern California. He died in 1981.
22. Edison Carneiro was a well-known Brazilian anthropologist. For a sample of his ideological statements regarding African culture, see the

section "African-Brazilian Perspectives on Pan-Africanism and Negritude" in Chapter 2 of this volume.

23. Later, after his return from exile, Ribeiro's support of the Afro-Brazilian movement became substantially more unequivocal and lucid.
24. *Quilombo* means maroon society.
25. *Cabresto* means reins. The traditional expression "voting by *cabresto*" indicates votes mandated by a local strongman.
26. After the Federal District was moved from Rio de Janeiro to Brasília, Rio de Janeiro City became Guanabara State. Today, it is the capital of Rio de Janeiro State.
27. These recent events are described in more detail in the "Editor's Epilogue" at the end of this chapter. In the Appendix to this chapter is found the text of Nascimento's inaugural speech as Secretary of State.
28. *Subúrbios* are working-class and poor communities, largely African-Brazilian, on the outskirts of the city.
29. General Eurico Dutra was President of Brazil from 1946 to 1950.
30. These struggles were represented by the civilian campaigns for social and economic justice and for cultural reforms, leading up to and during the administration of Jão Goulart, the constitutionally empowered reformist president deposed by the United States-sponsored military coup in 1964.
31. Due to the growth and autonomy of the Afro-Brazilian movement, and as a demand of Africans within Brazilian political parties, some of them, including the Communist Party, have modified this kind of behavior during the redemocratization process of the 1980s.
32. There is a mistaken tendency among enthusiastic African-American researchers from the United States to identify in the name of the Unified Black Movement a reality of unity that is not embodied in that organization. The MNU is only one among hundreds of Afro-Brazilian groups and does not by itself represent the African-Brazilian community and its concerns.
33. A *filha de santo* is an initiate in Afro-Brazilian religion.
34. Iyalorixá is the title given to an African-Brazilian female religious leader.
35. This refers to 1976, the time of the recorded interviews.
36. Since the 1970s, African religious worship has become fairly widespread in various regions of the United States. Religious authorities from South America, the Caribbean and Africa have established many of these houses of worship.

37. Works published in Portuguese, which document these events in more detail, are Nascimento's *The Genocide of Brazilian Blacks* (1978) and *Under Siege in Lagos* (1981).
38. In the context of these events in Nigeria, Colombia, and Panama, and of the Afro-Brazilian movement of this period, the work of Brazilian journalist Mirna Grzich deserves mention. Against great odds, she dedicated her efforts for some years to supporting the Afro-Brazilian movement. She was also instrumental in obtaining media coverage for its initiatives.
39. Created by the Sarney Government in 1988, as part of the Ministry of Culture, the Palmares Cultural Foundation was another significant victory of the Afro-Brazilian movement. Its first president, Carlos Moura, is now Cultural Attaché to the Brazilian Embassy in Cabo Verde. In the Collor administration, the Palmares Foundation escaped extinction but has been paralyzed by the eradication of federal cultural policy. Almost every other cultural agency has been extinguished (including the National Arts Foundation, Scenic Arts Foundation, Film Corporation, and others), and there are virtually no federal funds for arts or culture.
40. The Sixth Pan-African Congress (Dar-es-Salaam, 1974), the All-African People's Revolutionary Party Leadership Symposium (Washington, D.C., 1976), and the First Congress of Black Culture in the Americas (Cali, Colombia, 1977).
41. In the United States, by contrast, Quilombismo has been given serious and thoughtful attention by Afrocentric scholars like Molefi K. Asante and Maulana Karenga. Essays developing the idea were published in the *Journal of Black Studies* (Vol. 11, no. 2, December 1980) and in *African Culture: the Rhythms of Unity* (Asante and Asante, 1990).
42. As Governor of Rio Grande do Sul State (1958–62), Brizola had disappropriated the ITT and Bond and Share corporations. In 1961, he had successfully resisted an attempted military coup, intended to prevent Vice-President Jão Goulart's constitutional succession to the Presidency, by confronting the military with his State Guard and mobilizing nationwide popular resistance by radio broadcast.
43. See later section of this chapter entitled "Political Endeavors."
44. As Governor of Rio de Janeiro State (1983–87), Brizola instituted specific initiatives for the African-Brazilian community, as well as social, educational and health care programs benefitting Africans as the majority of the underprivileged and the poor.

45. Congressman Doutel de Andrade was an early co-founder of the Brazilian Labor Party (PTB) and close collaborator of Presidents Jão Goulart and Getúlio Vargas (the latter during his second term as democratically elected president). During the post–1964 military regime, Doutel was one of the most outstanding defenders of the rule of law. He also was instrumental in the founding and consolidation of the Democratic Labor Party (PDT), legitimate successor of the PTB, and its leader in the Congress from the 1987–88 Constitutent Assembly through 1990. He died in January 1991, shortly after his election to the Senate. Darcy Ribeiro, long an outstanding intellectual, writer, and anthropologist, founded the University of Brasília. He was later President Jão Goulart's Minister of Education. He was also Goulart's Chief of Staff. During his exile in France, Ribeiro was instrumental in raising the question of Native Americans' extermination in Brazil. During Governor Leonel Brizola's administration of the Rio de Janeiro State Government, Ribeiro was the main architect of the Integrated Centers for Public Education (CIEP) program, one of the outstanding achievements of post-dictatorship democratic government in Brazil.

Notes to Appendix of Chapter 1

1. *Axé* (ah-*sheh*) is the life-force or spiritual energy that imbues the cosmos according to African philosophy. To plant the *axé* of an Afro-Brazilian religious community is to lay the foundations that provide it with spiritual power, authority, and legitimacy.
2. For a more detailed account of these Constitutional measures, see the section entitled "Contemporary Afro-Brazilian Resistance" in Chapter 2 of this volume.

Notes to Chapter 2

1. Here we are referring, not to individual cases of intermarriage, but to a collective social phenomenon.
2. The escudo is the Portuguese currency unit.
3. For a more detailed explanation of the content of Quilombismo, see section entitled "Editor's Epilogue" in Chapter 1 of the present volume.
4. This conglomeration of *quilombos* (maroons) was the first free republic in the post-Columbian Americas. Palmares fought off armed colonial

aggression for more than a century (1594–1696), defending a multiracial, pluricultural, anticolonialist state governed and populated in its majority by Africans.

5. *Pardos* means mulattoes, roughly the equivalent of brown, except that most browns in Brazil class themselves as whites.
6. As foreign observers consistently remark, people with obviously African or Native American physical traits often class themselves as white, and very dark Africans as mulattoes.
7. The minimum wage in Brazil is so low and the inflation rate so high that it is conventional, rather than to speak of currency values, to cite wage levels in terms of units based on the current value of the minimum wage. For example, as we write these lines the value of the monthly minimum wage is twenty thousand cruzeiros (Cr$20,000.00), or about seventy United States dollars. A person who earns three minimum wages, therefore, will earn about US$210.00 this month. Two months ago, the currency value of the minimum wage was Cr$16,000.00, or the equivalent of about US$71.50. A very large proportion of Brazilians, even among those with steady jobs, earns less than the value of one minimum wage.
8. See National Survey Based on Domicile Samples (PNAD) (Rio de Janeiro: IBGE, 1982).
9. National Survey Based on Domicile Samples (PNAD) (Rio de Janeiro: IBGE, 1976).
10. During the period of redemocratization after the New State dictatorship of Getúlio Vargas (1937–1945), this Assembly was elected to write a new Brazilian Constitution.
11. Several Afro-Brazilian organizations are mentioned in Elisa Larkin Nascimento's *Pan-Africanism and South America* (1980) and in Abdias do Nascimento's *Brazil: Mixture or Massacre* (1989), but these lists are incomplete. They and others exaggerate the importance of the MNU, an organization founded in the aftermath of the 1978 demonstration, which now has local followings in some cities, but is not significant nationally. Since 1980, the Zumbi Memorial has emerged as the most outstanding national African organization.
12. Benedita da Silva (PT-RJ), Edmilson Valentim (PC do B-RJ), Carlos Alberto de Oliveira (Caó) (PDT-RJ), Paulo Paim (PT-RS).
13. This commission ultimately evolved into the Palmares Foundation, an Afro-Brazilian affairs body linked to the Ministry of Culture, which was legally constituted in 1990. The Foundation escaped extinction in early

1991, during the Collor de Mello administration's onslaught against federal cultural policy (in which bodies like the National Arts Foundation, the National Scenic Arts Foundation, and others were scrapped). Since then, however, it effectively has been denied resources and virtually ceased to function.

14. The African nations' diplomatic representatives in Brazil consistently have been present at the National Black Consciousness Day events, as have individual Africans. Among the first delegations from the United States was one headed by Congressman Mervyn Dymally and Prince Asiel Ben Israel, Extraordinary Ambassador of the African Israelite Hebrew Nation located in Dimona, Israel. Kwame Turé (formerly Stokely Carmichael), President of the All-African People's Revolutionary Party, climbed the hills of the Serra da Barriga in 1985, and a delegation of fifty or more African Americans from the United States participated in the National Black Consciousness Day celebrations in 1990.
15. See the section entitled "African Culture and Syncretism" in Chapter 3 of this volume, and Chapter 3 of Abdias do Nascimento's *Brazil: Mixture or Massacre* (1989) for more detail.
16. Statement made in debate transcribed in *80 Anos de Abolição*, special issue of *Cadernos Brasileiros* (Rio de Janeiro, 1968).
17. An interesting instance of the debate between Valladares and Abdias do Nascimento on this subject is found in *80 Anos de Abolição*, the same special issue of *Cadernos Brasileiros* (1968) cited supra. Excerpts are translated in Larkin Nascimento's *Pan-Africanism and South America* (1980:131–132).

Notes to Chapter 3

1. We use the term "Diaspora" in reference to all African populations, and their descendants, outside the home Continent.
2. We use the term "South and Central America" to designate the region from Mexico to Argentina, including the Spanish-speaking Caribbean. Although geographically Mexico is considered to belong to North America, the country identifies culturally, historically, and politically with South and Central America.
3. In English, Abdias do Nascimento's book *Brazil: Mixture or Massacre* (1989) includes brief descriptions of some of these *quilombos*. Richard Price's volume *Maroon Societies* (1983) deals with the Republic of

Palmares. Clovis Moura's untranslated work *Rebeliões de Senzala: Quilombos, Insurreições e Guerrilhas* (1972) provides a more thorough examination of Brazilian *quilombos.*

4. For more detail, see the "Pan-African Encounters" section in Chapter 1 of this volume and the book *Mixture or Massacre* (Nascimento, 1979).
5. Since 1988, Ambassador Awoonor has also represented Ghana in Cuba and at the United Nations.
6. See the section entitled "Afro-Brazilian Perspectives on Pan-Africanism and Negritude," in Chapter 2 of this volume, for more detail.
7. See Molefi K. Asante's classic works on Afrocentricity (1980, 1987).
8. Antonio Olinto's novel *The Water House* (1970) is an interesting literary treatment of this phenomenon.
9. As a result of pressure from Afro-Brazilian organizations and demographers in general, the 1980 census in Brazil incorporated these data for the first time in thirty years.
10. We are not speaking here of individual cases of intermarriage, nor do we defend biological purity of race, something which has never existed. What we refer to is a social phenomenon of domination, identifying African as inferior and therefore sexually exploitable and socially expendable.
11. Brazilian Marxist historians like Caio Prado (1966:130) attribute stimulation of European immigration to a supposedly objective economic reason, the alleged lack of work force, as if the emancipated Africans and their descendants did not exist or had no capacity for labor. Prado considers the European immigrants palpably superior to the preexisting mass of enslaved Africans. In fact, after the Golden Law abolishing slavery, Africans were displaced from the working class and left to marginal but structurally functional abject poverty.
12. For an account of the origin of this measure, see the section entitled "The Afonso Arinos Law Against Racial Discrimination" in Chapter 1 of the present volume.
13. The Portuguese were the first to invade and the last to leave Africa as colonialists. In the Americas, they were among the first to enslave Africans and the last to abolish slavery.
14. This Afro-Brazilian Affairs Commission ultimately evolved into the Palmares Cultural Foundation, legally constituted as part of the Ministry of Culture in 1990. The Foundation escaped extinction in early 1991, during the Collor de Mello presidency's onslaught against federal cultural policy, in which bodies like the National Arts Founda-

tion, the National Scenic Arts Foundation, and others were scrapped. Since then, however, the Palmares Cultural foundation has effectively been denied resources and virtually ceased to function.

15. *Axé* (ah-*sheh*) is the Brazilian orthography of the Yoruba word *àṣẹ*, meaning spiritual power or energy, the life force. Here, it refers to a permanent offering made on the *terreiro*'s foundation, establishing the house's source of spiritual power and legitimacy.
16. See the section entitled "African Perspectives on Pan-Africanism and Negritude," in Chapter 2 of this volume, for more detail.
17. See the Editor's Epilogue to Chapter 1 of this volume, "Memories from Exile," for a brief description of the Zumbi Memorial.
18. There are rare exceptions within the Evangelist church, including Congresswoman Benedita da Silva of the Assembly of God, who represents the Afro-Brazilian *favela* community and who defends religious freedom despite the position of her church.
19. Antonio de Oliveira Salazar was the dictator who controlled a right-wing police state in Portugal from 1928 until he suffered a debilitating stroke in 1968. He was succeeded by Marcelo Caetano, who had been his Minister for the Colonies. The Salazarist regime was finally brought down by a 1975 military uprising led by young officers motivated in large part by their disillusionment with Portuguese colonialist policies in Africa during the wars of independence.
20. The only exception is a tiny and economically insignificant business club in São Paulo called the Afro-Brazilian Chamber of Commerce, which consists essentially of one person and his not-so-successful business.
21. Nascimento; 1966, 1979; Larkin Nascimento, 1980.
22. See the section entitled "Afro-Brazilian Perspectives on Pan- Africanism and Negritude" in Chapter 2 of the present volume for more detail.
23. For a more detailed account of this incident, see the section entitled "Pan-African Encounters" in Chapter 1 of this volume.

Notes to Bibliographic Essay

1. In this context, we cannot fail to mention the work of Clóvis Moura, *Rebeliões da Senzala: Quilombos, Insurreições e Guerrilhas* (Rio de Janeiro: Ed. Conquista, 1972) and *O Negro: de Bom Escravo a Mau Cidadão?* (Rio de Janeiro: Ed. Conquista, 1977). Unfortunately, they are not yet translated into English.

2. Bastide, Roger and Florestan Fernandes, *Brancos e Negros em São Paulo*. São Paulo: Companhia Editora Nacional, 1959.
3. Octavio Ianni and Fernando Henrique Cardoso are among Fernandes' foremost followers. Oracy Nogueira, on the other hand, engages in a sophisticated elaboration of the Freyre model. Their works are not available in English.
4. We have been unable to ascertain whether this work has been published in English.

REFERENCES

Afrodiaspora Journal, Nos. 1-7. Rio de Janeiro: Afro-Brazilian Studies and Research Institute (IPEAFRO), 1983-1986.

Alakija, George. *The Trance State in Candomblé*, official contribution presented by the Brazilian government's delegation to the Second World Festival of Black and African Arts and Culture (Lagos). Brasília: Ministry of Foreign Relations, 1977.

Andrews, George Reid. "Race versus Class Association: the Afro- Argentines of Buenos Aires, 1850-1900," *Journal of Latin American Studies*, 10:2 (December), 1979.

Asante, Molefi Kete. *Afrocentricity*. Buffalo: Amulefi Press, 1980.

———. *The Afrocentric Idea*. Philadelphia: Temple University Press, 1987.

———. *Kemet, Afrocentricity and Knowledge*. Trenton: Africa World Press, 1990.

Asante, Molefi Kete and Kariamu Welsh Asante, eds. *African Culture: the Rhythms of Unity*, 2nd ed. Trenton: Africa World Press, 1990.

Azevedo, Thales de. "Os grupos negro-africanos," *História da Cultura Brasileira*. Rio de Janeiro: Ministry of Education and Culture, 1973.

———. *Democracia Racial: Ideologia e Realidade*. Petrópolis: Editora Vozes, 1975.

Bastide, Roger. *African Civilizations in the New World*. New York: Harper and Row, 1973.

———. *Estudos Afro-Brasileiros*. So Paulo: Editora Perspectiva, 1973.

———. *African Religions in Brazil*, 2nd ed., trans. by Helen Sebba. Baltimore: Johns Hopkins University Press, 1978.

Ben-Jochannan, Yusef. *Cultural Genocide in the Black and African Studies Curriculum*. New York: Alkebu-lan Books, 1971.

Brigagão, Clóvis. *Brazil's Foreign Policy: the Last Ten Years*. Stockholm: Institute of Latin American Studies Research Center, 1979.

———. *O Mercado da Segurança*. Rio de Janeiro: Nova Fronteira, 1984.

Brookshaw, David. *Raça e Cor na Literatura Brasileira.* Porto Alegre: Ed. Mercado Aberto, 1983.

Campbell, Horace, ed. *Pan-Africanism: Struggle Against Neo-Colonialism and Imperialism.* Toronto, 1975.

Capitaine, Fernando Winfield. "Notas sobre el Carnaval en una Comunidad Negra de Veracruz," *Cuadernos Afro-Americanos* I:1 (Caracas: Universidad Central de Venezuela, 1975.

Carew, Jan. *Fulcrums of Change: the African Presence in the Americas.* Trenton: Africa World Press, 1988.

Casimir, Jean. "Identificación del Negro en la Estructura de Clase: una Perspectiva Haitiana." Second Congress of Black Culture in the Americas, *Final Report.* Panama: Universidad de Panama, 1980.

Carneiro, Edison. *Ladinos e Crioulos.* Rio de Janeiro: Civilização Brasileira, 1964.

Cavalcanti, Pedro Celso Uchôa and Jovelino Ramos, eds. *Memórias do Exílio: Brasil, 1964-19??,* Vol. I. Lisbon: Editora Arcádia, 1976.

Clarke, John Henrik. "The influence of African Cultural Continuity on the Slave Revolts in South America and the Caribbean Islands." Presentation at Third International Congress of Africanists, Addis Ababa, 1973.

———. *Marcus Garvey and the Vision of Africa.* New York: Vintage Press, 1974.

———. "The development of Pan-Africanist Ideas in the Americas and in the Caribbean Islands." Presentation at Colloquium, Festac '77. Lagos: Festac International Secretariat, 1977.

Clington, Mário de Souza. *Angola Libre?* Paris: Gallimard, 1975.

Clytus, John. *Black Man in Red Cuba.* Coral Gables: University of Miami Press, 1970.

Coombs, Orde. "Mulatto Pride," *New York Magazine.* New York, June 26, 1978.

Davis, David Brion. *The Problem of Slavery in Western Culture.* Ithaca: Cornell University Press, 1966.

Degler, Carl N. *Neither Black nor White: Slavery and Race Relations in Brazil and the United States.* New York: Macmillan, 1971.

Diégues Jr., Manuel. *Africa in the Life and Culture of Brazil,* official contribution presented by the Brazilian government delegation to the Second World Festival of Black and African Arts and Culture (Lagos). Brasília: Ministry of Foreign Relations, 1977.

Diop, Cheikh Anta. *The African Origin of Civilization: Myth or Reality,* ed. and trans. by Mercer Cook. New York/Westport: Lawrence Hill, 1974.

———. *The Cultural Unity of Black Africa*. Chicago: Third World Press, 1978.

———. "Como vai, Anta Diop, meu velho irmão?," interview by Fred Aflalo, *Singular e Plural*, No. 1 (December), 1978.

Drake, St. Clair. "Diaspora Studies and Pan-Africanism," *Global Dimensions of the African Diaspora*, ed. by Joseph E. Harris. Washington: Howard University Press, 1982.

Duncan, Quince and Carlos Meléndez. *El Negro en Costa Rica*. San José: Editora Costa Rica, 1972.

Dzidzienyo, Anani. *The Position of Blacks in Brazilian Society*. London: the Minority Rights Group, 1971.

———. *The Position of Blacks in Brazilian and Cuban Society*. London: the Minority Rights Group, 1979.

———. *Nascimento and His Times: the Socio-Political Context of Afro- Brazilian Writing and Activity*. Manuscript in preparation, 1984.

———. *Afro-Brazilians and Brazilian National Image and Identity*. Working Paper in International Studies, No. 14. Minneapolis: University of Minnesota Institute of International Studies, 1988.

Edwards, Flora Mancuso. *The Theater of the Black Diaspora: a Comparative Study of Black Drama in Brazil, Cuba and the United States*. Ann Arbor: University Microfilms International, d.u. (Ph.D. Dissertation, New York University, 1975).

Entralgo, Elias. "La mulatización cubana," *Casa de las Américas* 36-37 (Special issue on Africa in America). Havana: Casa de las Américas, n.d.

Fernandes, Florestan. *The Negro in Brazilian Society*. New York: Columbia University Press, 1969.

———. *O Negro no Mundo dos Brancos*. So Paulo: Difuso Européia do Livro, 1972.

Figueiredo, Guilherme. "Apartheid, a Discriminação Racial e o Colonialismo na Africa Austral," in *Brasil, Africa e Portugal*, Special Issue of *Tempo Brasileiro*, No. 38/39. Rio de Janeiro: Tempo Brasileiro, 1975.

Fontaine, Pierre-Michel, ed. *Race, Class and Power in Brazil*. Los Angeles: UCLA Center for Afro-American Studies, 1985.

Fraginals, Manuel Moreno, ed. *Africa in Latin America*, trans. by Leonor Blum. New York: Holmes and Meier, 1984.

Franco, José Luciano. *La Diaspora Africana en el Nuevo Mundo*. Havana: Editora Ciencias Sociales, 1975.

Freyre, Gilberto. *The Masters and the Slaves: a Study in the Development of Brazilian Civilization*, trans. by Samuel Putnam. New York: Alfred A. Knopf, 1946.

———. *New World in the Tropics: the Culture of Modern Brazil.* New York: Alfred A. Knopf, 1959.

———. *The Mansions and the Shanties: the Making of Modern Brazil.* New York: Alfred A. Knopf, 1963.

———. *Casa Grande e Senzala,* 14th ed. Rio de Janeiro: José Olympio Editora, 1969.

———. "Aspectos da influência africana no Brasil," *Cultura,* VI:23 (October-December). Brasília: Ministry of Education and Culture, 1976.

———. "The Afro-Brazilian Experiment," *The UNESCO Courier* 5:10- 11 (August-September), 1977.

Friedemann, Nina S. *Ma Ngombe: Guerreros y Ganaderos en Palenque.* Bogotá: Carlos Valencia, 1979.

Geiss, Immanuel. *The Pan-African Movement,* trans. by Ann Keep. New York: Methuen, 1974.

Gonzalez, Lélia. "Uma retrospectiva da luta," submitted to *Afrodiaspora* for its forthcoming issue, No. 8. Rio de Janeiro: Afro-Brazilian Studies and Research Institute (IPEAFRO), 1992.

Graham, Richard, ed. *The Idea of Race in Latin America, 1870-1940.* Austin: University of Texas Press, 1990.

Guillén, Nicolás. "Nación y Mestizaje," *Revista Casa de las Américas,* special issue on Africa in America, No. 36-37, n.d.

Harris, Marvin. *Patterns of Race in the Americas.* New York: Walker and Co., 1964.

Hasenbalg, Carlos. *Race Relations in Post-Abolition Brazil.* Ph.D. Dissertation, University of California at Berkeley, c. 1976.

———. *Discriminação e Desigualdades Raciais no Brasil.* Rio de Janeiro: Edições Graal, 1979.

Herskovits, Melville J. *The New World Negro.* Bloomington: Indiana University Press, 1966.

Hoetink, Harry. *Slavery and Race Relations in the Americas.* New York: Harper and Row, 1973.

Ianni, Octavio. *Raças e Classes Sociais no Brasil,* 2nd ed. Rio de Janeiro: Civilização Brasileira, 1972.

Itamaraty. *Brazil 1966.* Brasília: Ministry of Foreign Relations, 1966.

Jackson, Richard L. *The Black Image in Latin American Literature.* Albuquerque: University of New Mexico Press, 1976.

———. "Mestizaje vs. Black Identity: the Color Crisis in Latin America," *Black World* (July), 1975.

Karenga, Maulana. *Essays on Struggle: Positions and Analysis.* San Diego: Kawaida Publications, 1978.

———. "Afro-American Nationalism: Social Strategy and Struggle for Community." Presentation at Colloquium of Second World Festival of Black and African Arts and Culture, Lagos, 1977.

———. *Introduction to Black Studies.* Los Angeles: Kawaida Publications, 1982.

———. *The Husia.* Los Angeles: Kawaida Publications, 1984.

Knight, Franklin W. *The African Dimension in Latin American Society.* New York: Macmillan, 1974.

Landes, Ruth. *The City of Women.* New York: Macmillan, 1947.

Larkin Nascimento, Elisa. *Pan-Africanism and South America.* Buffalo: Afrodiaspora, 1980.

———. *Pan-Africanismo na América do Sul.* Petrópolis: Editora Vozes, 1981.

Larkin Nascimento, Elisa, ed. *Dois Negros Libertários.* Rio de Janeiro: Instituto de Pesquisas e Estudos Afro-Brasileiros (IPEAFRO), 1985.

Levine, Robert M. *Race and Ethnic Relations in Latin America and the Caribbean: an Historical Dictionary and Bibliography.* Metuchen and London: The Scarecrow Press, 1980.

Lopes, Nei. *Bantos, Malês e Identidade Negra.* Rio de Janeiro: Forense Universitária, 1988.

Mattelart, Armando and Michelle. "Os Colonos do Apartheid," *Versus: Afro-Latino-América.* São Paulo (October), 1977.

Mellafe, Rolando. *Negro Slavery in Latin America,* trans. by J. W. S. Judge. Berkeley: University of California Press, 1975.

Moore, Carlos. *Castro, the Blacks, and Cuba.* Los Angeles: Center of Afro-American Studies, UCLA, 1988.

Mörner, Magnus. *Race Mixture in the History of Latin America.* Boston: Little & Brown, 1967.

———, ed. *Race and Class in Latin America.* New York: Columbia University Press, 1970.

Mortara, Giorgio. O desenvolvimento da população preta e parda no Brasil, *Contribuições para o estudo da demografia no Brasil,* 2nd ed. Rio de Janeiro: Instituto Brasileiro de Geografia e Estatística (IBGE), 1970.

Mosquera, Jesus Lacides, *El Poder de la Definición del Negro.* Ibague: Universidad de Tolima, 1975.

Moura, Clóvis. *Rebeliões da Senzala: Quilombos, Insurreições e Guerrilhas.* Rio de Janeiro: Conquista, 1972.

———. *O Negro: de Bom Escravo a Mau Cidadão?* Rio de Janeiro: Conquista, 1977.

Munanga, Kabengele. *Negritude: Usos e Sentidos.* São Paulo: Editora Atica, 1986.

Nascimento, Abdias do. *Sortilégio (Mistério Negro*. Rio de Janeiro: Teatro Experimental do Negro, 1957.

———. "An Open Letter to the 1st World Festival of Negro Arts," *Présence Africaine*, English ed. Vol. 30, No. 58 (April-June), 1966.

———. "Teatro Negro no Brasil: Uma Experiência Sócio-Racial," *Revista Civilização Brasileira*, Vol. IV, No. 2 (July), 1968. Reproduced in Spanish in the bilingual volume *Popular Theater for Social Change in Latin America*, ed. by Gerardo Luzuriaga. Los Angeles: UCLA Latin American Center Publications, 1978.

———. *Racial Democracy in Brazil: Myth or Reality?*, trans. by Elisa Larkin Nascimento. Ibadan: Sketch Publishers, 1977.

———. *Sortilege (Black Mystery)*, trans. by Peter Lownds. Chicago: Third World Press, 1978.

———. *O Genocídio do Negro Brasileiro*. Rio de Janeiro: Paz e Terra, 1978.

———. *O Quilombismo*. Petrópolis: Editora Vozes, 1980.

———. *Sitiado em Lagos*. Rio de Janeiro: Nova Fronteira, 1981.

———. *Combate ao Racismo*, Vols. 1-6. Brasília: Câmara dos Deputados, 1983-87.

———. *Brazil: Mixture or Massacre?*, 2nd ed., trans. by Elisa Larkin Nascimento. Dover: The Majority Press, 1989.

———. "Quilombismo: an Afro-Brazilian Political Alternative," Molefi K. Asante and Kariamu Welsh Asante, eds., *African Culture: the Rhythms of Unity*, 2nd ed. Trenton: Africa World Press, 1990.

———. *Orishas: The Living Gods of Africa in Brazil*, trans. by Elisa Larkin Nascimento. Trenton: Africa World Press, forthcoming.

Nascimento, Abdias do, ed. *Quilombo: Vida, Problemas e Aspirações do Negro*, Nos. 1-5. Rio de Janeiro: Teatro Experimental do Negro, 1949-1950.

———. *Dramas para Negros e Prólogo para Brancos*. Rio de Janeiro: Teatro Experimental do Negro, 1961.

———. *Teatro Experimental do Negro: Testemunhos*. Rio de Janeiro: Editora GRD, 1966.

———. *Journal of Black Studies* (special issue on African experience in Brazil), Vol. 11, No. 2 (December), 1980.

———. *O Negro Revoltado*, 2nd ed. Rio de Janeiro: Nova Fronteira, 1982.

Nascimento, Beatriz. "O conceito de quilombo e a resistência cultural negra," *Afrodiáspora Journal*, No.6-7, 1986.

Nkrumah, Kwame. *Consciencism: Philosophy and Ideology for Decolonization*. London: William Heinemann, 1964.

Nogueira, Oracy. "Skin Color and Social Class," *Plantation Systems in the New World*. Washington: Pan-American Union, 1959.

Nyerere, Julius K. *Ujamaa: Essays on Socialism.* London: Oxford University Press, 1974.

Olinto, Antonio, *The Water House.* New York: Carroll & Graf Publishers, 1970.

Ortiz, Fernando. "José Antonio Saco y sus ideas," *Revista Bimestre Cubana,* No.2, 1929.

Palmer, Colin A., *Slaves of the White God: Blacks in Mexico.* Cambridge: Cambridge University Press, 1976.

Pereda Valdés, Ildefonso. *El Negro en el Uruguay.* Montevideo: Instituto Histórico y Geográfico, 1965.

Pereira, José Maria Nunes. "O apartheid e as relações Brasil-Africa do Sul," *Cadernos Cândido Mendes: Estudos Afro-Asiaticos,* No. 14, 1987.

Pescatello, Ann, ed. *The African in Latin America.* New York: Alfred A. Knopf, 1975.

———. *Old Roots in New Lands: Historical and Anthropological Perspectives on Black Experiences in the Americas.* Westport and London: Greenwood Press, 1977.

Pierson, Donald. *Negroes in Brazil,* 2nd ed. Carbondale: Southern Illinois University Press, 1967.

Portella, Eduardo, ed. *Brasil, Africa e Portugal,* Special Issue of *Tempo Brasileiro,* No. 38/39. Rio de Janeiro: Tempo Brasileiro, 1975.

Porter, Dorothy B. *Afro-Braziliana: a Working Bibliography.* Boston: G. K. Hall, 1978.

Prado Jr., Caio. *A Revolução Brasileira.* São Paulo: Brasiliense, 1966.

Price, Richard. *Maroon Societies: Rebel Slave Communities in the Americas,* 2nd ed. Baltimore: Johns Hopkins University Press, 1983.

Queiroz Jr., Teófilo de. *Preconceito de Cor e a Mulata na Literatura Brasileira.* São Paulo: Editora Atica, 1975.

Rabassa, Gregory. *The Negro in Brazilian Fiction Since 1988.* Ann Arbor: University Microfilms International, 1977. (Ph.D. Dissertation, Columbia University, 1954.)

Rama, Carlos M. *Los Afro-Uruguayos.* Montevideo: El Siglo Ilustrado, 1967.

Ramos, Arthur. *The Negro in Brazil,* trans. by Richard Pattee. Washington, D.C.: The Associated Publishers, 1939.

Ramos, Guerreiro. *Introdução Crítica à Sociologia Brasileira.* Rio de Janeiro: Editora Andes, 1957.

Ribeiro, Darcy. "A America Latina Existe?," *Cadernos Trabalhistas,* Vol. I, No. 1. São Paulo: Ed. Global, 1979.

Rout, Leslie B. *The African Experience in Spanish America, 1502 to the Present.* Cambridge: Cambridge University Press, 1976.

Santa Cruz, Nicomedes. "Aportes de las civilizaciones africanas al folclore del Peru." Presentation at Colloquium: Negritude and Latin America, Dakar, 1974.

Sayers, Raymond S. *The Negro in Brazilian Literature*. New York: Hispanic Institute, 1956.

Senghor, Leopold. *Prose and Poetry*, trans. by John Reed and Clive Wake. New York: Oxford University Press, 1965.

Silva, Golberi do Couto e. *Aspectos Geopolíticos do Brasil*. Rio de Janeiro: Biblioteca do Exercito, 1957.

Skidmore, Thomas E. *Black into White: Race and Nationality in Brazilian Thought*. New York: Oxford University Press, 1974.

Soyinka, Wole. *Myth, Literature and the African World*. London: Cambridge University Press, 1976.

Tannenbaum, Frank. *Slave and Citizen*. New York: Alfred A. Knopf, 1947.

Thompson, Robert Farris. *Flash of the Spirit: African and Afro-American Art and Philosophy*. New York: Random House, 1983.

Toplin, Robert Brent, ed. *Slavery and Race Relations in Latin America*. Westport and London: Greenwood Press, 1974.

Turner, Doris. "Symbols in two Afro-Brazilian Literary Works: *Jubiabá* and *Sortilégio*," in *Teaching Latin American Studies (Presentations made at the First National Seminar on the Teaching of Latin American Studies)*. Latin American Studies Association, 1977.

Valladares, Clarival do Prado. "A defasagem africana ou Crônica do 1° Festival de Artes Negras," *Cadernos Brasileiros*, Vol. VIII, No. 36 (July-August), 1966.

Van Sertima, Ivan. *They Came Before Columbus*. New York: Random House, 1976.

Van Sertima, Ivan, ed. *African Presence in Early Asia*. New Brunswick: Journal of African Civilizations, 1985.

——. *African Presence in Early Europe*. New Brunswick: Journal of African Civilizations, 1985.

Vergara and Velasco, et al. "The Racial Composition of the Population of Colombia," *Journal of Inter-American Studies*, Vol. VIII, No. 2 (April), 1966.

Verger, Pierre. "African Religion and the Valorization of the African Descendants in Brazil," in *Faculty Seminar Series*, ed. by Olasope Oyelaran. Ife: University of Ile-Ife, Department of African Languages and Literatures, 1977.

Vianna Filho, Luis. *O negro na Bahia*. Rio de Janeiro: José Olympio Editora, 1949.

Wagley, Charles and Marvin Harris. *Minorities in the New World.* New York: Columbia University Press, 1968.

Westerman, George. *A Minority Group in Panama.* Panama: Liga Civica Nacional, 1950.

Whitten, Norman. *Class, Kinship, and Power in an Ecuadorian Town: The Negroes of San Lorenzo.* Stanford: Stanford University Press, 1965

———. *Black Frontiersmen: A South American Case.* New York: Schenkman, 1972.

Winters, Clyde Ahmad. "African Presence in Ancient Brazil." Submitted for publication in *Afrodiaspora.* Rio de Janeiro: Afro-Brazilian Studies and Research Institute (IPEAFRO), 1985.

LIST OF CHAPTER SUBTITLES

Chapter 1—Memories from Exile

Born in Exile	5
Childhood	6
A Young African and the Catholic Church	8
Education and Profession	9
Enlistment, Hope and Bad News	10
In the Army	12
Brazilian Black Front	14
The Footing	16
Integralism, Communism, and Prison	17
Afro-Campineiro Congress	19
Origins and Antecedents of the Black Experimental Theater	21
Convicts' Theater	23
The Black Experimental Theater (TEN)	24
Afro-Brazilian Democratic Committee	29
TEN: Headquarters and Censors	30
The Afonso Arinos Law	33
First National Congress of Brazilian Blacks	36
TEN's Newspaper *Quilombo*	37
Political Endeavors	38
Aesthetics, Christ, and the Black Arts Museum	40
Self-Criticism	42
The Excluded Ones	43
The Media, the Left and Africans	45
Dictatorship, Persecution, and Exile	48
Exile in the United States	49
Art and the Orishas	53

Pan-African Encounters 57
Perspectives 62
Editor's Epilogue 64

Appendix to Chapter 1 70

Chapter 2—Pan-Africanism, Negritude and the African Experience in Brazil

Introduction 83
Pan-Africanism and "Latin" America 84
African Presence in Brazil 87
Contemporary Afro-Brazilian Resistance 95
Afro-Brazilian Perspectives on Pan-Africanism and Negritude 102
Conclusion 116

Chapter 3—Africans in South and Central America

Introductory Remarks 121
General Considerations on Pan-Africanism 129
African Experience in South and Central America 137
Demographic Manipulation and Suppression of African Populations 143
The Miscegenation Illusion 147
African Culture and "Syncretism" 154
Brazil: Key Country in the African World 159
Pan-Africanism and the Afro-Brazilian Struggle 166
Conclusions 167

INDEX

ABI (Associação Brasileira de Imprensa), 25, 31
Abolition of slavery, in Brazil, 15, 19, 48, 52, 73, 89, 90, 93, 96, 97, 102, 149, 153; in South and Central America, 169; in the United States, 52
Abolitionist movement in Brazil ix-x, 8, 90
Abyssinia, 14. *See also* Ethiopia
Accra, Ghana, xii, 20, 61, 119
Adonias Filho, 41
"Aesthetic Prejudice" theory, 93–94
Affirmative action, 69, 152
Afonso Arinos Law against racial discrimination, Brazil, 33–36, 68, 152, 184
Africa, v-vii, ix, 15, 20, 46, 49, 57, 62, 63, 67, 88, 104, 113, 114, 121, 122, 124, 129, 131–135, 138, 140–142, 147, 159–165, 166, 167, 179, 184, 185
African, definition, 5n, 177
African-American, definition, xi
African Americans, v, xi, 56, 84, 85, 123; definition, xi, 85
African consciousness movements, vii, 122
African cultural unity expressed in African languages, 106
African culture, vi, viii, xi, xii, 20, 42, 51, 52, 54, 58, 72, 88, 105, 111, 113, 116, 123, 128, 133, 139–142, 146, 154–159, 175, 178, 183; and Liberation Theology, 158; and resistance movements, viii, 54, 96, 139–142, 154–155; repression of, in South and Central America and the Caribbean, 154; repression of, in Brazil, 57. *See also* Afro-Brazilian Culture
African Hebrews, 61
African identity, 103–108, 116–117, 133, 134, 136; in Brazil, *see* Brazil; in South and Central America, *see* South and Central America
African inferiority, theories of, *see* Inferiority
African Liberation Day, 52
African lingua franca, 85, 106. *See also* Ki-Swahili
African nations, *see* African states
African presence in Pre-Colombian America, 67, 84, 107, 123, 174
African religion, viii, xi, xii, 53–57, 154–159, 166, 174–175; and African freedom struggles, 54; and art in Brazil, xii, 53–57; and

Liberation Theology, 158; and slave rebellions, 140, 154–155; in the United States, xi, 179; repression of in Brazil, 57. *See also* Afro-Brazilian religion
"African stain" in Latin populations, *see* Black stain
African states, 122, 133, 167, 183
African world, vi, x, xi, xiii, 20, 57, 65, 84–86, 121–129, 136; language barriers in, 58–59, 85, 106, 125–126, 167
African Writers' Union, 59, 125
Afro-Brazilian Advisory Council or Afro-Brazilian Affairs Commission, Ministry of Culture, Brazil, 97, 102, 153, 184
Afro-Brazilian Congresses, 37, 135. *See also* First National Congress of Brazilian Blacks
Afro-Brazilian Culture, 54, 68, 74, 75, 78, 100, 127, 154–159, 175, 178; and resistance movements, 24, 28–29, 32–33, 40–42, 45–46, 50–51, 54–57, 64–66, 96. *See also* Afro-Brazilian religion
Afro-Brazilian Democratic Committee, 29–30
Afro-Brazilian religion, xii, 9, 42, 53–57, 59, 74, 108, 110–112, 115–116, 145, 154–159, 166, 175, 179, 181; and liberation struggle, 54–55. *See also* Candomblé, Macumba, Umbanda
Afro-Campineiro Congress, 15, 19–20
Afrocentric perspective, 66, 128, 133, 134, 136–137, 141, 142, 167, 173, 180
Afrocentricity, 103, 105, 116, 128, 133, 134, 184
Afrodiaspora Journal, 68, 149, 165
Aguiar, Ricardo Werneck de, 17, 28, 32, 178
Air Force, Brazilian, 14
Akan, 140
Akinjogbin, I. A., ix
Alabama, USA, viii
Alagoas State, Brazil, 90, 178
Alimata, Salambere, Minister of Culture, Burkina Faso, 61
All-African Peoples' Revolutionary Party, 52, 180, 183
Almeida, Rômulo de, 17
Alvares Penteado School, São Paulo, Brazil, 13, 14
Alves, Sebastião Rodrigues, *see* Rodrigues Alves
Alvim, Ricardo Cravo, 41
Amado, Jorge, 110–113, 115, 146, 156
Amazon River, 21
ANC (African National Congress of South Africa), 78, 165
Andes mountains, 21, 144
Andrade, Carlos Drummond de, 38
Andrade, Doutel de, 69, 180
Andrade, Mário de, 25
Anglo-American Corporation, South Africa, 164
Angola, 57, 61, 62, 147, 152, 161, 162, 163, 174
80 Anos de Abolição, special issue of *Cadernos Brasileiros*, see *Cadernos Brasileiros*
Anticolonialism, vi, 67, 84, 122, 123–124, 135, 162, 172, 182
Antiimperialism in Brazil, 17, 18
Antiracism, 20, 45, 60, 77, 92, 104, 107, 111; in Brazilian discourse,

116, 146, 148, 164; in "Latin" racial ideology, 92, 154. *See also* Nonracialism
Apartheid, 60, 148, 164, 165
APRA (political movement in Peru), 22
Aqualtune, 48
Arab world, 105
Araújo, Fernando, 26
Arequipa, Peru, 22
Argentina, 124, 138, 144, 159, 160, 170, 183
Arinos, Afonso (Afonso Arinos de Mello Franco), 34, 35
Army, Brazilian, *see* Brazilian Army
Aruanda, by Joaquim Ribeiro, 33, 55
Asante, Molefi K., xii, xiii, 59, 103, 137, 152, 184
Asantewaa, Yaa, 71, 121, 135
Assembly of God, *see* Evangelist Protestantism
Augustinian religious order, 8–9
Autochthonous Black Party, Argentina, 144
Awoonor, Kofi, Ghanaian Ambassador to the United Nations, 61, 124–125, 184
Axé, 55, 71, 73, 79, 117, 156, 168; definition, 181, 185
Azeredo, Albuíno, Governor of Espírito Santo State, Brazil, 76
Azevedo, Lima, MPLA representative in Brazil, 57, 62, 162

Bagley family, 50
Bahia State, Brazil, x, 8, 16, 31, 34, 37, 48, 55, 56, 71, 88, 89, 90, 102, 111–112, 116, 145–146, 149, 153, 154, 156
"Bahian whites," 34
Bakke decision, USA, 152
Balaio *quilombo*, Brazil, 89
Balogun, Ola, 59
Baoruco, 84, 139
Baraka, Amiri, 50
Barbosa, Ruy, Finance Minister of Brazil, 89
Barleta, Hugo, Argentine theater director, 23
Barquisimeto, Venezuela, 139
Barroso, Ari, Brazilian composer, 45
Bastide, Roger, 37, 172, 175, 185
Batista, Aída, 69
Batista, Nilo, Vice-Governor of Rio de Janeiro State, 70, 77
Bayano, King, 139
Beltrán, Gonzalo Aguirre, 138
Benário, Olga, 177
Benin, 138
Ben-Israel, Asiel, Prince, 60–61, 183
Bianco, Enrico, Brazilian stage designer, 27
Biko, Steve, 103
Bioho, Benkos, 84, 103, 139
Bissau, Guinea-Bissau, 20, 63
Black Angel, by Nelson Rodrigues, 32
Black Arts Museum, Brazil, 40–42, 48
Black Christ, 40–41, 46
Black Community Participation and Development Council, São Paulo State Government, Brazil, 97
Black Dance Workshop, Buffalo, USA, 52
Black Experimental Theater, 15, 21, 24–33, 36–37, 40, 42, 45, 48, 57, 96, 178

"Black Orpheus," by Jean Paul Sartre, 38
Black Orpheus, film by Vinicius de Moraes, 46
Black Panthers, 50
Black Power movement, 57
"Black stain" in Latin populations, 91, 170. *See also* Whitening ideology, Immigration
Blackfacing white actors in theater, in Brazil, 32, 46; in Peru, 21–22
Bluefields, Nicaragua, 60, 145
Blyden, Edward Wilmot, 103, 122
Bó, Efraín Tomás 21, 22
Bolivia, 22, 149, 159, 161
Bonzano-Simonsen coporate group, Brazil, 164
Borba, Osório, Brazilian journalist, 16
Bossa Nova musical trend, 46
Botelho, Egas, Police Commissioner, São Paulo, Brazil, 13
Brasília, 31, 179
Brazil, African identity in, 20, 25, 29, 64–67, 71–72, 73, 96, 105, 108; key country in the African world, 86, 129, 159–165; military regime of 1964 in, 5, 48, 57, 58, 59, 60, 159, 161–162, 173, 178, 179, 181; minimum wage in, 182; pre-Colombian African presence in, 123; white minority rule in, ix, 90, 149
Brazilian Army, 10–14, 23; racial discrimination in, 36
Brazilian Black Front, 14–16, 96
Brazilian Communist Party, *see* Communist Party of Brazil
Brazilian Constitution, *see* Constitution of Brazil
Brazilian Labor Party, *see* PTB
Brazilian National Congress, 40, 60; African-Brazilian representation in, 15, 34–35, 40, 53, 64, 68–69, 76, 97, 100–101, 111, 153; House Foreign Relations Committee, 60, 165
Brazilian Press Association, *see* ABI
Brazilian Socialist Party, 39
Brazilian Students' Theater, 26
Brigagão, Clóvis, 1
Brizola, Leonel de Moura, Governor of Rio de Janeiro State, Brazil, 40, 68, 69, 70, 75, 97, 180, 181
Brookshaw, David, 110, 175
Brown, Roosevelt, 58
Bruno, Ernani da Silva, Brazilian historian, 17
Buenos Aires, Argentina, 22, 23, 138, 144, 160
Buffalo, USA, 1, 52
Bugle of the Dawn, The, 15
Bullins, Ed, 50
Burkina Faso, 61, 168

Cabo Verde, 147, 161, 162, 180
Cabral, Amilcar, 64
Cabral, Pedro Alvares, 88
Cabral, Sadi, 28
Cabresto, 38, 179
Cabula, 154
Cadernos Brasileiros, 183
Caetano, Marcelo, Prime Minister of Salazarist regime in Portugal, 161, 185
Café Amarelinho, Rio de Janeiro, Brazil, 25, 31
Café Vermelhinho, Rio de Janeiro, Brazil, 31

Cali, Colombia, 60, 86, 145
California, 51
Callado, Antonio, 32
Câmara, Dom Hélder, Archbishop of Recife, Brazil, 17, 41
Câmara, Jaime, Cardinal Archbishop of Rio de Janeiro, 41
Câmara, José Sette, 147
Camargo, Aguinaldo, 20, 25, 26, 28, 29, 31, 36, 37, 45
Campinas, São Paulo State, Brazil, 15, 19
Campo, Diego de, 139
Campos, Geraldo, 19, 20, 33
Campos, Marietta, *see* Damas, Marietta Campos
Camus, Albert, 56
Canaan, 131
Canada, 78
Candomblé, 9, 32, 54, 63, 111–112, 145, 153, 157–158. *See also* Afro-Brazilian religion
Caó (Carlos Alberto de Oliveira), 75, 182
Cão, Diogo, 107
Capoeira, 69
Cardoso, Fernando Henrique, 186
Caribbean, vii, viii, xi, xiii, 58, 62, 84, 122, 125, 133, 137–143, 145, 154, 183. *See also* South and Central America
Carlos Chagas Foundation, 146
Carmichael, Stokely, 183
Carnaval, 12, 43
Carneiro, Edison, 36, 37, 38, 41, 113, 178
Cartagena, Colombia, 139
Carter, Jimmy, former President of the United States, 152
Casaldáliga, Pedro, Archbishop of Araguaia, Brazil, 158
Casimir, Jean, 139
Catete Palace, Rio de Janeiro, Brazil, 27
Catholic Church, 8–9, 41, 102, 154, 158, 169, 171
Catholicism, 8, 116, 155
Cauca River, Colombia, 145
Caxias, Rio de Janeiro State, Brazil, 31
Cayenne, French Guyana, 166
CEAA (Centro de Estudos Afro-Asiáticos), Rio de Janeiro, Brazil, 47
CEBA (Centro de Estudos Brasil-Africa), Rio de Janeiro, Brazil, 47
Censorship in Brazil, 16, 32–33
Center for Positive Thought, Buffalo, USA, 52
Central America, 22, 145. *See also* South and Central America
Cerqueira, Col. Nazareth, Rio de Janeiro State Secretary of Military Police, Brazil, 75
Césaire, Aimé, co-founder of Negritude poetic movement, 40, 58, 64, 102, 104, 106, 113, 116
Chaka, *see* Shaka
Checole, Kassahun, xiii
Chicago, USA, 35
Chico-Rei, 38
Chile, 138, 144, 159, 160
Chocó, Colombia, 145, 149
Christophe, Henri, 141
CIEPs (Centros Integrados de Educação Pública), 77, 181
Cimarrones, 67, 84, 138, 139, 140
Cinelândia, Rio de Janeiro, Brazil, 25

Cinque, Joseph, 122
Civil Guard, São Paulo, Brazil, 15, 39
Civil Rights Act, USA, 152
Clark, Ramsey, former Attorney General of the United States, 53
Clarke, John Henrik, x, 103, 123, 139, 141
Clash of cultures, 132–133
Class analysis, 37, 94, 129, 133, 172
Claudiano Filho, 31, 43
Collares, Alceu, Governor of Rio Grande do Sul State, Brazil, 76
Collor de Mello, Fernando, President of Brazil, 180, 182, 184
Colombia, 22, 59, 86, 87, 138, 140, 143, 144, 145, 153, 180
Colonialism, vi, 62, 66, 72, 86, 92, 104, 106, 122, 123, 125, 136, 147, 148
Columbia University, 50
Columbus, Christopher, 107
Communism, 12, 17–19
Communist Party of Brazil, 12, 16, 30, 34, 47, 97, 101, 177, 179
Compensatory action, antiracist legislative proposal, Brazil, 69, 98
Conceição, João, 45
Congo, 161
Congress of Brazil, *see* Brazilian National Congress
Congresses of Black Culture in the Americas, 86, 149, 153, 167. *See also* First, Second, Third Congress of (...)
Congressional Black Caucus, USA, 53
Connecticut, USA, 51
Constituent Assembly of 1946, Brazil, 33, 96, 182
Constituent Assembly of 1988, Brazil, 76, 97–100, 153, 181; Afro-Brazilian imput, 97–100, 101
Constitution of Brazil, 78
Constitutionalist Revolution of 1932, Brazil, 10, 11
Convicts' Theater, São Paulo, Brazil, 23–24
Copacabana, Rio de Janeiro, Brazil, 50
Corbisier, Roland, 17
Corrêa, Alfredo, African-Brazilian Army Lieutenant, 11
Corrêa, Captain Trifino, leader of *Intentona* rebellion, Brazil, 18
Correio da Manha, see *Morning Mail*
Costa, Haroldo, 31
Costa Rica, 60, 87, 145
Coutinho, Galeão, journalist, São Paulo, Brazil, 25
Coutinho, Jorge, African-Brazilian actor, 45
Couto e Silva, General Golberi do, 160
CPCs (Centros Populares de Cultura), Brazil, 46
Cruz, Nicomedes Santa, 137
Crypt Gallery, Columbia University, USA, 50
Cuba, 22, 28, 138, 140, 145, 174, 184
Cuffee, Paul, 122
Cuguano, Ottobah, 103
Cultural assimilation or amalgamation, 92, 108, 115, 126, 133, 135, 147, 155
Cumbes, 67, 84, 138, 139
Custódio, Aladir, 28

Dakar, Senegal, xii, 20, 57, 59, 81, 85, 113, 114, 125, 127, 166, 167
Damas, Leon, co-founder of Negritude poetic movement, 40, 103, 106
Damas, Marietta Campos, 40, 58, 116
Dantas, Raimundo Souza, 30, 41
Dantas, San Thiago, Minister of Foreign Relations, Brazil, 17
Dar-es-Salaam, Tanzania, 20, 58, 85, 166
Davila, José Campos, 60, 86
D'Avila, Roberto, Rio de Janeiro State Secretary for Environmental Affairs, 78
Davis, Asa, ix
DeBeers corporation, South Africa, 164
Delaney, Martin, 103, 122
Democratic Labor Party, *see* PDT
D'Evieri, Hugo, Peruvian actor, 21
Diaspora, 5n, 28, 58, 60, 85, 104, 121–129, 133, 166; concept of, 124 ; definition, 122n, 177, 183
Dictatorship in Brazil, *see* Brazil. *See also* New State Dictatorship
Diggs, Irene, 43–44
Dimona, Israel, 61, 183
Dionísio, Natalino, 26
Diop, Cheikh Anta, xi, 59, 67, 103, 105, 115, 131, 137
Diouf, Abdou, President of Senegal, 83
Djanira, Brazilian artist, 41
Dominican Republic, 87, 145, 159
Douglass, Frederick, 122
Drake, St. Clair, 141, 165
DuBois, Shirley Graham, 168
DuBois, W. E. B., vii, 64, 103, 121, 122, 123, 124, 168
Dunham, Katherine, 35, 38, 144
Dutra, Eurico Gaspar, President of Brazil, 36, 43, 179
Dymally, Mervin, United States Congressman, 53, 183
Dzidzienyo, Anani, 93, 113, 152, 172, 173, 174

Ecology, 67, 75, 142
Economic determinism, 129–132
Ecuador, 87, 138, 144, 149
Edwards, Flora Mancuso, 175
Egypt, vii, 107, 131
Ekemode, G. O., ix
Elísio, João, 32
Ellison, Ralph, 71
Emperor Jones, The, by Eugene O'Neill, 21, 26, 32, 45
Encounter on African World Alternatives, 85, 167
Encyclopedia Africana, 121
Engels, Frederich, 130
England, 125
Epictetus, ix
Escorel, Lauro, 17
Eshu, *see* Exu
Esmeraldas, Ecuador, 144, 149
Espírito Santo State, Brazil, 76, 154
Estado Novo, *see* New State Dictatorship
Ethiopia, vii, 14. *See also* Abyssinia
Ethnocentrism, 132–133
Europe, 25, 40, 46, 62, 73, 85, 124, 132, 136, 163
Evangelist Protestantism, 158–159, 185
Exile, 5, 39, 40, 47, 48, 49, 62, 64
Exu, 55, 61, 107
Exu Pelintra, 107

Fanon, Frantz, 64, 92, 147
Fauntroy, Walter, United States Congressman, 53
Favelas, 26, 40, 42, 74, 178, 185
Fávero, Flamínio, 23, 24
Federal Council on Culture, Brazil, 113
Fernandes, Florestan, 41, 49, 64, 172, 185
Ferreira, Bibi, 31, 178
Fespac (Festival of Pan-African Culture), xii, 81, 83, 126, 167
Fifth Pan-African Congress, 127
Figueiredo, Guilherme, Minister of Culture, Brazil, 148
Filha de santo, 50, 179
First Congress of Black Culture in the Americas, 60, 86, 145, 150, 151, 180
First National Congress of Brazilian Blacks, 15, 36–37, 96
First World Festival of Negro Arts, 57, 113–114, 127, 166
Five Times Slum, 46
Flamengo Beach Street, Rio de Janeiro, Brazil, 25, 29
Florida International University, Miami, USA, 81, 83
Folklore, 46, 54, 78, 114, 137, 146, 156
Footing, 16
Formiga, Minas Gerais State, Brazil, 7
Fraginals, Manuel Moreno, 169
Franca, São Paulo, Brazil, 6–11, 21, 38
France, 125, 181
Francis, Paulo, 32–33
Franciscan religious order, 8
Franco, José Luciano, 140
Frei Caneca Street penitentiary, Rio de Janeiro, Brazil, 18
Freire, Paulo, Brazilian educator and philosopher, 1
Frente Negra Brasileira, *see* Brazilian Black Front
Freyre, Gilberto, 109–110, 114, 146, 147, 175, 185
Friendly master stereotype, *see* Slave masters
Frobenius, Leo, 106

Galdino, José, 16
Galloti, Antonio, 17
Gama, Luiz, ix-x, 8, 38, 71, 90
Ganaderos, 138
Garça, São Paulo, Brazil, 20
Garcia, Léa, 31
García Lorca, 22
Garvey, Amy Jacques, 58
Garvey, Marcus, 15, 58, 64, 103, 122, 145
Genesis, 131
Genocide, 148
Georgia, USA, viii
Germany, 177
Ghana, xii, 61, 69, 70, 72, 119, 121, 124, 125, 138, 168, 184
Gilliam, Angela, 50
Góes, Fernando, 16, 25, 49
Goiás State, Brazil, 89
Golden Law of abolition in Brazil, 73, 184
Gonçalves, Marina, 31, 48
González, Lélia, 48, 60, 153, 173
Goulart, João, President of Brazil, 49, 179, 180, 181
Grande Otelo, 41
Greco-Roman tradition, 46
Greece, 46

Greek empire, 131
Grzich, Mirna, 180
Guadaloupe, 166
Gualberto, João, 20
Guanabara Palace, Rio de Janeiro, 69
Guanabara State, 39, 45, 178, 179
Guarnieri, Rossini Camargo, 16
Guimarães, Mário Mazei, 17
Guinea Bissau, 62, 147, 161, 162
Guyana, 140
Guzmán, Diego de, 84, 139

Haiti, 66, 135, 139
Hall, Prince, 122
Ham, 131
Hamenoo, Michael, Ghanaian Ambassador in Brazil, 69, 70, 72
Harlem, New York, USA, 50, 52
Harvard University, 51, 52, 56
Hasenbalg, Carlos, 173
Hausa, 89, 106, 177. *See also* Islam; Malê
Hayford, Casely, 121
Herbel, José, 25
Herrera, Larco, Vice-President of Peru, 22
Herskovitz, Melville, 169
Hispanic America, 148. *See also* South and Central America
Hispanics, xi
Hoetink, Harry, 171
Holy Orchid Brotherhood, 20–22
Honduras, 145
Hora, José Pompílio da, 36
Hotel Glória, Rio de Janeiro, Brazil, 43
Hotel Serrador, Rio de Janeiro, Brazil, 43–44
Howard University, 52
Hughes, Langston, 28
Human Rights Commission, New York City, 52
Hunter College, x

Ianni, Octavio, 186
IBGE (Instituto Brasileiro de Geografia e História), 74, 91, 94, 182
Ifa, 55
Ife, University of, Nigeria, ix, 59, 110
Ile Axé Opô Afonjá, 55
Ile-Ife, 20, 63
Ilé Iyá Nassô Oká, 112, 153
Immigration policy in Brazil, 90–91, 148–149, 161, 170, 184
Inferiority of Africans, theories of, 114, 129, 132, 135, 170
Inner City Cultural Center, Los Angeles, USA, 52
Institute of Black People (IPN), 61, 168
Integralism, 12, 17–19, 29–30, 39; definition, 12n, 177
Integralist movement, Brazil, 12, 17–19
Integrationist perspective, 27, 42, 47, 63
Intentona revolt, 12, 18, 19, 177
International Conference of Orisha Worship, 156
Invisible Man, by Ralph Ellison, 71
Iommi, Godofredo Tito, 21, 22
IPCN (Instituto de Pesquisa das Culturas Negras), Rio de Janeiro, Brazil, 47
IPEAFRO (Afro-Brazilian Studies and Research Institute), Rio de Janeiro, Brazil, 61, 68, 165

ISEB (Instituto Superior de Estudos Brasileiros), Rio de Janeiro, Brazil, 49
Islam, 155. *See also* Malê; Hausa
Israel, 60, 183
Issa, Alfredo, 16
Itamaraty (Ministry of Foreign Relations, Brazil), 45, 58, 143, 165, 166
Iyalorixá, 55, 179

Jackson, Richard L., 175
Jaguarão, Rio Grande do Sul, Brazil, 23
Jamaica, 58
James, C. L. R., 58, 64, 85, 86, 166
Jerônimo, 20
Jesus Christ, 8, 40, 41
Jim Crow, 96, 144
Johannesburg, South Africa, 56, 164
Jones, Pamela, 51
Jornal do Brasil, 38, 46
Judaeo-Christian tradition, 105, 131
Juqueri, 7

Karenga, Maulana, 59, 103, 134, 137, 180
Karucango, 38
Kawaida, 105
Kenya, 161
Killens, John O., 50
Ki-Swahili, 85, 106
Kitwe-Lusaka, Zambia, 148
Kubitschek, Juscelino, 31, 49

La Máscara theater group, 23
La Paz, Bolivia, 22
Lacerda, Carlos, 25, 45, 178
Lagos, Nigeria, 20, 59, 92, 110, 114, 166
Langston Hughes Center, Buffalo, USA, 52
Language barriers in African world, *see* African world
Larkin, Daniel, xiii
Larkin, Margaret, xiii
Larkin Nascimento, Elisa, v, xiii, 1, 35, 53, 60, 61, 81, 119, 128, 174, 182
"Latin" America, xi, 60, 83, 84, 87, 143, 166, 169, 170; slave system in, 147, 169
Latin American racial ideology, 86–87, 92, 126, 127–129, 136, 143, 146–154, 169–172
"Latin" identity, 86–87, 161
Leftist ideology, 28, 59, 129; in Brazil, 5, 28, 29, 37, 40, 46, 47, 59, 67, 101, 151
Legislative Assembly, Bahia State, Brazil, 112
Leite, José Correia, 15, 96
Leite, Luisa Barreto, 28
Lemba, 84, 139
Leonardos, Stela, 26
Levine, Robert M., 175
Liberation theology, 67, 158
Lima, Alceu de Amoroso (Tristão de Athayde), 41
Lima, Antonio Pereira, 39
Lima Azevedo, *see* Azevedo, Lima
Lima, Peru, 21–22, 137
Limón, Costa Rica, 60, 145
Lingua franca for African world, *see* African lingua franca
Linhares, Maria Yedda, Rio de Janeiro State Secretary of Education, Brazil, 77
Lisbon, Portugal, 1
Lívio, Tito, City Councilman, Rio

de Janeiro, Brazil, 45
London, England, 149
Lopes Filho, Napoleão, 21, 22
Los Angeles, USA, 52, 178
"Low color", 23
Luanda, Angola, 20, 61
Lumumba, Patrice, 64, 103
Luso-Tropicalism, 109, 147
Luz, Robson Silveira da, 47

Machado, Aníbal, 25
Macumba, 42. *See also* Afro-Brazilian religion
Mãe Senhora, 55
Magalhães Junior, R., 34, 44
Magno, Paschoal Carlos, 25, 26, 31, 43
Mahin, Luíza, 8, 38, 48, 71, 90
Malandro, 107
Malê, definition, 177
Malê revolts, 38, 48, 89, 90, 154–155. *See also* Slave rebellions
Maloney, Gerardo, 145
Mandacaru, 141
Mandela, Nelson, 78
Mangabeira, Octávio, 34
Maranhão State, Brazil, 16, 88, 89
Maria della Costa theater company, 32
Mariani, Clemente, 31
Maroon societies, v-vi, 67, 123, 135, 138, 141, 143;
and Pan-Africanism, 140–142; *See also* Cimarrones, Cumbes, Palenques
Martinique, 166
Marx, Karl, 140
Marxist ideology, 5, 35, 59, 94, 184; and Pan-Africanism, 129–136
Mato Grosso State, Brazil, 164
Mattos, Guiomar Ferreira de, 48
Medeiros, José, 28
Memmi, Albert, 92, 147
Memorial Zumbi, *see* Zumbi Memorial
Mercadante, Paulo, 30
Mestizaje, 87, 149
Mestizos, 171. *See also* Mulattoes
Mexico, 123, 124, 139, 140, 144, 170, 183
Miami, USA, xii, 81
Middletown, Connecticut, USA, 51
Miguel, King, 139
Military regime of 1964 in Brazil, *see* Brazil
Minas Gerais State, 7, 16, 25, 88, 89, 178
"*Mineiro* whites," 34, 35
Ministry of Culture, Brazil, 153, 180, 182, 184
Ministry of Education, Brazil, 25, 30, 41
Miscegenation, 60, 95, 109–110, 115, 126, 133, 135, 147–154, 170, 171. *See also* Race mixture
Miscegenation ideology, 84, 86, 108–110, 114, 126, 128, 135, 146, 147–154, 170–171
MNU (Movimento Negro Unificado), Brazil, 48, 173–174, 178, 182
Mondlane, Eduardo, 103
Moniz, Edmundo, Rio de Janeiro State Secretary of Culture, Brazil, 78
Montevideo, Uruguay, 23
Moore, Carlos, 58, 83, 174
Moraes, Vinícius de, Brazilian composer, 46
Morais, Marshall Mendes de, 39

"Moral personality" of African slaves in Latin America, 169, 171
Moreira, Thiers Martins, 31, 41
Morenidade, 87
Mörner, Magnus, 171
Morning Mail (Correio da Manha), 41
Mortara, Giorgio, 143
Mosquera, Jesus Lacides, 145, 149
Moura, Abigail, African-Brazilian composer, 27, 45
Moura, Almério de, 13
Moura, Carlos, President of Afro-Brazilian Affairs Council, Ministry of Culture, Brazil, 153, 180
Moura, Clóvis, 183, 185
Mourão, Gerardo Mello, 17, 21
Movimento Patrianovista, 16
Mozambique, 57, 147, 152, 161, 162, 163
MPLA (Movimento Pela Libertação de Angola), 57, 62, 162
Mulattization, 149
"Mulatto escape hatch" theory, 95, 171
Mulatto race, universal, *see* Universal race
Mulatto women, 40, 95, 109, 111, 148
Mulattoes, 25, 31, 63, 71, 94, 110, 136, 143, 170–172, 182
Müller, Felinto, 18, 177
Municipal Theater, of Rio de Janeiro, Brazil, 27–29, 32; of São Paulo, Brazil, 47
Museum of African and African-American Arts and Antiquities, Buffalo, USA, 52
Muslims, 155. *See also* Malê
Nabuco, Joaquim, 38
Namibia, 20, 60, 61–62, 68, 108, 161, 164, 165
Nascimento, Abdias do, v, ix, xiii, xii, 1, 40, 64–69, 70, 76, 81, 119, 128, 167, 173–174, 182, 183; speeches and bills of law in Congress, 68
Nascimento, Beatriz, 48
Nascimento, Edialeda Salgado do, 75
Nascimento, Elisa Larkin, *see* Larkin Nascimento, Elisa
Nascimento, Georgina Ferreira do, 6
Nascimento, José Ferreira do, 6
Nascimento, Milton, 158
Nascimento, Osiris Kwesi Larkin, 61, 125
National Alliance of Postal and Federal Employees, USA, 53
National Arts Foundation, Brazil, 182, 183, 184
National Black Consciousness Day, Brazil, 65, 69, 90, 101, 102, 108, 183
National Black Convention, Brazil, 33–36, 96
National Conference of Blacks, Brazil, 36
National Congress of Brazilian Blacks, First, *see* First National Congress of Brazilian Blacks
National Democratic Union, Brazil, *see* UDN
National Fine Arts Museum, Brazil, 41
National Language Institute, Angola, 61
National Liberation Alliance, Brazil,

12, 177
National Security Tribunal, Brazil, 18, 177
National Student Union, Brazil, *see* UNE
National Theater Service, Brazil, 31, 43
Nationalism, African-American, 103; Brazilian, 17
Native Americans, 66, 171; in Brazil, 73, 91, 92, 123, 181, 182; in South and Central America, 149
Native American cultural traditions, 67, 84, 87, 105, 123, 142, 156; in Brazil, 73, 123, 156
Native American deities, 156
Naziism, 27, 29, 161, 177
Neal, Larry, 60
Negritude, xii, 39, 49–50, 83, 84, 102–116, 184, 185
Negros de ganho, 138
Neto, Agostinho, President of Angola, 103, 162
Neves, Tancredo, President of Brazil, 97
New Lafayette Theater, New York, USA, 50
New Orleans, USA, viii
New State Dictatorship, Brazil, 14, 16, 29, 34, 177, 182
New World, v, 28, 51, 141
New York, USA, vii, 1, 49, 50, 52, 61
Newark, USA, 50
Newport, USA, vii
News media, 45–46, 98, 100
Newton, Huey P., 51
Nicaragua, 60, 145
Nigeria, ix, 58, 59, 62, 63, 69, 70, 72, 78, 110, 138, 159, 163, 180
Nile River and Valley, vii, 63
Nkrumah, Kwame, President of Ghana and Pan-African statesman, 64, 72, 103, 121, 122, 124, 129, 168
Nogueira, Hamilton, Brazilian Senator, 33, 35
Nogueira, Oracy, 150, 153, 186
Nonracialism or nonracism, ix, 87, 93, 109, 110, 147, 154, 171. *See also* Antiracism
Nubia, 72
Nyerere, Julius, President of Tanzania and Pan-African statesman, 58, 129
Nzinga, 64, 71, 103

O Globo, 28
O Jornal, 25
O Povo, 19
O Sítio do Pica-Pau Amarelo, 163
Oakland, California, USA, 51
Offensive, The, 17
Ofuatey-Kodjoe, W., vii
Ogun, xiii, 54, 59, 63, 140, 154
Old Testament, 131
Oliveira, Carlos Alberto de, *see* Caó
Olivella, Manuel Zapata, *see* Zapata
Olinto, Antonio, 184
Olusanmokun, Olu, Minister Plenipotentiary of Nigeria in Brazil, 69, 70, 72
Omegna, Nelson, 19
Omolu, 55
O'Neill, Eugene, 21, 26–28, 178
Oral tradition, 141
Orishas, 53–57 (esp. 54–55), 59, 107, 156, 157, 174
Oshogbo, Nigeria, 63
Oshun, 55, 59, 63, 112, 153

Ossaim, 54
Ouagadougou, Burkina Faso, 168
Oxossi, 154
Oyo, Nigeria, 63

Pabón, Francisco, 51
Padmore, George, 64, 121, 123, 135, 168
Paim, Paulo, 182
Palenques, 67, 84, 138, 139, 140
Palmares Cultural Foundation, 65, 180, 182, 184, 185
Palmares, Republic of, x, 26, 38, 48, 64, 65, 66, 71, 84, 90, 96, 108, 123, 135, 140, 141, 153, 158, 172, 178, 181
"Pan" movements, vi
Pan-Africanism, v-x, 72, 83, 84, 102–116, 119, 121–124, 128, 129–137, 140, 142, 166–168, 184, 185; definition, 123; language problem in, 106, 126
Pan-African Congresses, 86, 122, 124. *See also* Fifth Pan-African Congress; Sixth Pan-African Congress; Seventh Pan-African Congress
Panama, 65, 86, 142, 145, 153, 178
Panorama, 164
Panthers, Black, *see* Black Panthers
Pará State, Brazil, 89
Paraguay, 144, 149
Pardos, 91–92, 94, 182
Paris, France, 36, 107
Patrocínio, José do, 38
PDT (Partido Democrático Trabalhista), Brazil, 40, 53, 68, 181; Afro-Brazilian Secretariat of, 68, 75, 76, 79
Pedro II, Emperor of Brazil, 71
Pedro Mico, play by Antonio Callado, 32
Pedroso, Regino, 28
Pelé, 163
Pereda Valdés, Ildefonso, *see* Valdés
Péricles, 24
Pernambuco State, Brazil, 16, 88, 89, 141, 178
Peru, 21–22, 86, 87, 123, 137, 144, 149
Petraglia, Dr., 9
Petrobrás, 163
Philadelphia, USA, vii, xiii
Phoenix Theater, Rio de Janeiro, Brazil, 25, 31
Pierson, Donald, 147
Pigmentocracy, 150
Pinheiro, Israel, 31
Pinto, L. A. da Costa, 37
Pires, Dom José Maria, Archbishop of Paraíba State, Brazil, 158
Pires, Waldir, Governor of Bahia State, Brazil, 112, 153
Police persecution and brutality, 47, 57, 59, 74, 78, 112, 155
Pongetti, Henrique, Brazilian theater critic, 28
Porter, Dorothy, 175
Portugal, 58, 148, 161, 162, 177, 185
Portugal, Salazarist, 161
Prado, Caio, Brazilian Marxist historian, 184
Prado, Manuel, President of Peru, 22
Pratt, John, 35
Pre-Colombian Americas, African Presence in, *see* African presence in Pre-Colombian America
"Prejudice of mark" theory, 150

Présence Africaine, 57, 113
Prestes, Luis Carlos, 18–19, 34, 177
Pretos, 91–92, 94
Price, Richard, v, 141, 183
Princeton University, 52
Prison, 13, 17, 23–24
Process racism, 152
Protestant church, 102, 171. *See also* Evangelist Protestantism
Psychiatric institutions, 7, 56–57, 135, 155
PTB (Partido Trabalhista Brasileiro), 39, 40, 181; Black Affairs Department of, 68
Puerto Limón, Costa Rica, *see* Limón
Puerto Rico, 88, 145, 166
PUC (Pontifícia Universidade Católica), São Paulo, Brazil, 67

Queiroz, Teófilo de, 110
Quilombismo, 64–68, 70, 89, 105, 108, 142, 143, 181
Quilombos, 74, 78, 89, 96, 99, 100, 108, 123, 140, 158, 172, 181, 184; definition, 179; and Pan-Africanism, 140–142
Quilombo: Black Life, Problems and Aspirations, 37–38
Quitaúna Barracks, 10

Rabassa, Gregory, 175
Race mixture, 63, 86–87, 94, 108, 115, 147–148, 155, 171. *See also* Miscegenation
Race relations, 53, 87, 114, 149, 169, 171, 172
Raceless society, 135–136, 149
"Racial democracy," 16, 35, 45, 57, 62, 73, 86, 95, 100, 115, 126–128, 147–154, 163, 170, 172, 173
Ramos, Arthur, 36, 175, 178
Ramos, Guerreiro, 36, 38, 41, 93, 178
Ramos, Jovelino, 1
Rawlings, Jerry, 61
Rebouças, André, 71
Rebouças, Antonio, 71
Recife, Brazil, 37, 141
Record, Wilson, 135
Recruit, The, 12
Red Cross, 162
Red Lantern, 12
Revolutions of 1930 and 1932, Brazil, 10–12
Ribeiro, Darcy, 37, 40, 69, 178, 181
Ribeiro, Flexa, 41
Ribeiro, Joaquim, 33, 55
"Rigid descent rule," 171
Rio de Janeiro, Brazil, administrative status of, 179
Rio Grande do Sul State, Brazil, 16, 23, 76
Rodrigues Alves, Sebastião, 12, 13–14, 25, 29, 36, 37, 39, 68
Rodrigues, Ironides, 26, 31, 37
Rodrigues, Jaime de Azevedo, 17
Rodrigues, Nelson, 32, 178
Rodrigues, Nina, 93
Roman Empire, 131
Romano, Emílio, 18, 177
Rome, Italy, 85
Rufino, Joel, *see* Santos, Joel Rufino dos

Saco, José Antonio, 148
Salazar, Antonio de Oliveira, Prime Minister and dictator of totalitarian state in Portugal, 185

Salazarism, 18, 161, 177
Salgado, Clóvis, 31
Salgado, Plínio, Leader of Integralist movement, Brazil, 17
Salinas del Norte, Ecuador, 144
"Saline consciousness," 136
Salles, Francisco de Almeida, 17, 19
Salvador, Brazil, 102, 145, 157
Samba schools, 74, 158
Sampaio, Agur, 20
San Basilio, Colombia, 139
San Francisco, USA, 26
San José, Costa Rica, 60, 61
Sandoval, Fray Alonso de, 148
Santa Cruz, Nicomedes, *see* Cruz
Santa Rosa, Brazilian artist, 45
Santo Domingo, 138, 139
Santos, Arlindo Veiga dos, 15
Santos, Joel Rufino dos, 151
Santos, José Eduardo dos, President of Angola, 61
Santos, Isaltino Veiga dos, 15, 36
Santos, Nelson Pereira dos, Brazilian filmmaker, 41
Santos, Theodorico dos, 25
São Paulo city, 10–14, 19, 23, 25, 33, 60, 68, 86
São Paulo State, 6, 7, 8, 11, 15, 19–21, 35, 43, 47, 89, 96, 97, 146, 148, 154, 172, 185
São Paulo penitentiary, 23–24
Sarney, José, President of Brazil, 97, 164, 180
Sartre, Jean-Paul, 38
Sayer, Raymond S., 175
Scheibe, Karl, 51
School curricula, 66, 77, 98–100
"Scientific" socialism, *see* Socialism
Seale, Bobby, 51
Second Congress of Black Culture in the Americas, 60, 65, 86, 142, 145
Second World Festival of Black and African Arts and Cultures (Festac '77), 59, 92, 110, 114, 127, 166; Colloquium of, 59, 110, 166
Secretariat for the Defense and Promotion of Black People (SEDEPRON), Rio de Janeiro State Government, Brazil, 40, 69, 70–79
Segregation, 149
Segregationist racism, 152
Senate, Brazilian, 69, 101
Senegal, 62, 83, 109, 114, 166
Senghor, Leopold Sedar, President of Senegal and founder of Negritude movement, 40, 103, 107, 109
Senhor do Bonfim festival, Brazil, 154
Serafim, Arinda, 28, 31, 37, 48
Serra da Barriga, Brazil, 61, 65, 90, 108, 158, 178, 183
Sertima, Ivan Van, 67, 84, 103, 123, 136, 174
Seven Seven, Twins, 61
Seventh Pan-African Congress, 168
Shaka, 64, 135
Shango, 55, 63
Silva, Benedita da, 182, 185
Silva, Claudino José da, 34, 97
Silva, General Golberi do Couto e, *see* Couto e Silva
Silva, José, 28
Simon, Michel, 43
Simonstown, South Africa, 160
Singham, Archie, 53
Singular e Plural, 115

Sixth Pan-African Congress, 20, 58, 85, 123, 166, 180; Caribbean Steering Committee, 166; Planning Meeting, 58; Marxist-Leninist/"Scientific socialist" orientation, 167
Skidmore, Thomas, 91, 170
Slave masters, viii, 45, 88, 90, 109, 110, 131; friendly or benevolent master stereotype, 109, 170–171
Slave rebellions, vii, 38, 89, 90, 138–139, 154–155; and Pan-Africanism, vi-viii, 140–142. *See also* Cimarrones, Cumbes, Palenques, Maroon societies, Quilombos
Slavery, viii, ix, 7, 72, 110, 123, 130–132, 147, 169–171, 172, 184; in Africa, 132; in Brazil, 7, 52, 73, 88–89, 110, 154, 170; in South and Central America, 147, 169–171
Social Democratic Party (PSD), Brazil, 39
Social Labor Party, Brazil, 39
Socialism, 130, 135, 142; and Pan-Africanism, 129–136, 167; European, 66–67; "Scientific," 135–136, 167
Sodré, Moniz, 155
Sodré, Nelson Werneck, 1
Sortilege (Black Mystery) or *Sortilégio (Mistério Negro)*, play by Abdias do Nascimento, 29, 32
South Africa, 51, 60, 69, 76, 78, 108, 148, 149, 152, 160, 161, 164, 165
South and Central America, v, viii, xi, xii, xiii, 51, 83–86, 119, 121–129, 133, 137–154, 159, 160, 167, 169, 174, 175, 179; African identity in, 87, 147, 172; definition, 123n, 183; repression of African culture in, 154; white supremacism in, 87–88, 92–94
South Atlantic region, 159–162
South Atlantic Treaty Alliance, 160–161, 162, 164
Souza, Ruth de, 28, 31, 37, 43
Soviet Union, 178
Soyinka, Wole, 59, 64, 104–106, 136, 140
Spanish-speaking Caribbean, xi, xii, xiii. *See also* South and Central Americal; Caribbean
Spartacus, ix
Spirit House, Newark, 50
State University of New York at Buffalo; Puerto Rican Studies and Research Center of, 51
Statebuilding in Africa, 122
Steel band, Caribbean, 154
Sterilization, of African-Brazilian women, 74; of blacks in São Paulo, Brazil, 149
Studio Museum in Harlem, 52
Subúrbios, 42, 179
Sumac, Ima, 22
Sun, The, 45
Supreme Federal Court, Brazil, 24
Supreme Military Tribunal, Brazil, 19
Surinam, 140
Swahili, *see* Ki-Swahili
SWAPO (South-West Africa People's Organization), Namibia, 62, 69, 76, 165
Sykes, Bobby, 58
Syncretism, religious, 115, 128, 133, 154–159, 183

Tailors' Revolt, Brazil, 38, 89
Talmud, 131
Tanzania, 20, 62, 129
Teatro del Pueblo, Argentina, 23
Teer, Barbara Ann, 51
Teixeira, Ilena, 28
Teixeira Leite, R., 41
Temple University, xii; Department of African-American Studies, xii
TEN (Teatro Experimental do Negro), *see* Black Experimental Theater
Terencius, ix
Terreiros, 56, 57, 74, 155, 156, 157, 185
Theodoro, Helena, 48
Third Congress of Black Culture in the Americas, 60
Third World, 134, 160
Thompson, Robert Farris, 175
Tibério, Wilson, 25
Tietê Rowing Club, 47
Tiradentes, 13, 177
Titicaca, Lake, Bolivia, 22
Togo, 138
Toivo-ya-Toivo, Andimba, Secretary-General of SWAPO and Minister of Mines and Energy, Namibia, 62
Tomás, Antonio, President of Salazarist Portugal, 161
Toronto, Canada, 78
Torre, Haya de la, founder of APRA political movement, Peru, 22
Torres, Garrido, 17
Touré, Samory, 135
Tourinho, Mestre, 69
Trance, religious, 55
Traylor, Eleanor, 60
Trindade, Solano, 33, 38
Tulane University, 52, 56
Turé, Kwame, 183
Turner, Bishop Henry McNeil, 122
Turner, Doris, 111

Ucayale, Peru, 21
UCLA (University of California at Los Angeles), 52
UDN (União Democrática Nacional), 33
UERJ (Universidade do Estado do Rio de Janeiro), 68, 77
Uganda, 62, 63
Umbanda, 107, 158. *See also* Afro-Brazilian religion
UNE (União Nacional de Estudantes), 25, 29, 30, 31
UNESCO, 36, 57, 58, 61, 114, 116, 168, 169
UNIA (United Negro Improvement Association), 60, 145
Union of African Writers, *see* African Writers' Union
United League for Defense of the Negro Race, 127
United Nations, 61, 78, 162, 164, 183
United States vi-viii, xi, 15, 28, 30, 35, 43, 48, 49–53, 56, 57, 59, 62, 63, 85, 93, 94, 103, 122, 124, 148, 152, 159, 160, 171, 177–178, 179, 180, 182, 183
United States Congress, 53
Universidad Mayor de San Marcos, Peru, 22
Universal race or color, 86, 94, 136
Universal Races Congress, 149
Universalism, 127, 132, 135, 136
"Universalist" culture or civiliza-

tion, 108–109, 115
University of Brasília, 181
University of Ife, Nigeria, *see* Ife, University of
University of São Paulo Law School, 49
University of Southern California, 178
Uruguay, 144

Valdés, Ildefonso Pereda, 144
Valentim, Emilson, 182
Valladares, Clarival do Prado, 113, 115, 183
Valle, Laureano do, 38
Valle, Maria de Lourdes, 44
Van Dunem, Domingos, Angolan Ambassador to UNESCO, 61
Vargas, Getúlio, President of Brazil, 10, 11, 18, 26–27, 29, 173, 181, 182
Venezuela, 138, 139, 140, 144, 145
Vera Cruz, Brazil, 20
Vera Cruz, Mexico, 144
Verger, Pierre, 110, 114, 146, 147, 156, 157
Vianna, Oliveira, 93
Vivanco, Maestro, 22
Volkswagen do Brasil, 163
Voodoo, 140

W. E. B. DuBois Center for Pan-African Culture, Ghana, 61, 119, 121, 124, 168
Wagley, Charles, 171
Walters, Ron, 59
Washington, D.C., 52, 53, 58, 106
Werneck, Ricardo, *see* Aguiar, Ricardo Werneck de
Wesleyan University Center for the Humanities, 51
West Indies, vii, 123, 124. *See also* Caribbean
West Indians, 122, 144–145
Western civilization, 46, 67, 136, 137
Western world, vii, ix, 143
White supremacism, 37, 85–88, 92, 104, 105, 109–111, 123, 131, 132, 134, 136, 146, 147, 151, 170, 172–174, 178; in South and Central America, 86–87, 147–154; in Brazil, 90–91, 94, 96, 109, 115, 116
Whitening ideology, 90–91, 114, 148–149
Williams, Sylvester, 122
Windhoek, Namibia, 20, 61
Winters, Clyde Ahmad, 123
World Festivals of Negro Art and of Black and African Arts and Culture, *see* First World Festival and Second World Festival, respectively
World War II, 27
Wright, Richard, 135

X, Malcolm, 64, 103
X, Marvin, 50

Yale University, 52, 56; School of Drama, 51
Yanguicos, Mexico, 139
Yemanjá, 55
Yemoja, *see* Yemanjá
Yoruba, ix, 140
Young, Juan Raul, 21, 22

Zambos, 171
Zambia, 147

Zapata Olivella, Manuel, 60, 86, 145
Zé Capetinha, 38
Ziembinski, Zbigniew, 32, 178
Zimbabwe, 161
Zirimu, Pio, 59
Zózimo, 46
Zumbi, 26, 64, 71, 84, 90, 103, 108, 140, 168, 178
Zumbi Memorial, 61, 64, 65, 90, 108, 158, 182, 185